Camden Town Advanced

THE UK: BETWEEN TRADITION AND CHANGE

Politics, society and international relations

Erarbeitet von

Stephanie Claussen
Pamela Hanus
Christoph Reuter
Mirja Schnoor
Christian Seydel
Sylvia Wauer

Diesterweg

© 2015 Bildungshaus Schulbuchverlage
Westermann Schroedel Diesterweg Schöningh Winklers GmbH, Braunschweig
www.diesterweg.de

Das Werk und seine Teile sind urheberrechtlich geschützt. Jede Nutzung in anderen als den gesetzlich zugelassenen Fällen bedarf der vorherigen schriftlichen Einwilligung des Verlages. Hinweis zu §52a UrhG: Weder das Werk noch seine Teile dürfen ohne eine solche Einwilligung gescannt und in ein Netzwerk eingestellt werden. Das gilt auch für Intranets von Schulen und sonstigen Bildungseinrichtungen.
Auf verschiedenen Seiten dieses Buches befinden sich Verweise (Links) auf Internet-Adressen.
Haftungshinweis: Trotz sorgfältiger inhaltlicher Kontrolle wird die Haftung für die Inhalte der externen Seiten ausgeschlossen. Für den Inhalt dieser externen Seiten sind ausschließlich deren Betreiber verantwortlich. Sollten Sie bei dem angegebenen Inhalt des Anbieters dieser Seite auf kostenpflichtige, illegale oder anstößige Inhalte treffen, so bedauern wir dies ausdrücklich und bitten Sie, uns umgehend per E-Mail davon in Kenntnis zu setzen, damit beim Nachdruck der Verweis gelöscht wird.

Druck A[1] / Jahr 2015
Alle Drucke der Serie A sind im Unterricht parallel verwendbar.

Redaktion: Daniel Shatwell unter Mitarbeit von Charlotte Finn, Daniel Harnett, Dr. Verena-Susanna Nungesser, Daniel Walker und Chleona Young
Layoutkonzeption: Druckreif! Sandra Grünberg, Braunschweig
Illustrationen: Oliver Fuchs, Berlin
Herstellung und Umschlaggestaltung: Harald Thumser, Frankfurt am Main
Gestaltung und Satz: tiff.any GmbH, Berlin
Druck und Bindung: westermann druck GmbH, Braunschweig

ISBN 978-3-425-**74003**-4

Contents

Page	Theme	Text types	Skills training

1 Don't mention the war: Britain's relationship with Germany

Page	Theme	Text types	Skills training
6	**A** Getting started	• video clip	
9	Knowing your facts Anglo-German relations		

12	**B** Practice section	• newspaper comment
		• cartoon
			• Analyzing non-fictional prose
			  - tone
			  - communicative strategies
			• Analyzing cartoons
			• Writing: A letter to the editor

20	**C** Getting to the point	• newspaper comment	• Writing: Summary
23	**D** Mediation		• Writing: Drafting a magazine article

2 What is Britishness?: Citizenship, values and identity

Page	Theme	Text types	Skills training
30	**A** Getting started	• newspaper article	
32	Knowing your facts What it means to be British		

35	**B** Practice section	• drama	• Writing: Summary
			• Analyzing a drama
			  - stage directions
			  - choice of words/manner of speaking

41	**C** Getting to the point	• drama	• Comment: Discussing the relevance of certain criteria for establishing national identity

3 Them and us: Class matters in Britain

Page	Theme	Text types	Skills training
44	**A** Getting started		• Giving feedback • Describing pictures
46	Knowing your facts Class matters in Britain		
48	**B** Practice section	• newspaper articles • WikiHow • newspaper comment	• Writing: Summary • Comparing two different texts on the same topic
60	**C** Getting to the point	• newspaper comment	• Analyzing a non-fictional text - stylistic devices • Writing: A letter to the editor
62	**D** Speaking	• monologue • dialogue	• Presenting a character profile • Discussing different points of view in a group

Contents

Page	Theme	Text types	Skills training

4 Britain is great: The culture of Great Britain

Page	Theme	Text types	Skills training
68	A Getting started	• video clips • pictures	Describing pictures
71	Knowing your facts What's so great about Great Britain		

74	B Practice section	• novel extract	• Analyzing fictional texts:
			  - narrative perspective
			  - tone
			• Creative writing: Writing a report for a travel journal

80	C Getting to the point	• novel extract	• Analyzing fictional texts:
			  - narrative perspective
			  - characterization
			• Creative writing: Writing a dialogue

82	D Speaking	• monologue • dialogue	• Presenting an extract from a novel • Discussing an author's portrayal of casting shows

5 Awkward partners and a special relationship: Britain and the EU / Britain and the USA

Page	Theme	Text types	Skills training
88	A Getting started	• newspaper headlines • pictures • statements	• Describing pictures
91	Knowing your facts Britain and the United States of America Britain and the EU		
94	B Practice section	• political speeches	• Analyzing a speech - rhetorical devices • Creative writing: writing a speech
100	C Getting to the point	• political speech	• Checklist: Summary

6 God save the Queen: Political system in GB

Page	Theme	Text types	Skills training
102	A Getting started	• film scene • cartoons	• Listening to a discussion about the monarchy • Debating the end of the monarchy in Britain
104	Knowing your facts Political system in GB		

Contents

Page	Theme	Text types	Skills training
106	B Practice section	• film excerpts	• Analyzing film • Comment: Discussing what is important for the role of a modern monarch
112	C Getting to the point	• film excerpts	• Comment: Discussing whether historical events can be adequately presented in films

7 In or out: Devolution

Page	Theme	Text types	Skills training
114	A Getting started	• pictures • cartoons • video clip • podcast	
116	Knowing your facts A timeline of devolution		

119	B Practice section	• video clip
		• newspaper editorial
			• Analyzing a newspaper editorial:
			  - author's point of view
			• Analyzing a letter to the editor:
			  - rhetorical devices
			  - strategies
			• Writing: A letter to the editor

124	C Getting to the point	• newspaper editorial	
126	D Mediation		• Drafting an article based on a German-language source

8 The legacy of empire: Commonwealth and multiculturalism

Page	Theme	Text types	Skills training
128	A Getting started	• pictures • video clip	
131	Knowing your facts Commonwealth		
133	B Practice section	• picture • short story	• Analyzing fictional texts: - characterization • Giving feedback
141	C Getting to the point	• short story	• Creative writing: Writing a diary entry from the perspective of the narrator

6	Themes 1 – 8	
145	Skills	
175	Glossary – Literary terms	
182	Index – Names and terms UK*	

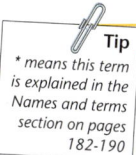

Tip
* means this term is explained in the Names and terms section on pages 182-190

1 Don't mention the war

Getting started

A1 **Think-Pair-Share:**
a) Individual work: Note down clichés about Germany and the Germans that you would expect to be confronted with abroad.

b) Pair work: Compare your ideas with a partner.

c) In class, identify the common clichés.

A2 a) Watch the TV clips from British commercials and share your first impressions.

> amused • appalled • shocked • angry • irritated • surprised • confused

b) Say why you feel this way.

c) Watch the clips again and note down which clichés about Germany and the Germans are presented in the clips.

> The music used in the Carling Black Label advert is taken from the film *The Dam Busters* (1955), which is about the British attacks during World War II on the dams of German water reservoirs using bombs that could bounce across the surface of the water.

Commercials: *Carling Black Label*

Citroën C5

A3 a) **Group work:** Study the materials A–E on pages 7 and 8 and arrange the points that are made about Germany and the Germans in a graphic organizer.

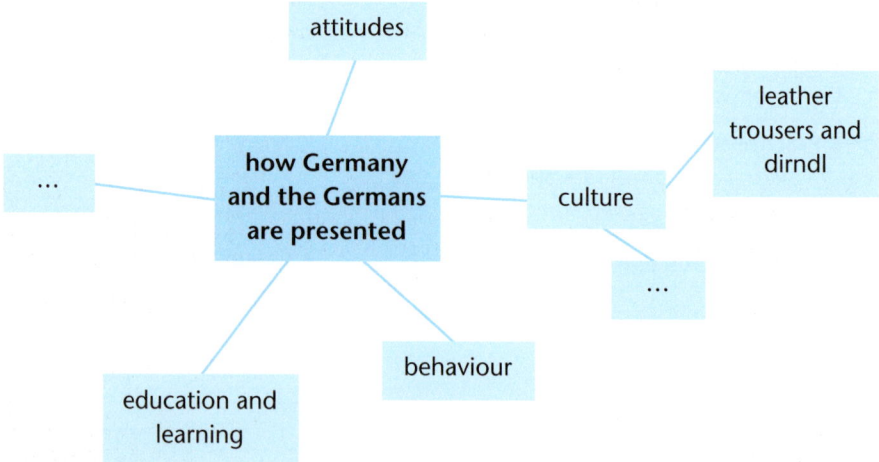

Don't mention the war: Britain's relationship with Germany

> **Info: Clichés, prejudices and stereotypes**
>
> A **stereotype** is a simplified and generalised understanding, usually of a person or a group of people, based on what you expect from them or have experienced with them. It is a kind of image that immediately arises in your imagination as soon as you hear a name, for example.
> Example: Germans wear leather trousers.
>
> A **prejudice** is used to refer to preconceived judgments of a group of people or a person because of personal characteristics such as race, gender, class, religion, nationality, etc. It refers to beliefs and attitudes that lack any real evidence and are difficult to change through rational argument. It tends to be negative and to discriminate against certain people.
> Examples: Unemployed people are just lazy.
>   Black people are better dancers.
>
> A **cliché** can apply to almost any situation, person or object. It is a concept that is not as clearly defined as the other two terms above. It represents a very simplified understanding of something that has become common among people of the same culture or background because this cliché has been used over and over again.

b) Group work:
- Look at the points in your graphic organizer and decide which definition from the info box they go with.
- Suggest what actual experiences/facts/observations they might be based on.

c) Present and talk about your findings in class.

A4 Choose two or three points you have identified in A3. Write a personal statement for an Internet forum in which such prejudices are discussed and present your view on how the British see Germany and the Germans.
Note: Although you may phrase your points humorously, don't forget to follow basic rules of politeness.

Example:
I'm amazed that an Englishman who has lived in Germany for some time can complain about ticket machines at German stations. As far as I know, you can always choose English as a language for the information on the computer screen. ...

Ⓐ Gary Lineker, former captain of England's national team:

> Football is a simple game; 22 men chase a ball for 90 minutes and at the end, the Germans always win.

Ⓑ British tabloid front pages during the Football World Cup 2010

Don't mention the war: Britain's relationship with Germany

> **Tip**
> * means this term is explained in the Names and terms section on pages 182-190

C

**Grant Hollings,
How German are you?**
(The Sun, 22 June, 2011)

DO you have a craving for sausage or get upset about bad timekeeping? Then you might actually be GERMAN.
Geneticists claim HALF of Brits could have German blood in them.
Up to 200,000 Anglo-Saxon immigrants came to south-east England in the Fifth and Sixth Centuries after the Romans left in AD410.
(...)

Germans we love
WIMBLEDON champ[1] Boris Becker, composers Beethoven and Johann Sebastian Bach, supermodels Heidi Klum and Claudia Schiffer, 99 Red Balloons singer Nena, Electropop pioneers Kraftwerk, inventor of the petrol-powered car Karl Benz, inventor of the diesel engine Rudolf Diesel, science genius Albert Einstein, fairy tale collectors the Brothers Grimm, car designer Ferdinand Porsche and our own Royal Family (King George V changed his name from Saxe-Coburg to Windsor during the First World War).

And some we're not so keen on
But for every popular German there is always … footie[2] diver Jurgen Klinsmann, who helped knock England out en-route to winning the 1990 World Cup, ruthless F1 champ Michael Schumacher and Kaiser Wilhelm II, whose support of Austria in 1914 led to the First World War.

D

Tim Collard, German efficiency: it works fine, so long as you bow your head and click your heels (*The Daily Telegraph*, 26 February, 2010)
No, I haven't forgotten all that's wrong with them; the unreflecting Euromania[3], the excruciating smugness, the impenetrable bureaucracy inaccessible to any form of common sense (…) – but it's a pleasant country with good beer and friendly folks and I always enjoy being there. In fact I'm doing so at the moment.
Traditionally, another perceived advantage was that at least Germany was a place where things actually worked. They certainly do, by comparison with dear old Blighty[4], but at a price.
Sometimes the price is merely that of inconvenience. When I arrived at Düsseldorf airport the other night, I extracted a wodge[5] of twenty-euro notes from a hole in the wall[6] and sallied forth[7] to get a train for the onward journey. At the railway station modernity was so far advanced that there was no actual ticket office in sight, just banks of automatic ticket machines. Finding the correct ticket on those was no picnic[8], but I got there in the end, and tried to pay. I discovered that the machines will not take 20-euro notes, only tens and fives, and of course they won't take foreign cards either. (…) But this station is attached to an international airport. Fortunately for the German taxpayer I found someone to split[9] my twenty, otherwise I would have had no way of catching my train without fare-dodging[10] (…).

E

Helen Pidd, German stereotypes: über-efficiency (*The Guardian*, 18 March, 2011)

They do seem to faff[11] about rather less than we do. According to statistics from the OECD*, your average German works 256 fewer hours a year than their British counterpart and yet gets a lot more done.
Plus while pretty much every other country in the western world was just trying not to go bust last year in the aftermath of the financial crisis, German labour productivity actually increased. Annoying, isn't it?
Well actually, it sometimes is. The downside of this efficiency is the bureaucracy that underpins it. Germans only manage to produce so much because they have a set of rigid, unbendable rules and they stick to them.

Everything has to be done exactly as prescribed – *und keine Ausnahmen* (no exceptions)! There is no point waving madly at the bus driver to let you on after he has closed the doors: the timetable leaves no time for compassion.
Of course the upsides are numerous: the streets are clean, houses are properly insulated and if a German *Bauarbeiter* (builder) says he will be there by 8am, you know he means it.
Just don't expect him to work a minute after five.

---

[1] **champ** = champion
[2] **footie** = football
[3] **Euromania** = (excessively) strong enthusiasm for Europe, particularly for a united Europe.
[4] **Blighty** = British slang term for 'Britain'
[5] **wodge** = *here:* of cash – a (large) stack of bank notes
[6] **hole in the wall** = *informal:* cash machine, ATM
[7] **to sally forth** = to go in a light and enthusiastic manner
[8] **to be no picnic** = to be difficult and challenging
[9] **to split (a banknote)** = *here:* to exchange for notes or coins of smaller denominations
[10] **fare-dodging** = travelling on public transport without having paid the required fare
[11] **to faff about** = to waste time by doing small and unnecessary things

Anglo-German Relations

"Forget two world wars and one World Cup […] geneticists reveal 50 per cent of Britons are GERMAN" – this headline from the tabloid newspaper *Daily Mail* from 21 June 2011 says a lot about the relationship between the peoples of Britain and Germany and about the history that connects them.

The 5th and 6th centuries: a shared ancestry

Recent studies have shown that many British and German people are closely related. They share a gene pool dating back to the 5th and 6th century AD, which was when many Angles, Saxons and Jutes – originally from modern-day Northern Germany and Denmark – invaded Britain and settled down there.

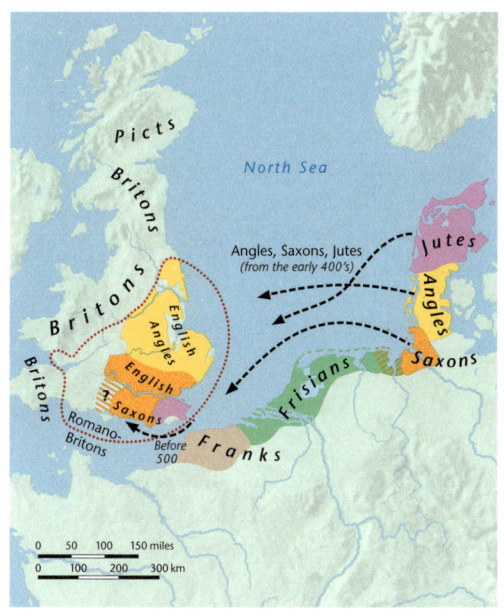

Modern English and German still share many words with similar sounds and meanings; for example *hoffen/hope, machen/make, zehn/ten* and *Apfel/apple*.
The migration of Vikings from Scandinavia (from around AD 800 to the mid-11th century) and Normans from Northern France (following the Norman Conquest in 1066) continued the process of foreign influence on the English language.

The Middle Ages and the early modern period

In subsequent centuries, most contact between the English and the Germans was based on the relationships between the monarchs and often concerned religious matters.
However, in 1714 a German royal dynasty, the House of Hanover, inherited the British throne. The German influence on the British monarchy therefore became much stronger during the 18th and 19th centuries, although the first of the Hanoverian monarchs, George I, was not particularly popular. He was considered to be too German and was accused of being hardly able to speak English, although this was not true; at least not in the latter years of his reign.

The 19th century

In 1837, Princess Victoria was crowned Queen of England. In 1840 she married Prince Albert of Saxe-Coburg-Gotha, a German nobleman. Although to attribute it to them alone would be to go too far, Victoria and Albert certainly helped to establish the German tradition of the Christmas tree in Britain.

At this time the relationship between Britain and Germany was an ambivalent one. At the level of the monarchy, there were close ties between the two countries. For example, the German Emperor Wilhelm II, who reigned from 1888 onwards, was Queen Victoria's grandson. However, towards the end of the 19th century there was a growing rivalry between the two countries. Although at the end of the 18th century Britain had been the birthplace of the Industrial Revolution, from the 1830s on, Germany's industry started to catch up with and in some sectors even to overtake Britain's. As Germany's industry started to develop, many German entrepreneurs imitated the British model; some going so far as to spy on their British rivals in order to try and catch up. Germany's economy was so successful – especially in certain new industrial sectors (e. g. electrical goods or chemicals) – that in 1887 Britain introduced a "Made in Germany" label to identify German products in the vain hope that consumers might prefer to buy British.

Additionally, Emperor Wilhelm II hoped to give Germany a more prominent role in interna-

Don't mention the war: Britain's relationship with Germany

tional affairs. Germany's bid to expand its colonies and its challenge to Britain's position as the leading naval power[1] led to a deterioration in the relationship between the two countries. This was not helped by Wilhelm's failure to forge an alliance with Britain.

The time of the two World Wars

Germany and Britain fought against each other in both the First and Second World Wars. However, after World War I, the British were among the first to realise that the terms of the Treaty of Versailles had probably been too harsh on the newly-established Weimar Republic. During the 1930s, hoping to prevent another war, the British pursued a policy of appeasement and gave in to or tolerated many of Hitler's demands. But in 1939, realizing that, no matter what they agreed to, Hitler would never be satisfied, the British changed their approach and on September 1st war was declared. Unlike the First World War, which had been fought mainly on the battlefields of Belgium and France, the Second World War was characterized by the ferocious attacks that Germany and Britain (with the help of America and the other Allies) made on each other from the air. The two countries aimed not only for targets of military or economical significance, but also for civilian targets, reasoning that such losses would break a country's morale. The effects were devastating and the Battle of Britain and the Blitz[2] are still remembered with a mixture of horror and pride in Britain today. Many cities in both countries still bear marks of the destruction that was caused, but the old animosity has subsided; Coventry and Dresden, both of which suffered particularly devastating attacks, are now twin cities[3].

After Germany's unconditional surrender at the end of World War II, the British were in charge of one of the four occupation zones into which the country was divided. Together with the US and the French zones, the British-occupied zone was one of the areas which became West Germany (officially the Federal Republic of Germany) in 1949. The British helped to rebuild Germany's infrastructure, including, for example, public broadcasting in the form of the NWDR, which was based on the model of the BBC. (Today this is the NDR and WDR as part of the ARD). Although West Germany was gradually given back most of its independence, the British still maintain a military presence in Germany, but the British army is due to leave by 2020 at the latest.

---

[1] **naval power** = a country with a large navy
[2] **the Blitz** = term taken from the expression *Blitzkrieg* and used by the British to refer to German bombing of British cities in WW2
[3] **twin cities** = *here:* two cities which have entered into an agreement usually intended to provide social, economic and touristic benefits to both

The post-war period

Whereas West Germany was a founding member of the EEC* (the European Economic Community, later to become the European Union), and joined in 1957, the UK only joined in 1973. The UK's entry was surrounded by expectations that an enlarged EEC would stimulate both the UK's and the other member states' economies. It followed long negotiations, especially with France, which was afraid of losing influence. The UK's relationship with first the EEC and then the EU has been a complicated one ever since. Whereas some member states have taken steps towards closer integration, for example by introducing the euro, most British politicians tend to interpret closer cooperation within the EU as an attack on British sovereignty and an attempt by the EU or its biggest member states, France and Germany, to gain power and influence over British affairs.

Aside from politics, Anglo-German rivalry has surfaced again and again in sports, especially in football. In 1966, teams from both countries competed against each other in the World Cup Final in London. England won the trophy after a controversial goal in extra time. However, in more recent years it has usually been the German team that has defeated the English in big tournaments. Germany was host nation to the 2006 Football World Cup and the way that it presented itself in this role helped to change the British perception of Germany. It established an image of Germany as a more open and modern nation than many British people had previously thought. Any Germans who feature prominently in the British media are also usually sportsmen and women; for example, former Wimbledon tennis champion Boris Becker still regularly appears on British TV. There are even a few Germans who have made a profession out of making fun of their Germanness and managed to become a success on the UK comedy circuit. The most well-known of these comedians is Henning Wehn.

Economically, both countries provide key markets and trading partners for one another. One particularly important area in which this is the case is the automotive industry. German cars have an excellent reputation for being highly reliable and technologically advanced and several historic British car manufacturers are now in the hands of German companies. Mini and Rolls Royce are owned by BMW and Bentley is owned by Volkswagen, for example. Furthermore, British tastes have influenced German culture; British pop music, films and TV programmes have been very popular in Germany for decades. Many British musicians continue to tour and kick off their careers in Germany, just as the Beatles did in 1960s Hamburg.

Optional tasks:

1) Visualize the changing relationship between Britain and Germany in a line graph.

    +
    ⎯⎯⎯⎯⎯⎯⎯⎯⎯⎯⎯⎯⎯⎯⎯⎯⎯⎯→
    −

2) Read the last paragraph again and concentrate on the everyday influence the English have on German lifestyle, culture, etc. Add another paragraph that gives more details on how British artists, products, etc. influence teenagers' lives in Germany today.

1 Don't mention the war: Britain's relationship with Germany

Practice section

Pre-reading

B1 **Pyramid discussion:** How would you describe the Germans in a realistic way? Choose five adjectives from the list that characterize the Germans best in your view and explain your choice. Go through the list first and look up any words you don't understand. Add any other adjectives you find more suitable.

> \+ trustworthy, trendy, open-minded, tolerant, innovative, sociable, amiable, clever, generous, humorous, reliable, sensitive, emotional, sensible, rational, spontaneous, liberal, efficient, punctual

> – self-centred, aggressive, serious, depressive, anxious, blunt, domineering, boring, racist, prejudiced, thrifty, loud, radical, narrow-minded, bigoted, perfectionist, critical, pedantic

Comprehension

B2 a) Read the text *These Strange German Ways and the Whys of the Ways*.

b) Divide the text up into meaningful units and sum each of them up in a heading or a sentence. Make sure that your heading/sentence captures the main message of the passage. Before you start, look at the examples for the first paragraph (ll.1–18) and decide which suggestion fits the passage best. Give reasons.

1. Who or what are the Germans?
2. The difficulty of self-assessment
3. The discrepancy between how the Germans see themselves and how others see them
4. The different definitions of what it means to be German

c) Outline how the author tackles the concept of stereotypes and questions their validity.

These Strange German Ways and the Whys of the Ways

Susan Stern

Oh! those Germans. Who and what are they? (…) If you yourself are one of them, you may think you have an inkling[1] of your Germanic essence, but – no offense – you probably don't.
5 For how many people know themselves well, not merely as individuals – difficult enough – but as part of a collective, as members of a nation? Especially when that nation is Germany, and self-knowledge is greatly hampered
10 by the Germanic trait of agonizing over everything, otherwise known as "worry-wartism", as well as by romantic self-delusion. Why, the Germans claim to see themselves as a bunch of melancholic, broody[2] thinkers and poetic phi-
15 losophers, whereas everybody else sees them as down-to-earth, hands-on[3], practical do-ers – that is, no-nonsense people who get things done. (…)

[1] **inkling** = a slight awareness, some idea
[2] **broody** = *here:* brooding
[3] **hands-on** = involved

Don't mention the war: Britain's relationship with Germany

Non-Germans – the Brits[1] and the French in particular – take a particularly fiendish delight in telling the Germans and the world who they think[2] the Germans are and what makes them tick. So-called experts write volumes on the subject, and just about everybody else seems to have some wisdom to contribute, more often than not unflattering. Misunderstood maybe, the Germans are definitely much-maligned. Which of us has not heard at some time or other that the Germans are … aggressive, pedantic, assertive, stiff, unapproachable, unfriendly, humourless – and so on? Even normally positive attributes such as "efficient" and "punctual" can quiver with negative vibes[3] when applied by the rest of the world to the Germans. A good number of the clichés in circulation can be written off[4] to fear or envy – or both, and in view of the (…) bellicose history of the first part of the 20th century, and the perceived almost indecent prosperity of West Germany in the second part, this is not too surprising. But – and now we come to the really tricky part – can we simply write off the clichés as completely unfounded, ignorant nonsense? Or is there something about "the Germans" which could lead the least prejudiced, most positively inclined observer to admit that the epithets might indeed contain some germinal[5] truth and reflect traits or characteristics that many people of German extraction[6] seem to share?

Clichés are by definition trite, and in our politically correct world, they've become unacceptable, even in attempts at humor. However, we shouldn't simply dismiss them. The reason they exist at all is because enough people over enough time have repeated much the same sentiments, and do this not because everybody chooses to perpetuate the same biased nonsense, but because these sentiments reflect some kind of perceived reality – that is, the way we see things. Moreover, the way we see things is itself a reflection of own psychic baggage[7] – our vision may be clouded[8] by our own feelings of insecurity or envy, for example. The Brits have never really forgiven the Germans for losing the war and then turning defeat into an economic miracle. In other words: ethnic stereotyping is essentially the boiling-down[9] of enormously complex perceived reality to a few conventional notions which are then applied uncritically and indiscriminately to anybody belonging to the species. Hell, according to one version of an old, tired joke, is a place where the cooks are all British, the policemen all Italian, the lovers all German, and the mechanics all French. And heaven? Just reshuffle the stereotypes.

Back to square one[10]. In our quest to figure out who and what the Germans are, we can't escape whatever-it-is that leads to the clichés, stereotypes and lousy[11] jokes. On the contrary – it's precisely that whatever-it-is, the elusive something I referred to above, that we need to capture in order to come up with a practical, useful description of the nation and its people – the quintessential Germans. We need to figure out just what makes the Germans tick. Above all, we need to determine what distinguishes them from everybody else and makes them Germans rather than Brits or Mexicans or Turks. In short, we're looking for the German core – something I call "Germanity".

But does Germany exist? Is it possible to lump all Germans together[12] and make global statements about them? The best answer is probably the German *jein* – a mixture of *ja* (yes) and *nein* (no). (…) There was a Federal Republic of Germany and German Democratic Republic, but no "Germany". I'm not about to delve deep into history here, but the psycho-socio-political vicissitudes (read: wars and their aftermath) of the amorphous middle European area often incorrectly referred to over the centuries as "Germany" has done nothing to help form and cement a firm German identity in its people. Particularly when abroad, Germans, unlike the Brits, the French, the Americans (…) tend not to consider themselves *first and foremost* as nationals of their country, but rather, as burghers of their communities: they define themselves more readily and happily as native sons and daughters of local states or cities.

---

[1] **Brits** = British people
[2] **what makes s.o. tick** = the feelings/ideas that make s.o. behave the way they do
[3] **negative vibes** = bad or negative energy
[4] **to write sth./s.o. off** = to give up on sth./s.o.
[5] **germinal** = in the earliest stage of development
[6] **of … extraction** = from or descended from natives of a country
[7] **psychic baggage** = memories of past experiences
[8] **to be clouded by** = to be complicated by
[9] **the boiling-down** = the essence
[10] **to go back to square one** = *here:* to return to the beginning of the argument or discussion, without having made any progress
[11] **lousy** = not very good
[12] **to lump together** = to put different things in one group, irrespective of whether they really belong together

Don't mention the war: Britain's relationship with Germany

Analyzing tone and communicative strategies

B3 In the text above, the author reveals her attitude towards stereotypes associated with Germans. When you take a closer look at how language is used to express an author's attitude, you analyze the tone of the text.

> **Info: tone**
> Generally speaking, the **tone** an author uses reveals his/her attitude towards his/her subject and towards the audience/the readers. It is created by a combination of different elements including the use of **stylistic devices**, the **choice of words** and **register**.
> Tone can be described, for example, as playful, serious, matter-of-fact/factual, ironic, light-hearted, humorous, provocative, scathing, academic, conversational, colloquial.
> The author may combine these different tones in one piece of writing.

a) Copy the grid. Go through the text and find expressions and sentences that fit the different kinds of tone in the grid.

light-hearted	academic/serious	colloquial
	"Or is there something about "the Germans" which could lead the least prejudiced, most positively inclined observer to admit that the epithets might indeed contain some germinal truth and reflect traits or characteristics that many people of German extraction seem to share?" (ll. 43-49)	

b) Look at your lists of expressions in the grid. Choose from the following suggestions to determine the effect the author wants to achieve by using the respective tone.
- not taking a topic seriously at all and making fun of those who do
- bridging the gap between author and reader by addressing him like a friend; reducing distance to the audience, giving them the impression that they are taking part in face to face communication
- presenting a serious topic in an easily digestible way, making the topic more easily accessible to the readership
- proving one's competence and insight into the topic, even into complex phenomena; presenting oneself as an expert
- highly critical of the topic or the views others might have on it
- clash between highly educated formulations and rather colloquial language may produce a tension that in itself produces a humorous effect

c) The use of stylistic devices contributes to the tone of a text. Identify the devices and match them with the descriptions of their function in the text.

Quote	Device	Function
Oh! Those Germans. (l. 1)	rhetorical questions	… breaks up the sentence and provides an explanation or a comment that may help avoid a misunderstanding, underlines conversational aspect
Who and what are they? (l. 1)	parathesis	… triggers associations of carrying heavy bags which become a burden and weigh you down, just like negative past experiences that are a psychic burden and may influence your way of seeing things negatively
– but no offense – (l. 4)	metaphorical language	… sounds almost exasperated, in despair about this never ending topic, since the Germans feature strongly on the political agenda, since stereotypes seem to be overruling the actual truth and might be an obstacle in a confrontation
Back to square one (l. 77)	exclamation	… reduces the sentence to its essential part, thus speeding up the text; here it is a reference to a rule in a parlour game, meaning that one has to start again from scratch > question not that easily answered > inference that there are no easy solutions/ that topic is more complicated
If you yourself are one … you may think (l. 2–3)	use of unifying pronoun	… serves as an introduction and makes the Germans sound like a very special species or some sort of prehistoric creature frequent use of … signals investigative intention of the author
psychic baggage (l. 61)	direct address	… involves the German readers directly thus making the topic more relevant to them, raising their interest since their perspective is specifically considered
In our quest … we can't escape (l. 77–79)	ellipsis/ incomplete sentences	… suggests that the author considers himself on the same level with the audience, providing a feeling of identity as both sides are involved in their search for relevant answers

d) Find additional examples in the text and explain their effect on the reader and how they contribute to the specific tone.

1 Don't mention the war: Britain's relationship with Germany

Analyzing communicative strategies

B4 **Group work:**

a) Analyze the language used by the author to express her views on German stereotypes. In your group, concentrate on either A or B. Start a grid for relevant passages/words from the text and their intended effect on the reader.

A Choice of words, especially the use of adjectives, adverbs and emotive verbs and nouns

Example	Function/effect
"*Misunderstood* maybe, the Germans are definitely *much-maligned*. …"	negative choice of words that creates compassion/refers to unfair treatment pointing out that the author does not agree with the stereotypes used for Germans …

B Rhetorical strategies, for example repetitions, use of examples, references to experts, quotations, use of inverted commas or italics, use of different personal pronouns (I vs. we)

Example	Function/effect
"Even positive attributes such as "efficient" and "punctual" can quiver with negative vibes"	it highlights the way in which seemingly positive labels are used in a derogatory way …

b) Present your findings in class.

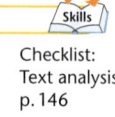
Checklist:
Text analysis
p. 146

B5 Use the information you have gathered to write your analysis:
Analyze how the author's language and tone make her view on German stereotypes clear.

Language support
Introductory sentence In her entertaining/ironic/… comment on how Germans are seen abroad/by foreigners/…, the author expresses her view on … (topic) … Stern makes it clear that … (the author's general opinion) … In order to relate her view to the readers, she chooses her examples and words carefully.
tone/register Her general tone/register is … in order to … (present herself as someone who …/present the topic in a … way so that …)
choice of words Furthermore, she emphasizes her message with the help of strong and emotive words that clearly show that … By using …, she presents the Germans/the habit of … as ridiculous/down-to-earth/likeable/eccentric/… This becomes particularly clear when she uses words like … as they reveal/underline/express … (continued)

16

Don't mention the war: Britain's relationship with Germany

Language support

stylistic devices
In order to … (make her way of presenting Germans more memorable/make the readers see the way Germans behave … more critically/sympathetically/…), the author employs various stylistic devices …
By using …, she highlights the point that …
By presenting … humorously, the author tries to draw attention to …

facts vs. opinion
In order to back up her statements on … , the author refers to …
By using adverbs such as … *(e.g. surprisingly)*/phrases like … *(e.g. I don't understand why)*, the author clearly indicates what her opinion is as she …
In order to disguise that she cannot refer to many actual facts as evidence, the author presents some of her opinions as if they were facts. …

Working with a cartoon

Comprehension

B6 Describe the cartoon on page 18.

Analysis

B7 Analyze how the cartoon's message is conveyed.

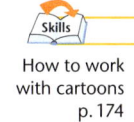

How to work with cartoons
p. 174

Checklist

For your interpretation include
✓ the text elements
✓ the visual elements
   • the setting
   • the characters and their actions/behaviour and facial expressions
   • the situation/context
   • the symbols.
Consider what might influence the cartoonist's point of view, e.g. his political beliefs, his nationality, the situation in which the cartoon was drawn.

Copy the grid below. Fill in the details and the corresponding effect.

category	detail/description	effect
Text elements		
Visual elements		
• setting		
• characters		
…		

17

1 Don't mention the war: Britain's relationship with Germany

visual element: characters
visual element: setting
visual element: blazing sun
text element: headline in newspaper
visual element: characters
visual element: characters
visual element: marks in the sand
text element: caption

"VE VILL OCCUPY ZE SUNBEDS HERE AT PRECISELY 5AM...!"

- group of middle-aged men, wearing Wehrmacht helmets or officer's hats, drawing symbols of strategic importance into sand; faces varying from determined and serious to gleeful and smirking
- "officer" uses stereotypical German-style English pronunciation to bark out commands
- middle-aged couple on beach loungers, evidently British, reading newspaper, facial expression: mouths turned down
- rhyme and layout seem to suggest British tabloid paper, derogatory about Germans
- a beach resort in the sunny south, hotel palm trees, probably Spain
- indicate planning with a high degree of organization and attention to detail
- indicates German toughness, ignoring extreme heat
- happy holiday makers in the background on hotel terrace

- provide contrast to the clash of nationalities in the foreground
- identifies couple on beach loungers as British
- refers to war and the Third Reich, men still plotting, obsessed with careful military-style planning instead of enjoying their holiday; movement of pointer and action of checking watch reveals military precision and zeal
- intensifies impression of their being totally engrossed in wartime memories/re-enactments
- represents classical battleground of British and German holidaymakers
- intensifies impression of Germans being very focussed
- shows displeasure with Germans and their behaviour on the beach
- parodies German aggressive, military-style communication

Don't mention the war: Britain's relationship with Germany

B8 Compare the cartoon's message to what Stern says about stereotypes. Explain to what extent the cartoon supports or contradicts Stern's view.

Language support	
similarities	*differences*
If you compare the cartoon and Stern's text, it is easy to see that they both share …	Whereas the cartoon focuses on …, the text presents Germans as …
Similarly, the text/cartoon expresses …	In contrast to …, the text/cartoon includes …
Both text and cartoon refer to the issue of …	The cartoon/text provides a more differentiated look at …
Although different means of highlighting the point of … are used, both texts emphasize the point that …	The cartoon/text shows more clearly …/ has a stronger impact on the reader by …

Comment/Creative writing

B9 Imagine you saw the cartoon in today's copy of The *Sun*. Write a letter to the editor of The *Sun* to express your opinion of the cartoon. Use the aspects gathered from Stern's article to back up your argumentation.

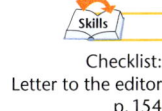
Checklist:
Letter to the editor
p. 154

• Don't use "Dear …"	Sir or Madam:
• Start by naming the article/cartoon you refer to and giving the reason for writing your letter.	Having seen the cartoon/article "…" in a recent edition of your newspaper, I would like to/I feel the need to point out … I am writing in response to the publication of the cartoon/article "…"
• State right away what you would like to praise/criticize about the article/cartoon.	As a firm believer in …/As a supporter of …, I totally agree/I see no reason why …
• Present your arguments in a structured form. • Refer to the original article/cartoon, but do not quote. • Go beyond the article/cartoon to explain why you share/oppose the author's point of view.	It is beyond doubt that … What you need to keep in mind is… Your article/cartoon raises the question of whether … The way I see it, … Although I understand why …, I cannot accept your overall conclusion that … I think you are mistaken if you believe … You overlook the fact that … You are absolutely right when you say that …
• End your letter with a strong statement, e.g. a final appeal or a strong expression of your opinion.	That is why I hope that you will keep drawing attention to … Therefore, we should be careful … Consequently, I strongly support your view …
• Close the letter by writing your name and place of residence.	John Miller London, England

1 Don't mention the war: Britain's relationship with Germany

Getting to the point

Pre-reading

C1 a) Choose one of the following topics and research it online. Prepare a short presentation of not more than five minutes.
Include some visuals to support your presentation.

1. The international popularity of Berlin as a tourist destination
2. The 2010 Football World Cup in South Africa: how the German and English teams performed and how the world reacted to the German national team
3. The intervention of western military powers such as Britain, France and the USA in Libya in 2011 and the German position on it at the time
4. The Fukushima nuclear disaster in 2011 and Germany's decision to give up on nuclear energy in 2011

b) Give your short presentations in groups.

Comprehension

Checklist:
Summary
p. 145

C2 a) Read the extract below and divide it up into three main parts. Then note down the main points for each part.
b) Summarize how Oltermann sees the present-day relationship between the British and the Germans. Use your notes from C2a).

Keeping up with the Germans

Philip Oltermann

As well as the cliché about Britain being stuck in the past, a line repeated again and again in the German press is that telling English people you are German can easily lead to a punch-up[1]. I have never got into trouble for telling people where I am from – once, on the top of a double-decker bus, I was confronted by a gang of menacing teenagers whose faces softened before my eyes when I told them I was from Germany: 'They've got marzipan there, haven't they? I love that shit!' Usually, the response used to be a polite, pitying silence. For the last two years or so, however, 'I'm German' has suddenly started to trigger an entirely different response: 'Germany? Oh, I *love* Berlin.' (…)

In the last five years, at least six of my friends have uprooted from London to Berlin. When I ask them why they prefer Berlin to London, the usual answers are either 'It's got so much history' or 'People in Berlin just know how to party', neither of which seems to make much sense, given that London doesn't particularly lag behind in the history department or the party stakes[2]. A rarer, more plausible explanation is that Berlin is simply a cheaper place to live, and more tolerant of creative and bohemian lifestyles. Indeed, whenever I've gone to visit friends there, the people I met were either writing novels, playing in bands, making documentary films or DJing in bars – or all of those at the same time. (…)

Those who didn't make it to Berlin in the last ten years just had to watch football to be reminded that Germany isn't quite the place it used to be. (…) I sat in a packed front room[3] in a flat in Finsbury Park[4] to watch England play Germany in the quarter-finals of the 2010 World Cup in South Africa. Of course Germany

[1] **a punch-up** = a fight
[2] **stakes** = point of comparison
[3] **front room** = downstairs living room or dining room which faces the main road
[4] **Finsbury Park** = place in London

20

won – nothing new there. What was new was the way in which they won, and the reaction among my English friends. The moment that summed up this change best happened in the seventieth minute of the match. Germany had already scored three to England's one, and the team in the red shirts was showing signs of frustration after having a perfectly clear goal disallowed. It's unclear whether it was lion-hearted courage or mere desperation that made England's barrel-chested defender John Terry desert his position and storm upfield to meet a cross from winger Joe Cole. The cross never arrived. Blocked by the German defence, the ball sailed back into the England half, putting defence midfielder Gareth Barry one-on-one with attacking midfielder Mesut Özil. Initially, it looked like the tall, muscular and athletic Barry was certain to reach the bouncing ball before the short and weedy twenty-two-year-old Özil. Two seconds later, Özil was five meters ahead of Barry, with the ball at his feet, making the Englishman look like a retired bobby chasing after a teenage delinquent. Özil passed for twenty-one-year-old Thomas Müller to score, and England found themselves at the receiving end of their highest defeat in World Cup history.

I turned around to look at my English friends, expecting angry faces and clenched fists. There was disappointment, for sure, but also the odd admiring nod of the head and a few sympathetic smiles. England, everyone agreed in the pub afterwards, had looked old, overhyped and overpaid, a collective of individuals without spark or spirit. Germany, on the other hand, looked young, fun, light-footed and confident in their new multicultural identity (…) Even though Mesut Özil and co. in the end failed to lift the cup, they had managed something their parents' and grandparents' generations had repeatedly failed at: to make the English like the Germans again. (…)

Other recent developments indicate that in spite of its apparent maturity, Germany can still be more of a dreamer than a doer. (…) Under the current coalition, Germany has abolished conscription into the military, considerably reduced the size of its army and refused to be drawn into a military conflict in Libya which Britain, France and the US entered with glee: a noble tendency, if the idea of a German military still makes you think about the Wehrmacht; naivety verging on hypocrisy if you consider that the country is also the world's third largest exporter of major conventional weapons, including to Middle Eastern countries like Saudi Arabia.

I was puzzled by how differently Germany and Britain reacted to the Fukushima Daiichi nuclear disaster caused by the Japanese tsunami in March 2011. In Britain, many concluded that the worst-case scenario had turned out to be not as bad as everyone had feared, and that nuclear power was therefore the safer and cleaner alternative to dirty coal power. In Germany, news from Japan triggered a return of the *'Atomkraft? Nein danke!'* slogans of the 1980s, a soaring Green Party and, eventually, the announcement that the country would shut down all nuclear power stations by 2022. It has led some critics to wonder if the Germany of the second decade of the twenty-first century is living in a childhood dreamworld where there is no war, free money and endless electricity. Being hopelessly idealistic strikes me as a lesser crime than being depressingly cynical, especially if that idealism might eventually translate into a successful renewable energy industry. And yet Germany can surely benefit from some constructive criticism from England, just as England can still learn from Germany. Perhaps that is the real lesson (…): that sometimes the value of the meeting isn't in the friendship, but in the criticism friends can give each other.

Don't mention the war: Britain's relationship with Germany

Analysis

Checklist:
Text analysis
p. 146

C3 Analyze Oltermann's use of language and explain what it tells the reader about his view of Anglo-German relations.
If you need help with this, follow these steps:
- Concentrate on one part of the text (see C2) and collect examples of how Oltermann tries to convince the reader of his way of seeing Anglo-German relations.
- Consider
  – the choice of words,
  – communicative strategies.

Comment

C4 **Group work (4): Placemat:**
a) Looking back at what you have read and heard about the relationship between the British and the Germans, comment on how fitting you find Oltermann's final statement that "sometimes the value of the meeting isn't in the friendship, but in the criticism friends can give each other".

b) After reading and commenting on all your partners' statements, agree on the three most important points that characterize Anglo-German relations.

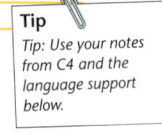
Tip: Use your notes from C4 and the language support below.

C5 Philip Oltermann works as a journalist for *The Guardian* and there have been several reviews and articles about his book in that newspaper.
Write a letter to the editor in which you comment on how he depicts present-day Germany.

Working with a cartoon/Comprehension

Checklist:
Letter to the editor
p. 154

C6 a) Look at the cartoon and say which topic mentioned in Oltermann's text it refers to.

b) Describe the cartoon.

Analysis

How to work with cartoons
p. 174

C7 a) Interpret the cartoon's message.

The Sun

Checklist:
Text analysis
p. 146

b) Compare the message of the cartoon and the relevant passage in Oltermann's text.

Mediation: Getting started

Pre-mediation

D1 a) **Think-Pair-Share:** Discuss which comedians/films/TV programmes you find funny and why.
b) Read the short article "German stereotypes: don't mention the sense of humour" published in the Guardian newspaper on 16 March 2011 and sum up its message in two to three sentences.
c) Compare the article's message to your discussions about what you find funny.
d) Discuss in class whether you recognize yourself in the way German humour is described in the article.

German stereotypes: don't mention the sense of humour

The Germans certainly enjoy a laugh – but not always at the same things as we British. Nor do they share our love of banter.

It is patronising, ethnocentric nonsense to suggest another nation has no sense of humour – especially if you lack the language skills to assess for yourself whether their jokes are amusing, or indeed translate your own witticisms for their benefit. Of course Germans have a sense of humour; it might just be different from yours.

Because of the wordplay involved, humour often gets lost in translation. Take this joke, printed in the Bild tabloid on Tuesday: Two mates are sitting at a table in the pub. One says to the other: "Tell me, do you sometimes get smog in your bedroom?"
"How come?" asks the other.
"A bad atmosphere and no traffic …" To get the joke, you have to know that the word for traffic *(verkehr)* can also mean sexual intercourse.

Some people have suggested that the rigid structure of the German language makes joke-telling difficult. For example, important verbs are withheld until the very end of a long sentence as soon as you insert a conjunction such as "because" or "if". Actually, though, this can help a comedian because it builds suspense. A good comic can lead an audience down one track, only to surprise them with an unexpected verb as the punchline.

If we must generalise, though, it is fair to say that Germans tend to take the mickey out of each other far less than Brits - and are fonder of putting the world to rights over a beer rather than engaging in mindless banter.

Mediation: Practice section

D2 a) Decide which of the following statements are true for mediation tasks:
1. Leave out unimportant information.
2. Imitate the language and register of the German original.
3. Reproduce the original type of text (e.g. comment, interview).
4. Only add information the addressee needs in order to understand cultural differences.
5. Focus on the requirements specified in the task.
6. Always keep the addressee in mind when writing your text.

b) Read the following mediation tasks 1–3. Concentrate on one of the tasks and note down

- what the situational context is,
- who the addressee is,
- what the focus of the task is, e.g.
- what kind of information you need
- to watch out for in the German original,
- what type of text you need to produce,
- what this means for the register of your text (e.g. formal, informal, colloquial).

c) Compare your results in small groups.

① Ihre Schule unterhält einen Schüleraustausch mit einer amerikanischen High School, der im Rahmen einer AG intensiv vorbereitet wird. Ms Kuehn, die Lehrerin, die den Austausch an der amerikanischen High School betreut, würde im kommenden Schuljahr gern einen behinderten Jugendlichen an der Austauschfahrt teilnehmen lassen. Sie hat sich an Ihre AG mit der Bitte gewandt, sie über die Integration behinderter Schülerinnen und Schüler an deutschen Schulen zu informieren.

Lesen Sie den Zeitungsartikel zur so genannten „Inklusion" behinderter Schülerinnen und Schüler an deutschen Schulen und fassen Sie dessen Aussagen für Ms Kuehn in einer Email zusammen.

② In Ihren Schulferien arbeiten Sie als Praktikant in einem international operierenden Unternehmen, das in Ihrer Region seinen Hauptsitz hat. Zeitgleich besuchen Auszubildende aus den ausländischen Niederlassungen die Konzernzentrale.
Sie haben die Aufgabe, im Rahmen eines allgemeinen Informationstags die Auszubildenden über die Konzeption des speziell in Deutschland verbreiteten „Duale Studiums" zu informieren und dessen Vorteile, aber auch Belastungen aufzuzeigen. Verfassen Sie ein Redeskript auf der Grundlage eines Zeitungsinterview mit zwei Unternehmern, die die Chancen und Risiken eines „Dualen Studiums" thematisieren.

③ Sie nehmen als freiwilliger Helfer im Bereich Pressearbeit an der Vorbereitung einer internationalen Sitzung des Europäischen Jugendparlaments (EYP) in Deutschland teil. Im Rahmen dieser Tätigkeit sind Sie dafür verantwortlich, für die englische Version der Veranstaltungshomepage einen Bericht über die Sitzung, ihre Thematik, die beteiligten Personen und ihren Ablauf zu verfassen, der in konzentrierter Form Nicht-Teilnehmer der Sitzung informiert, z. B. Pressevertreter und Ehrengäste. Als Grundlage dienen Ihnen zwei Texte der deutschen Website für die Veranstaltung, die sich speziell an die Teilnehmer und freiwilligen Helfer richten.

Don't mention the war: Britain's relationship with Germany

D3 a) Read the interview with Louise Brown and Philip Oltermann on pages 26–27. Find out how British and German humour compare to each other and sum the comparison up in a few sentences.

b) Read the mediation task carefully and, including what you know about the interview's content, identify

- what the situational context is,
- who the addressee is,
- what the focus of the task is, e.g. what kind of information you need
- to watch out for in the German original,
- what type of text you need to produce,
- what this means for the register of your text (e.g. formal, informal, colloquial).

Die Internetseite UK-German Connection Voyage, die deutsche und britische Jugendliche einander näherbringen möchte, unterhält ein Onlinemagazin, in dem junge Deutsche und Briten Artikel vor allem über das Verhältnis beider Völker veröffentlichen können.
Sie sind eingeladen, einen kurzen Zeitungsartikel für das Online-Magazin über die Gemeinsamkeiten und Unterschiede zwischen deutschem und englischem Humor und Umgang mit Sprache zu verfassen. Als Grundlage nutzen Sie ein Zeitungsinterview mit zwei Journalisten aus Deutschland und Großbritannien, die im jeweils anderen Land leben und arbeiten.

D4 a) Read the following passage from the interview and the three examples of notes below that students made. Decide which of the three fits the task best. Give reasons for your choice.

> **Oltermann:** Dazu kann ich auch eine Geschichte beisteuern. Meine Frau wollte sich kürzlich ein Kleid in einer Hamburger Boutique kaufen. Als sie es anprobierte, fragte sie die Verkäuferin, wie steht mir das Kleid? In England hätte es als Antwort geheißen, ‚that's very nice', auch wenn es nicht perfekt war. Diese deutsche Verkäuferin sagte ‚ganz nett', und meine Frau wusste sofort, es steht ihr nicht. Das ist deutsche Direktheit.

1. Germans tend to be very direct, also to strangers, e.g. when asking shop assistants for their opinion.
2. When Mr Oltermann's wife went shopping and tried on a dress, she asked the assistant for her opinion. The assistant said "quite nice" and so his wife knew that it did not look good.
3. German shop assistants tend to be more direct and less polite than English ones.

b) Go through the text and note down other points that are relevant to the task.

D5 a) Now think about the type of text you have to write. Decide which of the following you need to take into consideration.

> objective and matter-of-fact style • rhetorical devices • use of imagery • complex sentences • personal view • colloquial expressions • incomplete sentences • technical terms • slang • formal expressions • heading

b) Compare your results in class.

How to improve your mediation skills p. 170

D6 a) Use your results from the previous tasks to write a draft of the article for the online magazine.

b) Then go over your text again in order to improve it. Use the checklist below.

Checklist: Mediation

Content and structure:

✓ Include all the information from the original text that is relevant to the task.
✓ Structure your points in such a way that they fit the type of text you are expected to write.
✓ Make the content easy to understand for the people who are supposed to read it.
✓ Add explanations if there is any information that someone who is not from Germany cannot understand.
✓ Do not get lost in detail. Show that you can present the gist clearly.

Language:

✓ Make sure that your style and register fits the type of text and the addressee(s) you are writing for.
✓ Check your language for grammatical correctness and the right choice of words.
✓ Make sure that you express your ideas clearly and link sentences.

Von Martina Goy   *Die Welt, 14.07.2012*

Was deutschen und britischen Humor verbindet

Welt Online: Frau Brown, Herr Oltermann, es heißt, der Humor der Hamburger komme dem englischen ziemlich nahe. Stimmt das?
Louise Brown: Daran musste ich mich erst
5 gewöhnen. Hier in Hamburg ist es mir schon öfter passiert, dass mir jemand todernst etwas erzählt hat und ich erst beim Nachdenken habe ich gemerkt, dass es ein Witz war. In England ist man irgendwie eher darauf gefasst, dass
10 nicht alles ernst gemeint ist.
Philip Oltermann: Ich glaube, dass es in Deutschland sowieso viel mehr schwarzen Humor gibt, als viele Engländer denken. Das sieht man auch an dem Erfolg von Henning
15 Wehn, der als Deutscher durch englische Pubs zieht und dort mit seinen Witzen über beide Länder fast schon Kultstatus hat. Am meisten hat die Engländer überrascht, dass da ein Deutscher Stand-up-Comedy über sein Ich-bin-
20 deutsch macht.
Welt Online: Sind Sie gleich klar gekommen mit dem britischen Humor?
Oltermann: Die Frage wurde mir schon häufig gestellt. Britischer Humor hat ja in Deutschland
25 fast etwas Mystisches. Ich finde, so viel Ehrfurcht sollte man vor dem Witz der Briten nicht haben. Etwas Mut zu Galgenhumor und Surrealismus gehört schon dazu. Aber wer früher Monty Python-Filme geschaut hat, kann das.
30 **Welt Online:** Was ist mit Mr. Bean?
Oltermann: Diese Art von Humor ist heutzutage in England ziemlich out. Auch für Dinner for One kann man wenige Briten begeistern, der Sketch wurde ja noch nie im englischen

Fernsehen gezeigt. Ich glaube, inzwischen zeigt sich der britische Humor wieder mehr im Wortspiel als im Slapstick.

(…)

Oltermann: Man sollte die Attraktion von Traditionen nicht vergessen. Welche Faszination allein das englische Königshaus mit all seinen Geschichten auf die Deutschen ausübt, sieht man an den Quoten für die Übertragungen im Fernsehen. Egal ob Dianas Tod, die Hochzeit von William und Kate oder der Queen-Mum-Geburtstag, da ist man in Deutschland teilweise genauso vernarrt wie in Großbritannien.

Welt Online: Mal angenommen, das stimmt. Warum ist das so? Sehnen sich die Deutschen nach einem Königshaus?

Brown: Das würde ich nicht sagen, obwohl ich es häufiger von Deutschen gehört habe. Aber ich glaube, dass die Briten für die Deutschen schon etwas verkörpern, was sie selbst nicht sind.

Welt Online: Wovon reden wir? Exzentrik? Übersteigertes Selbstbewusstsein? Stolz sein auf eine Inselsicht?

Brown: (…) Exzentrisch? Vielleicht einfach gelassener. In London kann man, egal wie dick der Hintern ist, oder wie grau die Haare, mit einem knallpinken Minirock rumlaufen. In Hamburg ginge das so nicht. Generell glaube ich, dass man in London freier lebt als in Hamburg. Zumindest fühle ich mich dort freier. (…)

Welt Online: Herr Oltermann, Sie leben nun schon seit 15 Jahren in England. Wie deutsch sind Sie noch?

Oltermann: Ich habe inzwischen ein gespaltenes Ich. Einerseits habe ich noch typisch deutsche Werte und Vorurteile: Bei meiner Karriere wünsche ich mir Beständigkeit und Konstanz, und im Journalismus sehne ich mich nach Gründlichkeit und Tiefe. Kaum bin ich aber in Deutschland, kommen mir deutsche Nachrichten wahnsinnig steif und langatmig vor. Mir fehlt der englische Schwung und Witz.

Welt Online: Und Sie Frau Brown, was sind Sie? Schon deutsch oder noch englisch?

Brown: Ich bin seit meiner Jugend eine Pendlerin zwischen den Welten. In Hamburg fehlt mir das Lockere, der alltägliche Small-Talk, die Freundlichkeit. Als ich herzog, fand ich es schwierig, durch jene Schale zu dringen, die viele Menschen hier umgibt. Das änderte sich erst, als mein Sohn geboren war. Kinder sind ein Schlüssel zu den Herzen der Hamburger. Und dann die Direktheit, damit habe ich so meine Schwierigkeiten. ‚Sie sehen aber müde aus, Frau Brown!' – so etwas würde man als Begrüßung in einem englischen Büro früh am Morgen nicht hören.

Oltermann: Dazu kann ich auch eine Geschichte beisteuern. Meine Frau wollte sich kürzlich ein Kleid in einer Hamburger Boutique kaufen. Als sie es anprobierte, fragte sie die Verkäuferin, wie steht mir das Kleid? In England hätte es als Antwort geheißen, ‚that's very nice', auch wenn es nicht perfekt war. Diese deutsche Verkäuferin sagte ‚ganz nett', und meine Frau wusste sofort, es steht ihr nicht. Das ist deutsche Direktheit.

Brown: Andererseits gefällt mir, dass man hier weiß, woran man ist. Freundschaft heißt hier: Freundschaft. Oder im Beruf: Als ich in England etwas für eine britische Zeitung schrieb, hieß es: ‚das ist so ganz hübsch, aber ein paar Details könnte man noch ändern…' Auf Deutsch hätte das geheißen: ‚Bitte umschreiben!'

Don't mention the war: Britain's relationship with Germany

Mediation: Getting to the point

Pre-mediation

D7 a) Name the towns your home town is twinned with.
b) Talk about any trips to those twin towns or, alternatively, places you have visited on a school exchange.
c) Suggest what advantages such international contacts might offer.

Mediation

How to improve your mediation skills p. 170

D8 Use the tips from D6 to work on the following task:

Sie haben über eine professionelle Vermittlung einige Monate in einer britischen Gastfamilie verbracht und dort eine Schule besucht. Die dortige Deutschlehrerin würde gern einen Schüleraustausch mit Ihrer Schule beginnen und hat Sie gebeten, als Vermittler zu helfen. Ein Englischlehrer Ihrer Schule ist skeptisch, weil er nachfolgenden Artikel gelesen hat. Er möchte wissen, wie die Haltung der englischen Schule bzw. der Bewohner des Ortes zu Europa ist. Verfassen Sie eine Email an die Deutschlehrerin der englischen Schule, in der Sie – ausgehend von den Fragen Ihres Lehrers – in konzentrierter Form den Inhalt des Artikels und die Meinung des Autors über diesen Vorfall referieren.

Von Marco Evers, London   17. Dezember 2011, 16:11 Uhr

Ende einer Städtepartnerschaft

Die Europa-Monster aus Bishop's Stortford

Natürlich entscheidet sich das Schicksal Europas nicht in Bishop's Stortford, einem schmucken Ort mitten in England mit rund 35.000 Einwohnern.
5 Aber dieses leicht langweilige Städtchen ist gerade Schauplatz und Spiegel dramatischer historischer Ereignisse. Hier führt eine Riege seltsamer konservativer Lokalpolitiker eine Miniaturversion des Spektakels auf, das Premier
10 David Cameron auf der großen Bühne zum Besten gibt. Das Stück heißt: zum Teufel mit Deutschland, Frankreich und Europa.
Es ist Ende November. Noch streiten Berlin, Paris und London um die künftige Form von
15 EU und Euro-Zone, doch in Bishop's Stortford sind die Würfel längst gefallen. Bürgermeister John Wyllie schreibt Briefe.

Adressiert sind die Schreiben an die werten Amtskollegen der beiden Partnerstädte – Fried-
20 berg nahe Frankfurt am Main und Villiers-sur-Marne nahe Paris. Wyllie schreibt nicht, um die Kollegen einzuladen zu den üblichen Verbrüderungsfesten, Konferenzen, Jugendfreizeiten oder Austauschprogrammen. Er schreibt, um
25 ihnen die Freundschaft zu kündigen, nach 46 Jahren Sonnenschein.
Am 28. September 2012, so teilt Wyllie trocken mit, wird die Gemeinde alle Bande kappen mit den Schwestergemeinden. Gründe für den
30 Abbruch der diplomatischen Beziehungen nennt er nicht.
In Friedberg und Villiers herrscht seither ungläubiges Staunen. „Es ist ein Schrieb von nur einer Seite", sagt Friedbergs Bürgermeister

Michael Keller (SPD) fassungslos. Dabei seien die letzten Jahrzehnte „eine erfolgreiche Zeit gewesen". Natürlich sei das Konzept von Städtepartnerschaften etwas angejahrt, aber man hätte die Beziehung ja verändern und verbessern können. Und „das Mindeste" wäre doch ein Gespräch gewesen.

Für Keller ist der Fall klar. Hier habe ein konservativer Gemeinderat zeigen wollen, „was er von Europa hält". Nämlich nichts. „Bedauerlich" sei das, gefährlich sogar. „Systemrelevant sind in Europa nicht die Banken", mahnt Keller, „sondern die Kommunen." Und wenn es auf dieser Ebene nicht funktioniere, dann sei weiter oben im Gefüge erst recht Feierabend.

Bishop's Stortford grenzt an den Flughafen London-Stansted, aber es liegt außerhalb der Flugschneise. Ein ruhiger, wohlhabender Ort mit lauter Schieferdächern, einem niedlichen Flüsschen und fast ohne Arbeitslosigkeit. Er ist sich selbst genug. Mit dem Zug sind es 38 Minuten bis ins Londoner Finanzviertel, wo ein Großteil der Bewohner sein Geld verdient, auch Wyllie, der ehrenamtliche Bürgermeister.

Im Gemeinderat halten die Tories seit der Kommunalwahl im Mai eine allmächtige Mehrheit: Sie stellen 16 der 18 Mitglieder. Entsprechend kurz war der Prozess gegen Friedberg und Villiers.

Aussprache? Konsultation? Fehlanzeige. Der Entscheid kam „vollkommen überraschend", klagt Dave Smith, 68, pensionierter Elektro-Ingenieur, jetzt Vorsitzender des Partnerschaftsvereins mit seinen mehr als 100 zahlenden Mitgliedern. Seit 35 Jahren fährt Smith nach Friedberg („eine großartige Stadt"). Immer beglich er die Reisekosten selbst, wie alle Teilnehmer. Smith, die Völkerverständigung in Person, Bezwinger des Adolfsturms von Friedberg mit seinen mehr als 200 Stufen, kramt stolz ein Dokument hervor. Seit 1990 ist er „Träger des Ehrenschildes der Stadt Friedberg" – für seinen „persönlichen Einsatz für ein geeintes Europa", wie die Urkunde hervorhebt.

Jetzt zwingt ihn dieser Einsatz für Europa dazu, ausgerechnet gegen sein eigenes Stadtparlament in den Krieg zu ziehen. Es noch umzustimmen, wird ein schwerer Kampf, sagt Smith, „da darf man sich nichts vormachen".

So ist das eben mit den heutigen Konservativen, sagt Mike Wood, 66, das einzige Gemeinderatsmitglied von den europafreundlichen Liberaldemokraten. Tories seien „eigentlich normale Leute. Aber wann immer das Thema Europa aufkommt, verwandeln sie sich in eine Art Monster", sagt er.

Cameron hat sich jetzt an die Spitze seiner Europa-Monster gestellt und es bisher nicht bereut. Auf einmal erfreut sich der Premier bester Umfragewerte – und das, obwohl es eigentlich gerade nicht gut läuft für seine Regierung. Die Wirtschaft rutscht wieder in die Rezession. Mehr Leute sind arbeitslos denn je in den vergangenen 17 Jahren. Die Inflation liegt bei fast fünf Prozent. Doch alle schlechten Nachrichten sind wie vergessen, seit Cameron sich als EU-Rebell gebärdet.

Natürlich war Wyllie, Bürgermeister von Bishop's Stortford, noch nie in Friedberg oder Villiers. „Leider", sagt er. Ihm bleibt alle Aufregung um die Kündigung der Städtepartnerschaft vollkommen unverständlich. Heute flögen austauschwillige Schüler doch lieber nach China, Russland oder in die USA, aber „mangels Interesse" doch eher nicht nach Deutschland.

Um Europa jedenfalls, so beteuert Wyllie, sei es ihm bei der Entscheidung keineswegs gegangen. Auch Geld habe keine Rolle gespielt, Städtepartnerschaften kosteten ja ohnehin kaum etwas.

Worum ging es dann?

Wyllie ist durch und durch Tory, und das bedeutet: von Grund auf argwöhnisch gegenüber allem, was vom Kontinent kommt und Kooperation im Schilde führt. Er sagt dazu nur dies: „Uns war es einfach wichtig, das Thema Städtepartnerschaft zu entpolitisieren."

2 What is Britishness?

Getting started

A1 a) **Placemat:** Write down what you consider to be essential elements of German identity. Comment on your partners' ideas and agree on a final list of the top five features.

b) Compare and discuss your results in class.

c) You have 30 seconds. Write down what you consider to be typically British. Now organize the information in a mind map.

A2 In 2012, the British public celebrated both Queen Elizabeth II's *Diamond Jubilee* after 60 years on the throne and the Olympic Games in London. These events are often referred to as part of the *Great British Summer*. In this context, 100 people from the UK were interviewed about what being British means to them. Here are six examples to read and listen to.

a) Read Tom Stinchcombe's statement and listen to the statements of the other people. Identify those people who see themselves as British. Give reasons why they see themselves as British and what "Britishness" means to them.

b) Add any new aspects concerning "Britishness" to your mind map from A1.

c) Now consider those who do not feel British. Explain why that is the case.

Tom Stinchcombe, 23, student
Hastings, East Sussex
I'm originally from Bristol, but am now at the University of Brighton studying media and sociology. I consider myself British rather than English. Scotland, England and Wales need to stick together. We're not a big country. I don't relate much to the Queen and her jubilee. Britishness means living under a democracy and having the freedom to do what you want with your life. The Queen may not embody Britishness, but Parliament does. It's a unique institution. The way they debate must look out of control when people in other countries see it, but it's all part of how we run our country. The economic situation worries me and capitalism as we know it isn't working to everybody's benefit, so business as usual is no longer acceptable. But there is still much to admire in this country. We are more questioning and more secular than the US, and have true freedom of speech. It's important for my generation not to buy into the Britain-in-decline idea.[1] Instead of waging wars, we should be in the forefront of things like finding alternative fuels. We should be an ideas bank for the world.

David Sinclair-Benstead, 67, retired hospital chef Stratford, east London

Karen May, 50, assistant front-of-house[2] manager Stratford-upon-Avon, Warwickshire

David Singh, 43, souvenir shop owner Edinburgh, Midlothian

Michael McDowell, 35, investment manager Belfast

Alicia Jones, 16, student Caernafon, Gwynedd

---

[1] the Britain-in-decline idea = the idea that the general social and economic situation in Britain is becoming progressively worse
[2] front-of-house = the part of a theatre which is accessible to the public

What is Britishness? Citizenship, values and identity

A3 a) Read the following newspaper article published at the end of the Summer Olympics 2012 in London. State how the author assesses the question of Britishness at that point.

b) The author claims that, for him, the Olympics felt "like a turning point" (l. 55). State what he associates with Britain as it was before the Olympics and after.

c) Compare his view with the statements you read and listened to before (A2). Explain whose view comes closest to Tim Lott's view.

The Independent, August 12, 2012

Tim Lott: We have surprised ourselves – and our potential is unlimited

Over the past several generations we have been a nation obsessed with "who we are". Countless books and television series have appeared to address the question. (…) But perhaps the Olym-
5 pics more than any other event for a generation (…) has raised the question, and writ[1] in larger letters than ever before. And for once (…), I think we truly have some answers, and those answers are very encouraging, and somewhat
10 surprising.

There is a sense in which it is impossible to say what a nation "is" any more than it is possible to say who a person "is". Both polity and individual are a fleeting, shifting mass of influences,
15 changes, and cross-currents, both historical and contemporary. Both are about hopes and fears as much as facts, and both feature widely contradictory poles hard to reconcile.

A year ago, we were reeling under the impact of
20 the riots. Only last week, a gang of youths was imprisoned for their attack on a restaurant in Notting Hill, west London. Put that together with our long-standing economic and political struggles, the spotlights on corruption among the
25 police, the financial sector, the press and the politicians, and we have, until the past few weeks, not had much to celebrate about ourselves.

But perhaps this is because we have been, characteristically, looking in the wrong place. (…)
30 Yes, we've applauded ourselves through the Queen's Jubilee, but this is a parading of an institution, not a nation of people. And our occasional sporting successes in, say, cricket or rugby have been marginal and sectional. The Olym-
35 pics have been different. It is truly a theatre of the citizens, not the subjects, of the UK and we have surprised ourselves in many different ways. We have discovered that we can make things work: even Swiss newspapers have admired our
40 clockwork efficiency. We have discovered that we are deeply, well, nice. (…)

I would now joyfully include the Scots and the Welsh in this definition of national personality, because the Games also brought home some-
45 thing else that has lately become counter-intuitive: that we are, truly, a United Kingdom, not just a drifting set of disparate nations making their own way. (…)

The Games showed us to be a nation – again,
50 surprisingly – at ease with itself. Our multicultural character felt very natural and unforced now, deeply and uncontroversially part of who we are. And this was expressed in joy and happiness that truly took foreign observers aback. (…)
55 For me, the Olympics feels like a turning point, a moment in which for the first time since our decline from empire, we felt genuinely self-confident. For the first time I can remember, we like ourselves.
60 We're surprised that we like ourselves, but we like liking ourselves too. And I don't think we're going back to the old self-hating people we thought we were a few weeks ago in very much of a hurry.

---

[1] writ in larger letters than ever = made more obvious than ever

What is Britishness? Citizenship, values and identity

What it means to be British

If you ask yourself what constitutes Germanness, you realise how difficult it is to define one's national character – even more so if a state like the UK is made up of different countries – England, Wales, Scotland and Northern Ireland – with rather strong regional identities. What is more, there might be at least some differences between what someone considers characteristic of one's own country or
5 what someone abroad associates with that particular country. At the end of the day, Britishness is what people believe it to be, especially in contrast to what they consider typical of Great Britain in contrast to other countries.

1 a) Before you read on, answer the following questions as best you can:
1. What do you think are the best characteristics of British people as a whole?
2. What do you think are the worst characteristics of British people as a whole?
3. What is Britain's national drink?
4. What is Britain's national dish?

b) Now look at the statistics and compare the actual answers of the British public to yours. Say what reflects your expectations and what does not.

The following statistics are based on a survey that was carried out by Ipsos Mori in 2012:

Tip
* means this term is explained in the Names and terms section on pages 182-190

Knowing your facts

WHAT IT MEANS TO BE BRITISH/ BRITISH VALUES/ CHARACTERISTICS/ FOOD&DRINK

1 Overall, which two or three of the following, would you say makes you most proud to be British?
Base: All who are British (931)

	%
Our history	45
The NHS*	37
British Army/armed forces	36
The Royal Family	28
Our culture and arts	24

2 From this list, please tell me which two or three, if any, you think are the best characteristics of British people as a whole.
Base: All

	%
Good sense of humour	45
Friendly	34
Tolerant to all sections of society	30
Hard working	28
Polite/good manners	26

3 From this list, please tell me which two or three, if any, you think are the worst characteristics of British people as a whole.
Base: All

	%
Drink too much	50
Ignorant of other cultures	33
Complain too much	23
Lazy	20
Intolerant to different sections of society	19

What is Britishness? Citizenship, values and identity

4a Which, if any, of the following is your favourite drink?
Base: Split sample (528)

4b Which, if any, of the following would you say is Britain's national drink?
Base: Split sample (466)

	4a	4b
Tea	38	65
Beer/lager	14	22
Coffee	14	4
Wine	11	2
Fizzy drinks e.g. Coke, Lemonade	7	2

5a Which, if any, of the following is your favourite dish?
Base: Split sample (521)

5b Which, if any, of the following would you say is Britain's national dish?
Base: Split sample (455)

	5a	5b
Roast beef and Yorkshire pudding	33	31
Curry	15	8
Fish and chips	9	41
Full English breakfast	9	13
Pasta	9	*

Britishness, however, consists of more than what this survey shows. All kinds of behaviours, habits, symbols or simply icons that nearly everyone identifies as typically British contribute to this notion.
Another way to find out about what is understood by Britishness is to look at what British institutions teach visitors to understand what is typical of the UK. Here are some points from a slightly humorous overview on the BBC America website.

1. What Brits want to talk about

When we chat to strangers at bus stops, it's likely that the weather will get top billing,[1] but not because we're particularly enamored by meteorological happenings. It's just easy to roll out a stock conversation[2] we've rehearsed all our lives. In fairness, Americans talk about the weather too, but theirs does tend to be more varied and compelling than drizzle and light misting. With friends, meanwhile, topics range from TV, dogs and football to that-toff[3]-Cameron and which high-profile person died recently. We seek intimacy by trying to make our co-conversers laugh rather than share emotionally (see below).

2. What Brits don't want to talk about

Our "feelings" are not up for discussion, unless we're confiding in someone we inherently trust, like the family Labrador. Money is also a danger zone. Only known eccentrics reveal how much they make or what they have in the bank. You might, however, allude to your riches by boasting about exotic holidays or nod[4] at your impoverishment by "forgetting" to buy a round.[5]

3. What Brits laugh at

We like our funnies dry and dark or silly and strange. What might seem unsettling to Americans is nectar[6] to us. We love to see people fail, whether it's falling on their face or crumbling[7] emotionally. Most Britcom-literate Americans know this already – and might feel similarly disposed[8] – but if you want to educate a novice, point them at Steptoe and Son*, Fawlty Towers*, Father Ted*, Blackadder*, League of Gentlemen*, Peep Show* and This is Jinsy*.

[…]

6. Brits love an underdog[9]

We consider ambitious, confident overachievers to be loathsome creatures who need knocking[10] down to size. I think this is one of the few Britishisms that Americans, who openly covet and laud success, find genuinely baffling. We do quite like back-of-the-pack, A-for-effort types[11], so long as they greet their eventual success with humbleness so extreme it borders on self-flagellation.[12]

Knowing your facts

[1] **to get top billing** = *here:* to be given the most attention
[2] **stock conversation** = the conversation that a person always makes
[3] **toff** = *informal:* an unflattering term for a posh person

[4] **to nod at sth.** = *here:* to briefly draw attention to sth.
[5] **to buy a round** = of drinks
[6] **to be nectar to so.** = to be very enjoyable for so.
[7] **to crumble emotionally** = to display (excessive) emotion and lose self-control
[8] **to feel disposed** = to like sth.; to want to do sth.
[9] **underdog** = person expected to fail
[10] **to knock so. down to size** = to make so. realize they are not as important as they think they are
[11] **back-of-the-pack, A-for effort type** = so. who takes part in a competition and tries hard but often isn't successful
[12] **self-flagellation** = self-inflicted punishment

2 What is Britishness? Citizenship, values and identity

[13] **to creep so. out** = to make s.o. feel very uneasy
[14] **saccharine** = here: excessively sweet, artificial and insincere
[15] **all bets are off** = anything is possible; it's not possible to make future predictions
[16] **booze** = slang: alcoholic drinks

7. Why Brits might seem cold and uptight

American style sincerity creeps[13] us out. Gushing is acceptable behavior in waterfalls, not humans. Even our speeches at weddings and funerals are about affectionate humiliation, not swooping, saccharine[14] declarations. We find this kind of conduct, and premature displays of openness, disingenuous and untrustworthy. Understandably, some Americans view our unquenchable desire to mercilessly mock those we love as unkind and call our resistance to public displays of earnestness inhibited.

8. Why all bets are off[15] when we're drunk

Disregard any of the above if the Brit in question has consumed more lager than they have blood, which for most of us is once or twice a week starting from mid-adolescence. Booze[16] allows us to loosen[17] our laces and, temporarily, become huggers[18] who want to tell their friends how much they love them. Of course, there's a tacit understanding that this kind of nauseating carry-on[19] will be airbrushed from history as soon as sobriety arrives.

Knowing your facts

[17] **to loosen one's laces** = to relax in an informal setting
[18] **hugger** = so. who wants to hug other people a lot
[19] **carry-on** = undesirable behaviour

2 Go through the survey and the text and note down six sentences that express what is part of Britishness. You can choose the points that you find most convincing, special, funny or based on clichés.

3 a) Look at the postcard "Brain of Britain". Describe it and explain in your own words which characteristics are associated with being British.
b) **Group work:** Compare your findings and discuss what the overall message of the postcard is supposed to be.

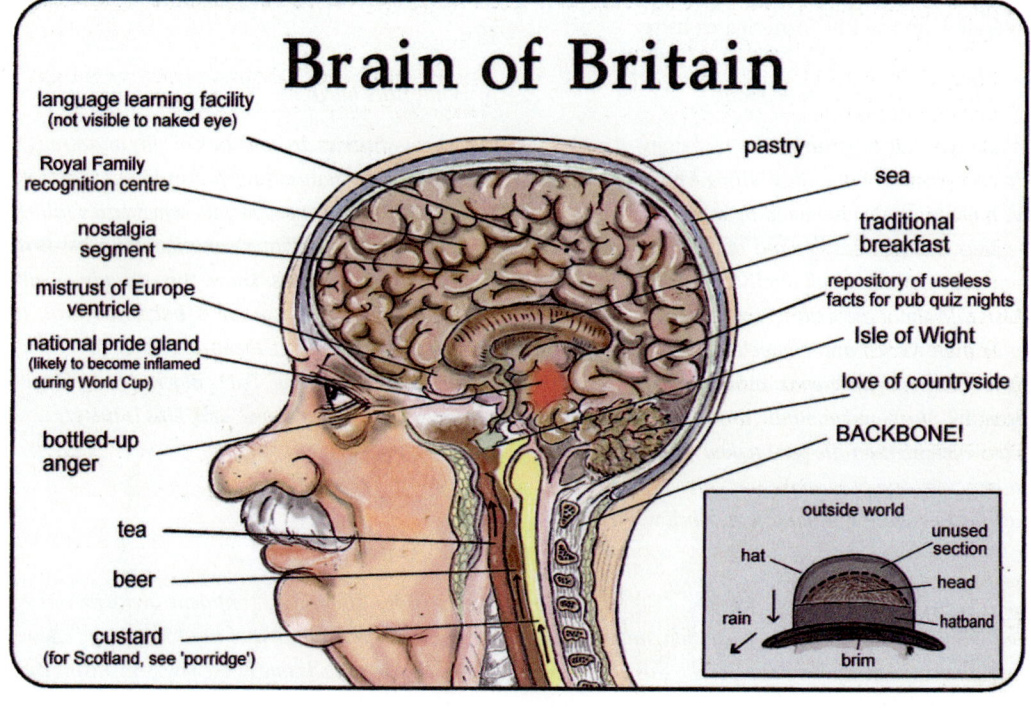

34

Practice section

Pre-reading

B1 Read the first extract from the play "Pyrenees" by David Greig.

a) While reading, note down the questions that come to your mind.

b) **Pair work:** Find possible answers to your questions.

The Proprietor Is the gentleman in trouble? He's been very quiet. He comes down from his room every morning and sits on the terrace. He looks at the mountain. Bernard-Marie comes by in the afternoon to check he's still here. He talks to him. Bernard-Marie is struggling with inner demons,[1] don't tell him I told you that, and I think he likes to talk things through with an Englishman. I don't count. If you ask me, the man's a pilgrim. When they found him he was clutching a scallop shell. In all likelihood he's a pilgrim who's had a nervous breakdown, got lost in the snow, and … now here he is. I play chess with him. He's a poor chess player, but no one else here plays at all so … He pays for the room by the day. He doesn't complain. I'll be sad to see him go. Do you have an idea who he is? I don't want to know. If he's done something awful, I don't want to know.

Anna What makes you think he's done something awful.

The Proprietor How old do you think he is?

Anna I don't know, late fifties …?

The Proprietor Do you know any man, or any person for that matter, but let's be more specific, do you know any man, any man at all who has reached the age of fifty without at any stage in his life having done something awful. Some awful act, or failure to act, which he regrets bitterly. Some act which could come back to him nightly and bring beads of sweat to his forehead. Some act which he would yearn to erase.

Anna Well, I don't know.

The Proprietor Take it from me.

Anna But people … sometimes people are ashamed of perfectly reasonable things. Maybe he wanted to erase something that happened to him. Something he was a victim of.

The Proprietor Perhaps. I hope you're right.

Anna And people are capable of good.

The Proprietor Sporadically.

Anna So, you know, he's just as likely to have done good things, to be a good person, a person whom someone loves. Someone who someone else needed, needs even.

The Proprietor What are the chances?

Anna Do you speak to him about this?

The Proprietor No. Of course not. I play chess with him. That's all. Really. He's been the perfect gentleman.[2] Can I bring you a pot of coffee?

Anna Thank you.

> **David Greig** (b. 1969) was born in Glasgow and brought up in Nigeria. He returned to Scotland in his teens and later studied English and Drama at Bristol University. He has been noted as one of the most prolific and most productive modern British playwrights. His plays often deal with how people are connected, especially in an increasingly globalized world.

[1] inner demons = personal emotional issues
[2] to be the perfect gentleman = (of a man) to behave politely and respectfully in the company of a woman

Comprehension

B2 a) Read the second extract from the play on pages 36–38 and note down
- what you find out about the three characters (the proprietor, Anna and the man),
- how they seem to be related,
- what the problem is that they want to solve.

b) Use your notes to write an introductory sentence for a summary.

> **Tip**
> The entries and exits of characters usually mark the beginning/ending of passages. Similarly, a change of setting and topic in the dialogue mark the beginning of a new passage.

2 What is Britishness? Citizenship, values and identity

B3 a) Read the extract again and divide the text up into sections.

b) In a grid, make notes for each section to sum up the most important points. Example:

Line(s)	Content
ll. 1–xx (→ The P exits (2nd time))	Anna and the proprietor talk about the mysterious man; the proprietor is of the opinion that he must be British, Anna feels unsure about the situation
ll. x–xy	…

Language support
Verbs für summarizing a dialogue
to mention
to insist
to disagree
to complain

Checklist: Summary p. 145

B4 Use your notes to write a summary.

The Proprietor Shall I ask him if he wants anything?
Anna Leave him just now.
The Proprietor Do you have any inside
5   information?
You must have an idea.
The British police must have an idea.
Has he done something awful?
No I actually don't want to know.
10 **Anna** Really I'm only here to establish if he's our responsibility.
Once I've done that I'll be out of your hair.[1]
The Proprietor Oh, he's definitely British.
I'll go further than that. He's English. I'd put
15   my shirt on it.[2]
I haven't lived in England since I was a tiny boy.
Who'd want to?
Really.
20 I occasionally go to London on business.
Dearie me.[3]
But I can tell an Englishman when I see one.
We still carry a certain bearing.[4]
Wouldn't you say?
25 **Anna** I don't know. I'm not an expert. I'm just … I'm really just a … it's quite an unusual job for me, in fact. It's not part of my regular duties.
(…)

30   *The Proprietor exits.*
He returns with a tray and a coffee.
He puts it down in front of her.
The Proprietor Will there be anything else?
Anna No. I'm fine. Thank you. This is fine.
35   Thank you.
The Proprietor remains for a moment
Anna takes out her purse.
She takes out some money, offers it to him.
Thank you.
40 **The Proprietor** It's not necessary to offer me a gratuity. I am the proprietor, madam.
Anna Oh, I'm so sorry.
The Proprietor If there's nothing else.
Anna No. No. I'm fine. I'm sorry.
45 **The Proprietor** It's not necessary to be sorry for offering me a gratuity, madam.
Anna Right. Silly.

The Proprietor exits.
The Man comes back over to Anna and sits
50 *down.*
The Man I've been thinking.
I'm wondering if I might be from Bristol.
Or at least the West Country*.
Cheltenham, or Swindon, or Gloucester.
55 **Anna** Right.
The Man It's the landscape. It's … soft, and I do seem to have a sense of low hills, woodland and mists … which is –

[1] **to be out of so.'s hair** = to be gone and therefore no longer causing a nuisance to s.o.
[2] **I'd put my shirt on it** = I'd bet everything I have on it.
[3] **Dearie me** = Oh dear; expression of negative sentiment
[4] **to carry a certain bearing** = to have a sophisticated and distinguished manner

What is Britishness? Citizenship, values and identity

Anna You don't have a strong accent.
60 **The Man** That doesn't necessarily mean anything.
I may have lost the accent.
Or else I may be – you see I have money – maybe I'm middle-class.
65 Perhaps I'm a person from the West Country* but with a standard accent.
R.P.[5]
Neutral.
Anna I suppose it's worth following up.
70 **The Man** There's something else as well.
As I was standing there, smoking, and by the way I'm convinced now that I am a smoker, I saw a woman walking on the pasture. The woman from room one hundred and eight.
75 She was walking down the path towards the … what's that word – stream. And I had a feeling …
Anna The undertow.[6]
The Man That's right. And I thought to
80 myself, 'There she is, walking the downs[7].' The word 'downs' came to me. From nowhere.
But that's a West Country word, isn't it?
Anna You might be right.
85 **The Man** It might be nothing.
…
I just started to get a picture of myself.
As a boy, amongst a soft landscape.
And growing up, and needing to leave.
90 A sense of myself as a sailor, of some kind.
Of the pull of the sea.[8]
And a feeling that life held more for me.
Adventure.
Dolphins – a picture of dolphins amongst
95 the foam at the prow of a fast-moving boat.
The company of men.
It's all very vague, but …
What do you think.
(…)
100 **Anna** I was just thinking – about the breakfast – you mentioned you had the full English?
The Man You're worried about my health again.
Anna Well – yes – smoking, cholesterol …
105 No, it's just I wondered – the full English breakfast.[9]
I wondered.

Is that what you've had every morning.
The Man Since I've been here.
110 **Anna** I just wonder if that – might mean you're English. If you see what I mean.
The Man I do.
Anna You're a man who eats a full English breakfast. That's your preference.
115 **The Man** Although I always dither[10] over the continental.[11]
Anna Maybe in your previous – maybe – before – maybe –
The Man Maybe.
120 But then – what if I was the sort of man who ate a continental breakfast out of concern for my health but deep down had always wanted to eat a full English? That would explain the dithering.
125 **Anna** You're right.
It's probably nothing.
The Man For example.
I've shown a marked[12] preference for coffee.
Even though they offer tea here.
130 But that's not very English, is it?
To drink coffee?
Anna Well, these days … I don't know, I drink coffee myself and I'm English. Well, as I say, Welsh.
135 **The Man** Welsh.
Anna Yes.
The Man If you hadn't said, I'd never have guessed.
Anna People don't.
140 **The Man** Where from in Wales?
Anna You wouldn't know it.
The Man I suppose not.
Anna To be honest, I say I'm Welsh, my father came from Wales. I was actually brought up
145 in Essex.
So … whatever that means.
And then I went to school in Yorkshire.
Nuns.
And then I went to university in Brighton.
150 And then I joined the Diplomatic Service, so I've lived in Tel Aviv and in Gaberone and now here I am in France.
But if pressed
I think of myself as Welsh.
155 Whatever that means.
Something of a pause.

[5] **R.P.** = received pronunciation; a way of speaking British English which is seen as using standard pronunciation in the UK
[6] **undertow** = strong current, hidden deep beneath the surface of the water and moving in the opposite direction to the water above
[7] **(the) downs** = *here:* a large grassy and slightly hilly area
[8] **the pull of the sea** = the longing that some people (esp. sailors) feel to return to the sea
[9] **full English breakfast** = a breakfast of bacon, sausage, fried egg, baked beans etc. traditionally eaten in England
[10] **dither** = *here:* hesitate due to uncertainty
[11] **continental (breakfast)** = a breakfast of cold meats, cheese, bread rolls, croissants, jam etc
[12] **marked** = *here:* strong

What is Britishness? Citizenship, values and identity

Let's carry on.
I mean, there isn't much more to do.
I think we've established that you're Eng-
160   lish.
Quite possibly from the West Country.
Probably middle-class, professional.
At some point you may have worked on the sea.
165   We have some material on tape for the forensic experts to study. I think it's a safe bet that you're the responsibility of the British Embassy.
The Man   I can't argue with that.
170   **Anna**   All I need to do now, really, is to establish some details about your arrival here. And then I have everything I need.

B5   a) **Pair work:** Focus on one of the passages from the extract (ll. 1–XX; ll. XX–XY; ll. YY–ZZ):
Read your passage and note down what you learn about the two characters in your passage.
b) In class, compare your first impressions of the characters.
c) Read the info-box on stage directions and explain what the advantages or disadvantages of stage directions may be.

Info: Stage directions

In addition to the lines of the dialogue, many dramatic texts also include stage directions. These are additional words or sentences by the playwright – usually written in brackets or italics – that are supposed to help with performing the play. Not every playwright includes stage directions in his text. Even if there are stage directions, they can vary considerably – both in the amount and in the content. They can range from very basic information on when certain characters are supposed to enter or exit the stage to highlighting pauses or describing a character's supposed facial expressions, gestures and posture or the tone of his/her voice. Stage directions can also be used to give a detailed description of the setting and therefore the stage design.

Example from Peter Nichols' play *A Day in the Death of Joe Egg*

BRI comes on without warning. Shouts at audience.
BRI: That's enough! *(Pause. Almost at once, louder.)* I said enough! *(Pause. Stares at audience. He is thirty-three but looks younger. Hardly ever at rest, acts being maladroit[1] but the act is skilful. Clowning may give way to ineffectual hectoring and then self-piteous[2] gloom.)*
Another word and you'll all be here till five o'clock. Nothing to me, is it? I've got all the time in the world. *(Moves across without taking his eyes off them.)* I didn't even get to the end of the corridor before there was such a din all the other teachers started opening their doors as much as to say what the hell's going on there's SOMEBODY'S TALKING NOW! *(Pause, stares again, like someone facing a mad dog.)* Who was it? You? You, Mister Man? …

---

[1] **maladroit** = *formal:* clumsy
[2] **self-piteous** = behaving as if your situation is worse than other people's and that people should feel sorry for you

d) **Pair work:** Go through your passage again add stage directions that reflect your understanding of the text and show how the characters feel.
e) **Group work:** Stage a dramatic reading of the whole extract based on your stage directions.
f) Discuss how the dramatic reading has improved your understanding of the characters and their relationship to each other.

What is Britishness? Citizenship, values and identity

Analysis

B6 At the end of the scene, Anna concludes that "it's a safe bet that you're the responsibility of the British Embassy" (ll. 166–168).
Analyze the extract to show how the characters come to this conclusion.
In order to do that, examine
- each character's assumptions about the man's identity. Also consider how they approach the question (logic? intuition?).
- what qualifies someone as being British in their view

These tips can help you organize your work:

a) It is helpful to look at each character's input, approach to the question and views on Britishness separately first. In order to do that, find relevant passages from the text for each character.

b) Examine how their choice of words and manner of speaking reflect how convinced they are of their conclusions.

Language support:

Very convinced ⟵⟶ not quite sure

is, has, …	modals like might, should, ought to …
statements	questions
words like definitely, surely, certainly	words like maybe, probably, possibly, presumably …
expressions like I know, I am certain that, …	expressions like I believe, I suppose, …

c) Organize your findings in a grid:

	Anna	The Proprietor	The Man
their assumptions about the man's identity		is convinced that the man is English – "I can tell an Englishman when I see one" (l. 22) – he uses his intuition, does not give reasons for his assumption …	
their ideas about what qualifies someone as being British			a certain landscape he feels connected to because of his origin (cf. l. 56) …
how convinced they seem to be of the conclusions they reach and how this is reflected in their choice of words and their manner of speaking	not very convinced: frequent use of the word "maybe" (l …) …		

B7 Now you can write a text analysis. Analyze how the characters – including the man himself – see the man's identity.

Creative writing

B8 In her function as an employee of the British Consulate, Anna has to report back to her superiors. Write her formal letter in which she explains her judgement concerning the man's identity.

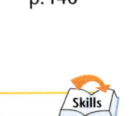

Skills
Checklist:
Text analysis
p. 146

Skills
Checklist:
Formal letter
p. 152

2 What is Britishness? Citizenship, values and identity

Getting to the point

Pre-reading

C1 a) Read scene two of David Edgar's play "Testing the Echo". Test yourself and write down the answers to as many questions as you can.

b) Discuss which questions should or shouldn't be asked in order to establish whether someone should be granted citizenship of a country.

C2 a) Stage a dramatic reading of the extract. Divide the class into two groups – seven students who take over the roles of the characters and the rest as the audience.

b) Describe the effect this scene has on you as a member of the "audience".

Scene Two

Citizenship tests. Actors come on to the stage, barking questions at the audience. Gradually, an instrumental version of 'Jerusalem*' fades up behind them.

Teresa Who is head of the Church of England?
Farzana How many members are there in the Welsh assembly?
Syrus What is the distance from John O'Groats* to Land's End*?
Teresa Choose either kilometres or miles.
Robert What is the main function of the Council of Europe*?
Kirsty Tip: Do not confuse the Council of Europe with the Council of the European Union*.
Sushil How can you find a dentist?
A moment.
Ian Should a man be allowed to lock his wife or daughter in the house in order to prevent her disgracing him in public?
Robert Where does the word 'Canada' come from?
Ian What are the first three words of the US constitution?
Sushil When did the Danish women's national handball team win the world championships?
Farzana Name three low, German, mountain ranges.
A moment.
Kirsty What are the *two* key features of the civil service?
Teresa What *two* rights are limited to US citizens?
Syrus What did Johannes Gutenberg invent?
Ian What proportion of the UK population lives in Northern Ireland?
Sushil Why does the flag have thirteen stripes?
Robert List three ways in which you can protect the environment.
Farzana Why did the Huguenots come to Britain in the sixteenth and the eighteenth centuries?
Kirsty Which German composed the famous 'Ode to Joy' at the end of his Ninth Symphony?
Robert Which province has the most bilingual Canadians?
Teresa Name one of the authors of the Federalist Papers?
Syrus How would you react if your adult son said that he was homosexual?
Ian/Farzana Who do you go to if you have problems with your neighbour?
Enter an Asian woman in her thirties, dressed neatly in a blue suit, with a clipboard. She is an ASSISTANT REGISTRAR.

David Edgar (b.1948) was born in Birmingham and studied drama at Manchester University. After starting a career as a journalist, he became a full-time writer at the age of 24. He has frequently worked with the Royal Shakespeare Company during his career. His plays are often concerned with the different ways private and public life interact.

Comprehension

C3 Read scenes 23 and 24 from "Testing the Echo". Describe the situation and explain what the characters do.

Scene Twenty-Three

Child's bedroom. MAHMOOD *still there.* The WEBSITE *is testing* TETYANA.

Website The first type of question involves selecting one correct answer from four options.
Tetyana/Website Where is the Prime Minister's official home in London?
Website Downing Street*, Parliament Square, Richmond Terrace, Whitehall Place.
Tetyana I suppose to know this?
Website The next type of question involves deciding whether a statement is true or false. Citizens of the UK can vote in elections at the age of eighteen. True or false.
Tetyana True.
Website The next question type involves selecting two correct answers from four options. You should not select more or fewer answers than this!

Scene Twenty-Four

ESOL[1] *class.* EMMA (the teacher), TOBY, HALIMA, JASMINKA, BABA, RANJIT, DRAGOSLAV *and* NASIM.

Ranjit If you ask me, community is most important as a common bond of people share one place.
Emma And 'society'? What is the difference between community and society?
Pause.
'Between.' This or that. The difference of that from this.
Jasminka In my view maybe society … is many small, add up to big.
Emma You mean that all our communities/ add up -
Toby Our diverse communities.
Emma Good, good. And what about diversity?
Pause.
Well, in my opinion …
She waves round the class.
Baba ESOL class.
Emma Exactly. Indian, and Serbia, the Congo …
Gesture to JASMINKA.
Jasminka Kosova.
Emma Of course. And/Egypt …
Dragoslav (*muttered in Serbian*).
Nema zemlje Kosovo. [There is no country called Kosovo.]
Emma In English please, and I've missed somebody …
Dragoslav I say that Kosovo is not a country.
Emma Good example. Many differing opinions.
Dragoslav Forgive me say this, please.
Emma Which is what happens when you have diverse communities.
Halima I am so very sorry but is my opinion … I come to this country not for community diversity.
Emma Came. Go on.
Halima Good free of speech and assembly and religion, oh yes please. But most big matter, most …
Toby Important thing.
Halima Yes, important thing is government. I am from Somalia.
Emma Well, point taken. And 'values'. What are values?
Ranjit I think if you ask me …
Emma Yes?
Ranjit Values is all the words.
Emma 'Respect.' 'Freedom.' 'Justice.' Yes. Great point.
Pause.

---
[1] **ESOL** = English for Speakers of Other Languages

What is Britishness? Citizenship, values and identity

Are there any values that aren't there?
Slight pause.
Baba Religion.
Jasminka Parliament Westminster.
Emma Well, democracy's a value.
Toby Equality.
Emma Good. What is equality?
Ranjit Everybody is the same.
Emma Treated the same. So, for example, in this college, men and women are all paid the same for doing the same job. Paid equally.
Pause. The learners look at each other.
Except for Toby, who's a volunteer, so he doesn't get paid anything. Aaah.
All *(echoing)* Aaah.[2]
Halima Beg pardon.[3] You mean you pay same as Mr Chlebowski?
Emma Is this so terrible?
Halima But you have husband.
Emma Do you think that makes a difference?
Pause.
Ranjit In UK, the most rich person is the Queen.
Emma Some people think we shouldn't have a queen. That the monarchy – having kings and queens – is rather old-fashioned and outdated. Perhaps some of you agree with that?
The learners look at each other.
Well, fair enough. As Halima reminded us, you'll all be swearing oaths to be loyal to the Queen. So, moving quickly on to 'Justice' and 'Respect' …
TOBY *nudges her.* NASIM *is holding up her handout.*
Ah, Nasim.
Nasim You say we must take these pictures home.
Emma Yes, to choose the right words from the list.
Nasim I cannot take these pictures home into my house. Forgive me please.
She stands, takes the pictures to EMMA, *and hands them to her.*
Emma Well, if …
Nasim *(turning to* DRAGOSLAV*).* You are Serbia?
DRAGOSLAV *nods.*
So many of my people die in Bosnia and Kosova.

[2] **Aaah** = said with long, falling voice to show sympathy; can be used ironically
[3] **beg pardon** = *here:* polite way of showing you disagree with what so. has said. Correct usage = beg your pardon.

Analysis

C4 Analyze the way the characters speak and behave and how that reflects their ideas, values and reasons for becoming British. Consider both the dialogue and stage directions.

Comment

C5 In the Citizenship test and the ESOL class, the immigrants are confronted with a number of facts and values that are considered relevant to becoming British. Assess how important and justified you feel these criteria are for establishing Britishness.

3 Them and us

Getting started

A1 a) Get into groups of four (home group). A British journalist asks you to name and describe the different social groups within German society in a few words. Answer spontaneously.

b) Watch the video and compare the interviewees' answers with your own from A1a). Speculate about reasons for their reactions.

www.diesterweg.de/cta/74003/links

A2 **Jigsaw:** Get into four expert groups with at least one student from each home group: watch your video(s).

a) In key words note down the main aspects mentioned.

b) Watch your video again and write down useful phrases and/or words related to the topic "class".

c) Compare your findings with those of the other members of your expert group and add any missing information to your own.

Group 1: "What is the working class?"
www.diesterweg.de/cta/74003/links

Group 2: "What is the middle class?"
www.diesterweg.de/cta/74003/links

Group 3: "What is the upper class?"
www.diesterweg.de/cta/74003/links

Group 4: "You can change your class" and "Class doesn't matter any more."
www.diesterweg.de/cta/74003/links

A3 Get back into your home groups (see A1). Each expert presents his/her results.

a) First consider in what way your findings are related and then discuss how you can best present the results of your group work on a poster.

b) Create a poster using as many of the new words and phrases as you can.

c) **Gallery walk:** Study the other posters and discuss which of them best illustrates the results.
Consider the following questions: Is it well-structured/concise/comprehensive/informative/precise/clear/well-designed …?

d) In class, discuss to what extent the results shown on the posters can be related to German society.

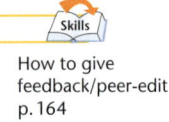

Skills
How to give feedback/peer-edit
p. 164

Them and us: Class matters in Britain

3

> **Tip**
> * means this term is explained in the Names and terms section on pages 182–190

Skills
How to describe pictures p. 172

A4 Many people in Britain would recognize this photograph, taken in 1937 outside the ground where an Eton* vs Harrow* cricket match was taking place. It has been used repeatedly in the media, and even on book covers.

a) Describe the photo in detail.

b) List features of the boys' clothes and body language which indicate differences in class.

c) **Freeze frame:** in groups of five bring the photograph to life and voice each boy's thoughts.

d) Comment on how well your classmates' freeze frames illustrate the relationship(s) between the boys.

A5 a) Read the extract from Ferdinand Mount's "Mind the Gap: The New Class Divide in Britain" (2005) and find a suitable title.

b) Find pictures of the fashion items mentioned in the text, find an appropriate place on your poster and stick them on.

c) Explain why Mount speaks of "a class system in clothes" (l. 28–29). Relate your findings to the photograph.

[…] Now let us take a cross-section of passers-by in a London street today and begin to sort them. First, there are the men in standard lounge suits'[1], from Austin Reed* or Cecil Gee*. They will be hatless and wearing pale shirts and darkish ties. Their shoes may be polished. These men, we assume, will be working in banks, insurance offices, law firms or the civil service.

Then we see men who are on average somewhat younger, in baggy Armani-type[2] suits with loafers[3] on their feet. Their shirts are likely to be of a darker colour and half of them won't be wearing a tie. These are sometimes described as belonging to the New Class. They work in the media, advertising, PR[4], graphic design or publishing. They too will be hatless.

Then we can see men in track-suits, or track-suit bottoms and T-shirts if fine, or until recently shell suits[5]. They will be wearing trainers and possibly a baseball cap or a hoodie[6] of the type traditionally worn by serial rapists. If the wearer is under 25, the baseball cap may be worn reversed, and he may also sport[7] an earring. All ages may well be shaven-headed.

Don't we have here the makings of a class system in clothes at least as strongly marked as the dress code of the 1930s? I am not confident enough to trace a similar system in women's clothes of either period, except to say that the similarities in style (not in quality or cut of cloth) between women of different classes in any period usually seem to us more strongly marked than their differences. In the late 1920s, for example, every woman from the Duchess of York (later the Queen Mother) downwards will be wearing a cloche hat. My grandmother, no fashion plate[8], is wearing one as she strides over the grass between my uncle and my grandfather in the photograph I mentioned. Ten years later, women of all classes will be switching over to turbans; skirt lengths similarly go up and down according to the dictates of fashion rather than social class.

[1] **lounge suit** = a man's smart suit (jacket and trousers) of the sort usually worn in a business environment
[2] **Armani-type** = cut in the style of suits made by the exclusive Italian fashion house Armani
[3] **loafers** = smart-casual shoes of a type sometimes worn with modern business dress
[4] **PR** = Public Relations
[5] **shell suit** = a type of suit, originally intended for sports use, often made from brightly coloured and shiny synthetic material and very popular in the 1980s
[6] **hoodie** = sweatshirt with an attached hood
[7] **to sport** = to wear
[8] **no fashion plate** = not very attractive

Them and us: Class matters in Britain

[9] **straight** = *here:* heterosexual
[10] **Guards officers** = officers of Guards regiments of the British Army

Even if you concentrate on the young – who are famously addicted to an international classless style of dress – you can still find class markers today, fainter perhaps but not entirely erased. For example, straight[9] upper-class young men these days will certainly possess several pairs of jeans, but on top, instead of a T-shirt, they will wear a polo shirt or a casual Friday* shirt from Boden*. And instead of a leather jacket, incongruously they will sometimes sport with their jeans a boating jacket* of the type worn by Guards officers[10] in summers long gone by. There are complicated feelings at work here, perhaps a desire to be both hip and cool and at the same time keep their distance and retain a separate group identity. At the weekend in London, upper-class men of all ages may still dress as if they were going for a walk in the country – tweed jacket, corduroys often of a lurid canary colour, and even a flat cap*.

A6 a) Consider what fashion items and brands might be regarded as indicators of social status in Germany. Compare them with those in Britain.

b) Find more class indicators other than fashion.

Class matters in Britain

The social structure of the United Kingdom has historically been highly influenced by the concept of social class, which still affects British society in the early 21st century. Traditionally British society was categorized into three different classes, the *upper class*, the *middle class* and the *working class*. As the middle class has over time become the largest group, it is sometimes further divided into three sub-categories: *the upper-middle, the middle-middle and the lower-middle class*.

Although a precise definition of class is problematic, some factors are usually seen as defining indicators for the determination of class:

- family background: aristocratic, academic, uneducated, …
- education: public school* or state school*; grammar* or comprehensive* school; Oxbridge*; no further education, …
- occupation: government official, factory worker, doctor, hairdresser, …
- income: high (starting at £ 60,000 a year), low (less than £ 8,000 a year), …
- housing: estate, detached*, semi-detached*, terraced* houses, high-rise tower blocks, …
- life-style: sports, clothes, hobbies, …
- language: regional accents, choice of words, register, …

Here are more detailed characteristics for each of the classes:

Upper Class:
- by far the smallest group
- mainly aristocracy and landowners:
  - the nobility: royal family, Viscount Linley, Duke and Duchess of Kent, Earl of Glasgow, Baron Trefgarne, …
  - the landed gentry; they are the typical "country gentlemen" who own and administer land

Upper-middle class:
- top managers, CEOs, high-ranking government officials, business executives, barristers, …
- important stratum in society with a lot of influence in politics, administration, business, civil service, engineers, the world of finance.

Them and us: Class matters in Britain

Middle-middle class:
- professionals (e.g. doctors, architects, solicitors, teachers, etc.), highly-skilled employees, lower and middle management, …

Lower-middle class:
- biggest stratum of British society
- lesser officials, owners of small businesses, office workers, skilled workers like builders and electricians, …

Working class:
- factory workers, waiters, shop assistants, the so-called semi-skilled
- cleaners, rubbish collectors, farm labourers, the unskilled
- close family and community ties
- more separated from the other groups than in other countries
- "us against them"-attitude towards the other groups
- hardest hit by unemployment

In 1998, the British Prime Minister at the time Tony Blair* famously proclaimed the end of the British class system by saying: "We're all middle class now." Although the traditional British social divisions into upper, middle and working class are indeed out of date in the 21st century as they no longer reflect modern occupations or lifestyles, results of a recent study point to an even more complex class system.

A survey of people around Britain carried out by the BBC in 2011 and published in 2013 came up with seven new classes that reflect British society today. Here they are in alphabetical order:
- elite: 6% of the population
- emergent service workers: 19% of the population
- established middle class: 25% of the population
- new affluent workers: 15% of the population
- precariat: 15% of the population
- technical middle class: 6% of the population
- traditional working class: 14% of the population

Tip
For more information on class see pages 62–63

3

Them and us: Class matters in Britain

Practice section

Pre-reading

B1 a) You are going to read a newspaper article about the British working class, middle class and upper class.

Pair work: look at the words and expressions taken from the article. If necessary, consult a dictionary. Then speculate about which class they might refer to. Give reasons.

snobbery	ostentatious	camaraderie	lineage and acreage	to gate someone
	to ooze entitlement	detached	to squeeze into sth.	pebble-dash
fastidious chatelains	cleanliness	crockery	to suck rags	affluent	unsullied
	posh	blowsy plants	money was tight	proletariat	pecking order
	semi-detached	inferiority complex	showy	to fraternize	collieries
	natural solidarity	shipyards	terraced homes	impecunious	enclave

b) Read the headline and the first paragraph on each class. Identify the text type by using the list below.

> editorial • column • news item • press release • letter to the editor • comment • review • personal • account • report • interview

---

The Independent

Three views from across Britain's class divide

Working-class camaraderie, Fifties middle-class suburbia and the complications of life in the upper-classes
By Kevin Maguire, David Randall and Matthew Bell
Sunday, 20 March 2011

Working-class

*There's nothing romantic about poverty, but **Kevin Maguire** regrets the passing of genuine social camaraderie*

[…] Money was tight in our family in South Shields*
5 on Tyneside* in the 1960s and 1970s. Eight of us, two parents and six kids (I was the third), squeezed into a three-bed council house*. Dad was a miner, and

Kevin Maguire (right) regrets the fading of solidarity in the working-class community he knew in his youth

mam[1] got up early to clean houses in the posh bit of town and worked in the then Wright's biscuit factory.

We were bought new clothes at Christmas, Easter and the end of the six-week summer holiday to go back to school [...]. Holidays, abroad or here in Britain, were for mythical figures we read about in the Daily Mirror* or watched on TV. But we didn't suck rags and it wasn't the hole in the road with a piece of tarpaulin [...].

I do, however, grimace a little recalling how we once had no writing paper for my homework. Thankfully, the impecunious working class cherished cleanliness: I handed in the sums on a Kleenex* tissue. Back then we just got on with life like everybody else on the Whiteleas estate*. There was no self-pity, no hang-ups[2] and no inferiority complex[3]. We were working class. I don't recall any pride or shame in that. It was what we were. End of.[4]

I'm wary of peering through rose-tinted spectacles to that era when I prefer lying on a settee in my centrally heated sitting room enjoying the footie[5] on subscription Sky Sports to huddling around the coal fire and watching a cheesy[6] soap on BBC.

Yet there was a genuine sense of community, a natural solidarity that the working class created and which a more affluent middle class, which celebrates the individual, never experienced. The mines and shipyards of South Shields produced industrial workers who knew they needed to work and strike together, creating a camaraderie which extended beyond clocking-off[7].

I, like every lad I knew, feared the man who knocked on our door complaining we'd broken a window or woken him while he tried to sleep after the night shift, because our parents sided[8] with him. Similarly the teacher who complained about bad behaviour at school would find parents who sided with them instead of a dad who wanted to knock[9] the living daylights out of them in the playground.

Working-class values survive and indeed flourish in parts of our country, although they're in retreat. The closure of big workplaces, including the collieries and shipyards, is a factor. Toiling in twos and threes in small businesses will never engender the collective values of, for example, a thousand men hewing coal half a mile down into the earth and four miles out under the North Sea. The deliberate marginalisation of trade unions by successive governments and employers has played its part, too, denting the confidence of individuals by isolating them instead of bringing workers together.

[...] A sizeable number who think – or at least tell pollsters[10] – that they're middle class must be on wages in socio-economic groups that even Ed Miliband* would not include when he extends the squeezed middle to include everyone he hopes will vote Labour.

Perhaps the X Factor* generation feels there's something embarrassing about being working class. The comment attributed to Maggie Thatcher* about how a man older than 26 using a bus must be a failure may be apocryphal, but she, John Major*, Tony Blair*, Gordon Brown* and, for obvious reasons, Buller Boy* David Cameron* champion the deceit of a classless Britain even though inequality has never been greater.

[...] Class isn't whether you call a mid-day meal dinner or lunch or a toilet a lavatory, but life chances. That includes how long we live, when a bloke in the grittier[11] parts of Glasgow may die 13 years earlier than a resident of well-heeled[12] Kensington and Chelsea. Class should matter more in politics than it does, yet it's shunned[13] by politicians. They are happy to talk about gender, race and sexuality, and then run away from discussing, let alone confronting, a major dividing line in society.

I regret the fading of solidarity in the working-class community I knew in my youth.

What I regret most, however, is the conspiracy to avoid class as an issue because it's convenient for an influential, powerful and wealthy few to pretend it doesn't exist. And so a far larger number of people become confused about who and what they are and, most importantly of all, how to make Britain fairer.

Kevin Maguire is associate editor (politics) of the 'Daily Mirror'

---

[1] **mam** = mum
[2] **hang-up** = a feeling of fear, embarrassment or anxiety about sth.
[3] **inferiority complex** = an strong feeling of being worth less than other people
[4] **End of.** = end of story (i.e. there's nothing more to say)
[5] **footie** = *informal:* football
[6] **cheesy** = lacking style or quality
[7] **to clock-off** = to mechanically or electronically register that one is finishing one's working day
[8] **to side with so.** = to support so. in a dispute or argument
[9] **to knock the living daylights out of so.** = to hit so. very hard
[10] **pollster** = person or organization who asks a lot of people their opinion about sth.
[11] **gritty** = *here:* more deprived
[12] **well-heeled** = comfortably wealthy
[13] **to shun sth.** = to avoid sth.

Them and us: Class matters in Britain

Middle-class

Fifties suburbia was all unwritten rules and snobbery. **David Randall** *recalls an almost lost world*

Class, to me, always means crockery and, in particular, the "workmen's cups" in which my mother served tea to handymen and the like. Their existence ensured no working-class lips soiled the family's utensils, and they were even kept on a separate, lower, shelf. If that makes my mother seem an intolerable snob, you hadn't met our neighbours. Several would greet workmen with the news that, on no account, was the loo to be used. Should the need arise, these fastidious chatelaines[1] would add, there are excellent facilities at the pub up the road. Thus were their avocado-coloured ceramics[2] unsullied by the proletariat.

This is how it was in the Fifties and Sixties in Worcester Park, a Tudorbethan* enclave laid out in the 1930s. On one side of the railway line were mainly terraced homes, which gradually, as you crossed towards our side of the tracks, shaded into semi-detacheds, which became larger and larger and, finally, detached. Our road, Edenfield Gardens, was the local Mason-Dixie Line*: on our side of the street, semi's[3]; on the other, detached[4]. Fraternising was frequent, but tensions were there. My brother struck perhaps the smartest blow in our road's muted class war when an especially appalling woman announced to him that her husband had booked a family holiday in the Canaries, then an ostentatious luxury. "Oh," he replied, "our milkman's just come back from there."

The detached homes had a certain type of name – "Tall Trees", or "Hilltops" – suggesting to the distant correspondent they commanded several choice Home Counties* acres. (Another, "Pantiles", was treasured by us, if only because we enjoyed removing the "L" from time to time.) Ours merely had a number, one of many signs that you had not quite "arrived", others being net curtains, pebble-dash[5] and garden gnomes. Front gardens in our road had to be neat (otherwise you were letting some unseen side[6] down), but not showy[7]. The place for the trays of blowsy plants bought at the local nurseries was the back garden, not the front. That would have been vulgar.

This was part of the unwritten Common Law* of the suburbs, adherence to which ensured no one thought you common. The dos and don'ts of the suburban Sunday featured strongly, which was strange because, apart from the church organist two doors down, we knew no one who was anything other than irreligious. Thus, on the seventh day, we boys could play in the garden, but not outside. You could saw, but not hammer. You could raise[8] a frame for runner beans, but not your voice. And bonfires were for Saturdays.

It was, then, a childhood of grammar school* and golf club, of steak-house meals and two-star hotels. Its watchword[9] was a lack of adventure – both socially (I knew no one you could remotely call working class), educationally (there were but three books in the house) and sexually. When I was 14 or so, I started meeting a girl in the park. She had dark hair, and was pretty as a picture[10]. Unfortunately, like most pictures, she was also painted, and, to my parents, any girl wearing make-up at the age of 14 was plainly up to no good[11]. Alas, I was gated[12], and the opportunity to find out if they were right was lost. You might think an upbringing so narrowly middle class was ideal preparation for Cambridge, but it wasn't. Suddenly, I was mixing, and competing, with the products of public schools*. They oozed entitlement, but often lacked real self-confidence, the giveaway being their anxious probing to discover where you went to school, how much your parents had, etc. Old boys[13] from the really big schools were

David Randall graduates from University

---

1 **fastidious chatelaines** = women who expect everything to be perfect in their homes down to the last detail
2 **avocado-coloured ceramics** = bathroom suites in a shade of green very popular in the 1970s
3 **semi's** = short for semi-detached houses
4 **detached** = *here:* of a house: sharing no walls with its neighbours
5 **pebble-dash** = a substance made of cement combined with lots of small pebbles which is spread over the outside walls of a house
6 **to let the side down** = *informal:* to work less hard than the people who you are working with
7 **showy** = brightly coloured and attractive
8 **to raise** = *here:* to put up
9 **watchword** = a word or phrase which expresses an attitude or intention
10 **pretty as a picture** = very attractive
11 **to be up to no good** = to intend to do sth. wrong or secret
12 **to be gated** = to be grounded; to be not allowed to go out
13 **old boys** = former pupils of a boys' public school

not like this, and my best friend in college was an old Harrovian*. His parents bought him a Bentley* for his 21st. They had even more money than my girlfriend's parents, who had homes in three counties. But it was always hard, for all their consideration, to feel anything other than a poor relation when visiting. "Do you ride?" one of my girlfriend's relatives once asked, a question, I immediately realised, not designed to find out if I had a bicycle.

I graduated, joined the local paper, and immediately fell in love with the first person I interviewed. She was a nurse, her father a clerk of works[14], and her mother a woman who, at 13, was an under-house parlour maid[15]. When we told my parents we were engaged, you could have cut the atmosphere[24] with a special atmosphere cutter. The following morning, my mother brought me tea. "We thought you'd do better for yourself than that," she said. How wrong she was. Within a few months, they had fallen[25] for her nearly as completely as I had – proof, I like to think, that there are, even for inhabitants of the Worcester Parks, forces more powerful than class.

[14] **clerk of works** = a manager on a building site who makes sure that work is carried out properly and safely
[15] **under-house parlour maid** = the deputy to the house parlour maid in a smaller household. The parlour maid cleaned living areas and served refreshments.
[16] **one could cut the atmosphere** = the atmosphere was very tense
[17] **to fall for so.** = to fall in love with so.

Upper-class

Silly voice, pink shirt, **Matthew Bell** *is definitely posh. But the higher you go, the more complicated it gets*

The trouble with class is you only know what you're given. In my case, that was an expensive education and a decent grounding in bridge[1]. Oh, and I do like vintage cars. In fact I own a couple. According to my colleagues, that makes me "posh". Never mind, they say, when I ask what the similarities are to Victoria Beckham*. You own a 1923 Delage* – of course you're posh.

Well, I'm the first to admit I have a silly voice. And I do own a pink shirt. But to be a member of the upper classes takes more than that. There's clearly still an elite in Britain, one not defined by influence or wealth. So how come nobody in today's poll defines themselves as upper class? One reason could be that the upper classes don't do market research. Another, that to label yourself upper class is a sure-fire sign that you're not – unless you're Julian Fellowes*, in which case you modestly insist you're at the bottom of the top. The poshest people I know were busy estuarising[2] their accents in the sixth form. It doesn't help that the gradations of class become impossibly complex at the top, where money and power increasingly jostle[3] with lineage and acreage. David Cameron* has all four, which to many makes him the definition of upper class. And yet, in certain drawing rooms, he is irredeemably middle class – his father a stockbroker, his mother a magistrate.

In the end, class is relative. We are born into certain positions on various pecking orders[4] – wealth, education, civility – of which we gradually become more aware. The hope is that we can die somewhere else on those scales if we wish. In the meantime we're left with a problem of terminology. Yes, I started out more fortunate than some, though every sports day, when elaborate picnics would emerge from F&M hampers*, it was evident that I was by no means the luckiest. Because as Joanna Lumley* put it, you don't have to be posh to be privileged.

[1] **bridge** = card game beloved by the upper classes
[2] **to estuarise** = to change the accent to mimic a lower-class style of speech known as "estuary English"
[3] **to jostle** = to compete
[4] **pecking order** = hierarchy

Comprehension: Summary writing

B2 A model approach: How to summarize a text.

A summary of a text is for someone who has not read the text but needs to know the essence of what it is about. If you want to identify the main elements of a newspaper article, you will need to answer these wh-questions:

Who	is the author?	
When	was the article published?	
Where	was it published?	} introductory sentence
What	type of article is it?	
What	topic does the article deal with?	
What	is the content of the article?	
What	is the author's opinion or point of view?	

Study the following step-by step approach on how to summarize Randall's personal recount of middle-class life. You will then have to write a summary of one of the other two accounts.

a) Read the text carefully and highlight key words and/or key sentences.

b) Divide the text into sub-sections

c) Find an appropriate sentence or some keywords to summarize each sub-section.

d) Answer the wh-questions above using key words.

e) Write an introductory sentence using your answers to the first five wh-questions.

f) Write the main body of the summary.

highlighted key words and/or key sentences	sub-sections and summaries
Middle-class *Fifties suburbia was all unwritten rules and snobbery. David Randall recalls an almost lost world* Class, to me, always means crockery and, in particular, the "workmen's cups" in which my mother served tea to handymen and the like. Their existence ensured no working-class lips soiled the family's utensils, and they were even kept on a separate, lower, shelf. If that makes my mother seem an intolerable snob, you hadn't met our neighbours. Several would greet workmen with the news that, on no account, was the loo to be used. Should the need arise, these fastidious chatelaines would add, there are excellent facilities at the pub up the road. Thus were their avocado-coloured ceramics unsullied by the proletariat.	a clear separation between the classes: the middle-class is not willing to share crockery or toilets with members of the working-class

Them and us: Class matters in Britain

highlighted key words and/or key sentences	sub-sections and summaries
This is how it was ==in the Fifties and Sixties== in Worcester Park, a Tudorbethan enclave laid out in the 1930s. On one side of the railway line were mainly ==terraced homes==, which gradually, as you crossed towards our side of the tracks, shaded into ==semi-detacheds==, which became larger and larger and, finally, ==detached==. Our road, Edenfield Gardens, was the local Mason-Dixie line: on our side of the street, semi's; on the other, detached. Fraternising was frequent, but tensions were there. My brother struck perhaps the smartest blow in ==our road's muted class war== when an especially appalling woman announced to him that her husband had booked a family holiday in the Canaries, then an ostentatious luxury. "Oh," he replied, "our milkman's just come back from there." The detached homes had a certain type of name – "Tall Trees", or "Hilltops" – suggesting to the distant correspondent they commanded several choice Home Counties acres. (Another, "Pantiles", was treasured by us, if only because we enjoyed removing the "L" from time to time.) Ours merely had a number, one of many ==signs that you had not quite "arrived"==, others being ==net curtains, pebble-dash and garden gnomes==. Front gardens in our road had to be neat (otherwise you were letting some unseen side down), but not showy. The place for the trays of blowsy plants bought at the local nurseries was the back garden, not the front. That would have been vulgar.	types of houses as class indicators: terraced for working-class; semi-detached and detached for middle-class differences within the middle-class middle-class indicators: • names for upper middle-class homes • features such as net curtains for the lower middle-class
This was part of the ==unwritten Common Law of the suburbs==, adherence to which ensured no one thought you common. ==The dos and don'ts of the suburban Sunday== featured strongly, which was strange because, apart from the church organist two doors down, we knew no one who was anything other than irreligious. Thus, on the seventh day, we boys could play in the garden, but not outside. You could saw, but not hammer. You could raise a frame for runner beans, but not your voice. And bonfires were for Saturdays.	• certain rules of behaviour on Sundays …
It was, then, ==a childhood of grammar school and golf club, of steak-house meals and two-star hotels==. Its watchword was a ==lack of adventure== – both ==socially== (I knew no one you could remotely call working class), ==educationally== (there were but three books in the house) and ==sexually==. When I was 14 or so, I started meeting a girl in the park. She had dark hair, and was pretty as a picture. Unfortunately, like most pictures, she was also painted, and, ==to my parents, any girl wearing make-up at the age of 14 was plainly up to no good==. Alas, I was gated, and the opportunity to find out if they were right was lost.	• a boring and unadventurous life in every respect … • make-up on young girls seen as immoral.

highlighted key words and/or key sentences	sub-sections and summaries
You might think an upbringing so narrowly middle class was ideal preparation for Cambridge, but it wasn't. Suddenly, I was mixing, and competing, with the products of public schools. They oozed entitlement, but often lacked real self-confidence, the giveaway being their anxious probing to discover where you went to school, how much your parents had, etc. Old boys from the really big schools were not like this, and my best friend in college was an old Harrovian. His parents bought him a Bentley for his 21st. They had even more money than my girlfriend's parents, who had homes in three counties. But it was always hard, for all their consideration, to feel anything other than a poor relation when visiting. "Do you ride?" one of my girlfriend's relatives once asked, a question, I immediately realised, not designed to find out if I had a bicycle.	differences between the middle-class and the upper-classes: • privileged • very wealthy • expensive hobbies like horse-riding
I graduated, joined the local paper, and immediately fell in love with the first person I interviewed. She was a nurse, her father a clerk of works, and her mother a woman who, at 13, was an under-house parlour maid. When we told my parents we were engaged, you could have cut the atmosphere with a special atmosphere cutter. The following morning, my mother brought me tea. "We thought you'd do better for yourself than that," she said. How wrong she was. Within a few months, they had fallen for her nearly as completely as I had – proof, I like to think, that there are, even for inhabitants of the Worcester Parks, forces more powerful than class.	to the initial disappointment of his parents, Randall falls in love with a working-class girl

The **introductory sentence** of a summary should include the author, title, type of text, the place and date of publication, and the main idea.

Here is an example:

In this extract from the article "Three views from across Britain's class divide", published in "The Independent" on 20th March 2011, David Randall recounts his suburban middle-class upbringing by differentiating between the classes and making fun of class distinctions as he perceives them.

The **main body** of the summary, which connects the highlighted passages and the summaries of the sub-sections. Your main body could begin like this:

For Randall, who grew up in the 50s and 60s, a clear separation between the classes became obvious through his mother's and other middle-class members' unwillingness to share crockery or the toilets with people from the working class. According to the author, …

Them and us: Class matters in Britain

B3 Divide the class into two groups. Each group should work on one of the other two sections of the article.

a) Read your section of the article carefully and highlight key words and/or key sentences.

b) Divide your part of the article into sub-sections.

c) Answer the wh-questions using key words.

d) Find an appropriate sentence or keywords to summarize each sub-section.

e) Write an introductory sentence.

B4 Compare your introductory sentence with those of others in your group and agree on the best one. Write a new one if necessary.

B5 Now write the main body of the summary of your extract.

It needs to be clear in your summary that the article presents the author's personal and subjective view. The following phrases and the checklist will help you to achieve this:

Skills
Checklist: Summary p. 145

Language support	
The author believes … claims … emphasizes … states … points out …	*From the author's point of view, …* *According to the author/(name), …* *The author is of the opinion that …*

Checklist
- ✓ Use the simple present (careful: as the article is a personal account, some passages will have to be written in the simple past).
- ✓ Focus on essentials and leave out details.
- ✓ Don't quote from the text. Use your own words.
- ✓ Don't start analyzing the text.
- ✓ Don't give your personal opinion.
- ✓ Use connectives to link your sentences.

B6 **Pair work:** Find a partner who summarized a different section of the article. Read each other's summaries and identify major differences between the working class and the upper class as stated in the article.

3 Them and us: Class matters in Britain

Info: chav
The term "chav" has been the subject of much controversial discussion in the British media. Some commentators see its use as typical of class snobbery, of the upper and middle classes looking down on the lower classes. Others say that chav culture is not necessarily lower class but rather an easily identifiable aggressive attitude or behaviour which deserves to be criticized or parodied.

Comprehension

B7 a) Read the wikiHow article "How to become a Chavette".

b) Here are four introductory sentences. Choose the most appropriate and explain your choice.

1. In an ironic fashion the text from the website "wikiHow" deals with steps one should undertake to become a chavette.
2. The article, taken from the web page "wikiHow", is about a woman who wants to become a chavette.
3. Based on stereotypes the text from the website "wikiHow" gives ironic advice on how to become a chavette.
4. The text from "WikiHow" is very ironic and gives us a few good tips on how to change our lives.

c) Discuss your choices in class.

d) **Pair work:** Tell each other what characterizes chavs/chavettes.

B8 Analyze the tone of the text.

How to Become a Chavette (Female Chav)   wikiHow
                                                              _____ to do anything

You've decided that you want to become a chavette. Maybe it's because all of your friends are chavettes, or you realized you are one deep down. Whatever the reason, it's your choice.

Step 1 • Look Like a Chavette

1 Clothes: Invest in some skin tight leggings, most likely black ones. These are a 'must have' favourite – particularly among chubby[1] chavettes (usually young mums aged between 14 and 25). Remember in summer to get your toes out. Chavettes love to show their dirty, badly fake-tanned feet in their Primark* £1.99 sandals. A baby in a pram could also be classed as a piece of clothing among most chav colonies.

2 Make-up: Wear lots of liquid black eyeliner, liberally coated mascara (3–4 coats should do it) and *really* fake-looking false eyelashes from Superdrug*. Foundation is a must and should be reapplied frequently throughout the day – a nice tangerine/orange complexion is a chavette staple, as is a ridiculous fake tan. Blusher isn't usually used (much too healthy looking) and neither is a coloured lipstick. Stick to a death-pale concealer on the lips or legit death-pale lipstick – even better make it a white shade. Apply liberally.

3 Hair: Chavs were *once* known to have long hair tied into a side ponytail or bun, but now, it has been updated. Be addicted to your hair straighteners. You can never be too chav to straighten the f*** out of your hair. Dye your hair either bleached blonde, jet black (classic chavette!) or that red-purpley colour that has since been made popular amongst chavettes by well-known X-Factor* celebrities.

4 Jewellery: Chav etiquette calls on how one must look as rich as possible, even though this ironically makes them look really poor. Gold earrings from Argos* were once a firm must, but now the 'Cash-4-gold'* shops have spread around Great Britain like wild fire[2] – so chavs have resorted to selling off their Argos Gold jewellery (as well as gold family heirloom jewellery – stolen from their nan's[3] house and other pensioners) for a few quid, thus the chav-style has evolved onto Primark gold, Primark gold being fake – as with any high-street jewellery. High-street jewellery isn't 'chav' – but wearing lots of it at the same time is. Layer it, wear as much jewellery as much as possible, and remember fake diamantes should be heavily embellished on belts, hats, and belt-buckles etc.

---

[1] **chubby** = slightly fat
[2] **like wild fire** = very quickly
[3] **nan** = *informal:* grandmother

Them and us: Class matters in Britain

Step 2 • Get the Attitude

1. Chew chewing gum as much as possible.
2. Spit on the floor.
3. Swear in every sentence, especially the 'F' word.
4. Get to know the chavvy music e.g. Tinie Tempah or the majority of Ibiza mega-mixes.
5. Decide whether you are a racist chav or chav trying to fake being of black descent. Both are prominent in the complex chav kingdom depending on where you live.
6. Listen to music really loud on your earphones in the street, on the bus, or in your zuped up[4] chav-car. If the latter – windows down, even if it's freezing cold.
7. Shout a lot in public. Intimidation is key to chav-power.
8. Drink cans of Coke in the street (even better Stella*) and eat a bar of chocolate or crisps for snack time if you're at school. Never bring packed lunches – starve yourself and smoke where possible.
9. Be addicted to your phone/facebook. One must keep on top of[5] estate gossip and politics.
10. Most chavs have a stark need to reproduce, and it is drilled into them from childhood that it is the only reason to live – how else can you make money without having a job. Be benefit savvy[6].

[4] **zuped up** = *souped up*: fitted with after-market accessories and modifications, such as large exhaust canisters blue LED lighting, lowered suspension and large sound systems
[5] **keep on top of sth.** = *here*: obtain all the important information about sth.
[6] **savvy** = *informal*: knowledgable

Tips

- Don't go round declaring that you're a chav, they'll soon realize you're a fake and jump[7] you.
- Try to get a chav boyfriend, it will bode well[8] for you if you do this. Remember, single chavettes are seen as nothing but the local estate lesbian.
- To improve your chances of getting a chav boyfriend, put out on the first date (preferably at the bus station) or at a party.
- If you're rich – wear Ugg* boots at parties; leopard print ones in particular. These are seen as formal attire amongst the breed. Don't ever say you bought them with your own benefit-money – just say you stole them from a stupid cow[9] you smacked earlier, and laugh.
- Being clever is for geeks – so try to lower your IQ and for God's sake never admit to reading a book for fun.
- Swear frequently.
- Attack people frequently.
- Random tattoos are a nice touch. Be sure to get these out in the summer.
- Socialize at local chav hot-spots: the job centre, sexual health clinic, bus stations (as already mentioned) and McDonalds.

[7] **to jump so.** = to violently attack so.
[8] **to bode well** = to be a sign that sth. good will happen
[9] **cow** = *here, offensive*: an insulting term for a woman

B9 Read Polly Toynbee's article (on pp. 57–58) on chavs taken from "The Guardian".

Polly Toynbee

The Guardian, Tuesday 31 May 2011

Chav: the vile word at the heart of fractured Britain

Fostering the loathing of a feral underclass allows public resentment to be diverted from those above to those below

That word slips out. This time it was used by a Lib Dem peer* on the Equality and Human Rights Commission. Baroness Hussein-Ece tweeted: "Help. Trapped in a queue in chav land. Woman behind me explaining latest East Enders* plot to mate while eating largest bun I've ever seen." When challenged, she said she hadn't meant chav in any derogatory way. Of course not.

57

Them and us: Class matters in Britain

But take a look at the venomous class-hate site ChavTowns to see what lies beneath.

She would presumably never say nigger[1] or Paki[2], but chav is acceptable class abuse by peo-
15 ple asserting superiority over those they despise. Poisonous class bile is so ordinary that our future king and his brother played at dressing up and talking funny at a chav party mocking their lower class subjects.

20 Wrapped inside this little word is the quintessence of Britain's great social fracture. Over the last 30 years the public monstering of a huge slice of the population by luckier, better-paid people has become commonplace. This is lan-
25 guage from the Edwardian* era of unbridled snobbery. When safely reproduced in Downton Abbey*, as the lady sneering at the scullery maid or the landowner bullying his workers, we are encouraged to look back smugly as if these
30 shocking class differences were long gone. The form and style may have changed – but the reality of extreme inequality and self-confident class contempt is back.

That brief period between 1917 and 1979,
35 when British wealth, trembling in fear of revolution, ceded some power, opportunity and money to the working classes is over. There is now no politics to express or admit the enormity of what has happened since the 1980s – how wealth and
40 human respect drained from the bottom to enrich and glorify the top.

Public perception of the shape of society has been so warped that most no longer know how others live, where they stand in relation to the
45 rest, who earns what or why. By deliberate misrepresentation, drip, drip, week after week, the powerful interests of wealth deliberately distort reality. The best weapon in the class armoury fosters loathing of a "feral underclass" – its size
50 vague and never delineated, relying on anecdotes of extreme dysfunction, of which any society has plenty. One sneer cleverly elides millions of low-earning workers in equal chav contempt for all living on an estate, drawing any benefit
55 – even if in work – as cheats, addicts and layabouts. That's the way to divert resentment from those above, to those below.

[…]

Anecdotes smearing all on housing benefit* or
60 tax credits[3] help make the working class disappear. In his 1997 triumph, Tony Blair* declared class over, we're all middle class – except for a "socially excluded" lumpen rump[4]. "The new Britain is a meritocracy[5]," he declared – not as a
65 future goal but as a fact. So who are the 8 million in manual jobs and the 8 million clerks and sales assistants who make up half the workforce?

In my book Hard Work, I reported on the remarkably strong work ethic of those in jobs
70 paying little more than benefits, the carers and cleaners doing essential work well, despite lack of money or respect. In Unjust Rewards, David Walker and I charted how since the decline of the unions people have lost their bearings on class
75 and incomes: the mega-wealthy are clueless about ordinary earnings and even the poor are misled into thinking their pay is quite middling[6].

Aspiration and social mobility are the useful mirage, laying blame squarely with individuals
80 who should try harder to escape their families and friends, instead of seeking great fairness for all. It suits life's winners to pretend this is a meritocracy: we well-off deserve our luck, anyone can join us if they try.

---

[1] **nigger** = *extremely offensive:* very derogatory term for a black person
[2] **Paki** = *extremely offensive:* very derogatory term for an Asian person
[3] **tax credits** = a reduction of the tax payments made by people on a very low income
[4] **lumpen rump** = poorest social class in a society
[5] **meritocracy** = a society in which people prosper according to the skills and ability which they possess
[6] **middling** = average

Analysis: Comparison

B10 Compare the two texts on chavs. Take the following categories into consideration:
- text type
- content and message
- tone
- reliability
- effect on the reader

In order to prepare for your comparison, complete the table on page 59:

Checklist: Text analysis p. 146

Them and us: Class matters in Britain

Two texts on Chavs				
	"wikiHow"	reference and lines	"The Guardian"	reference and lines
text type	ironic online advice page			
message			Britain is still a class-ridden society with the better-off looking down on the less well-to-do.	"The form and style may have changed – but the reality of extreme inequality and self-confident class contempt is back." (ll. 31–34)
tone of text	ironic, exaggerated	"Most chavs have a stark need to reproduce, and it is drilled … live." (ll. 30–32)		
reliability			argumentative, analytical	"Poisonous class bile is so ordinary that our future king and his brother played … subjects." (ll. 17–20)
effect on reader	amusement, disgust	"Chavettes love to show their dirty, badly fake-tanned feet." (ll. 7–8)		

You can now write a comparison of the two texts by using the information from the table. Here are some examples:

Introductory sentence
The two texts "How to Become a Chavette", published on the wikiHow online advice page, and Toynbee's Guardian article "Chav: the vile word at the heart of fractured Britain", published in 2011, both deal with the social phenomenon of so-called chavs. …

Comparison
Although the wikiHow text gives a comprehensive insight into chav characteristics, it cannot be taken seriously because the advice given is highly ironic and exaggerated (see lines XXX). By contrast, the Guardian article …
Toynbee essentially claims that Britain is still a class-ridden society with the better-off looking down on the less well-to-do. This becomes clear when she states that "[t]he form and style may have changed – but the reality of extreme inequality and self-confident class contempt is back." (ll. 31–34). In contrast to that, the wikiHow article ….

> **Language support**
> in comparison with/ to sth.
> while …/ although …
> In contrast to/with sth.
> By contrast, …
> …, whereas …
> except that
> However, …
> Similarly, …

Comment

B11 Comment on whether the baroness' tweet "Help. Trapped in a queue in chav land. Woman behind explaining latest East Enders plot to mate while eating largest bun I've ever seen." was totally uncalled for and why or why not she should apologize publicly. Refer to both texts.

Checklist: Comment p. 148

3 Them and us: Class matters in Britain

Getting to the point

Comprehension

C1 Read the following article from "The Guardian" in which the well-known British journalist Polly Toynbee takes on the myth that 'social class is dead'. Then summarize the main points of her arguments.

Checklist: Summary p. 145

Analysis

C2 a) Explain why Toynbee thinks it dishonest to claim that class is dead.

b) Analyze the stylistic devices she uses and explain their effect with regards to the journalist's intention.

Checklist: Text analysis p. 146

Comment/Creative writing

C3 In her article Toynbee quotes the writer Richard Wilkinson as saying: "Boosting social mobility without addressing income inequality is like trying to diet without worrying about calories." Explain what is meant by this statement and then comment on it.

Checklist: Comment p. 148

or

Write a letter to the editor supporting or contradicting Toynbee's view on class in Britain. Base your arguments on what you have learned about this topic so far.

Checklist: Letter to the editor p. 154

Polly Toynbee   *guardian.co.uk, Monday 29 August 2011 22.00 BST*

Money busts[1] the convenient myth that social class is dead

Britain likes to pretend it has moved on: but birth determines our destiny and income more now than it did 50 years ago

Class is a dangerous subject, taboo in mainstream politics. The riots brought out a rash[2] of comment implying that there is one great, respectable middle class and an inexplicable underclass beneath, quite unconnected to what's been happening to wages, incomes and the stretching of social bonds.

Britain is adopting the American political dishonesty of disguising ever-widening income differences by calling nearly everyone "middle class". More than 70% now call themselves "middle" – because that's the way politics has led and because, post trade unionism, people no longer know where they stand on the earnings scale.

The convenient political myth says class is dead. Downton Abbey* deference is no more, and look how differences among the young meld into universal estuary* and mockney*. Classlessness may be modern and hip – yet birth determines destiny more certainly than 50 years ago. Never mind Hyacinth Bucket* niceties of napkins over serviettes, class matters more not less than it did, and it needs saying loudly.

I have been making a BBC radio series, The Class Ceiling, which starts this week. Before setting out I asked everyone I came across if they had a story about class: everyone has – either working class people confounded by middle

---

[1] to bust a myth = to expose a commonly held belief as not true
[2] a rash of sth. = *here*: a lot of instances of sth. happening in a short period of time

class snobbery, or privileged children embarrassed by being posh. Pretence, shame, pain, guilt, anger – the stories tumble out. Scratch below the surface denial and class is everywhere, as I found in making these programmes.

Nobody in the BritainThinks poll* admitted to being "upper", so you have to gauge what people mean from who's talking. Those calling themselves "middle" stretch from euphemisms for the highly privileged – the 7% with children in private schools – all the way to families struggling on the edge to pay a half-mortgage on an ex-council house. Only 24% call themselves working class now. Where once the label was a badge of pride (67% claimed it in 1988) now those self-defining as working class say despondently that it only means "poor" and "low-paid" these days.

Of course people sense how far birth still determines fate: those who make it from humble beginnings are admired because rags to riches stories are so rare. The great majority of those in professions and good jobs were born to them. My father was a writer and journalist: would I be writing this if I hadn't had a head start? The successful are smug if they deny their luck, either in birth or other good fortune, including talents. Too often "effort" is overclaimed and luck ignored by those eagerly justifying their class and income advantage over the very hard-working low-paid.

[…] Labour shies away from crude class attack, probably wisely saying it's not where you come from but what you stand for that matters – though they might point out the frequent synergy between them. New Labour* was so afraid of being cast as a cloth cap*, northern party of dying industries that Tony Blair* proclaimed "the class war is over". He chose to end the war, not class. He could have galvanised the great majority that have been cheated by an overweening super-class but thought it electorally necessary to mimic the Tory myth of the undifferentiated big-tent[3] "middle".

My series touches little on the party politics of class, exploring instead the social realities beneath. Why do people falsely believe class is fading? Because the postwar years did see an exceptional upward surge, as a great increase in white collar and middle managerial jobs changed a two-thirds working class society into two-thirds middle class: it's worth noting it happened not via education but the changing labour market. Then social progress stopped – a study comparing the fate of children born in 1958 with those born in 1970 shows the latter more hermetically sealed into the social class of their birth.

British children's achievement is more closely linked to parental status than in most developed countries. Only 21% of children from families in the lowest fifth of incomes get five good GCSEs, against 75% from the richest fifth. Class trajectory is almost set before they get to school. Usha Goswami, a Cambridge University neuroscientist, explains how much the first year of life shapes the brain, babies thriving according to the love, language, empathy and intellectual stimulation they receive. All parties now talk about the importance of early years, yet we invest least in the youngest.

And all parties avoid one inconvenient fact raised by Oxford's John Goldthorpe: social mobility goes both ways. If poorer children rise up, some from higher classes must fall. Room at the top is limited, and there is little prospect of another 60s-style surge in good jobs. Politicians pretend "it's not a zero sum game[4]", but ask recent graduates discovering good jobs don't multiply to greet more well-qualified applicants.

Class is a tangled web of education, taste, history and illusion – but follow the money, and income matches class pretty accurately. GDP has doubled since 1978, but only the top 10% have seen incomes grow at or above that rate, twice as fast as the median and four times faster than the bottom 10%. As universities minister David Willetts has honestly acknowledged, "Western societies with less mobility are the ones with less equality too." When the income gap is wide, few cross the class divide, so remedies may lie less in schools than in the society they reflect.

As Richard Wilkinson, co-author of The Spirit Level, says, "Boosting social mobility without addressing income inequality is like trying to diet without worrying about calories." Avoiding the word class, all parties instead urge social mobility. But they never say why we should bother swapping round which people are mega-rich and which are dirt poor, when it's the unjust gulf in wages and rewards that does the social damage.

---

[3] **big-tent** = a political party's policy of permitting a broad range of views and attitudes amongst its members

[4] **zero sum game** = mathematical representation of a situation in which one party's gains or losses are exactly matched by the losses or gains of the other party, ensuring that the figure obtained by subtracting total losses from total gains is always zero.

3 Them and us: Class matters in Britain

Speaking: Class

In 2011, the BBC carried out a survey of people around Britain. After studying the data, the BBC developed a set of seven class categories that reflect British society today.

D1 a) Look at some of the questions of the actual survey and identify which criteria for defining class they were based on.

b) Discuss how the answers to these questions are related to class.

What is your annual household income after taxes?
Total income for you/spouse/significant other
☐ Under £10k[1] ☐ £10–25k ☐ £25–50k ☐ £50–100k ☐ Over £100k

Do you own or rent a property?
Value of all property owned/mortgaged by you/spouse/significant other
☐ Own ☐ Rent
☐ Under £125k ☐ £125–250k ☐ £250–500k ☐ Over £500k

Do you have any savings?
Pensions, shares, ISAs etc
☐ None ☐ £0–10k ☐ £10–25k ☐ £25–50k ☐ £50–100k
☐ Over £100k

Which of these people do you know socially?
Select all the people who you know
☐ Secretary ☐ Nurse ☐ Teacher ☐ Cleaner
☐ University lecturer ☐ Call centre worker ☐ Electrician ☐ Solicitor
☐ Farm worker ☐ Office manager ☐ Postal worker ☐ Scientist
☐ Lorry driver ☐ Accountant ☐ Shop assistant ☐ Artist
☐ Chief executive ☐ Software designer

Which of these cultural activities do you take part in?
Select all of the activities you do sometimes or often
☐ Go to stately homes ☐ Go to opera ☐ Listen to classical music
☐ Listen to jazz ☐ Listen to rock/indie ☐ Watch dance or ballet
☐ Watch sports ☐ Go to the theatre ☐ Exercise/go to gym
☐ Go to gigs ☐ Socialise at home ☐ Go to museums/galleries
☐ Do arts and crafts ☐ Play video games ☐ Listen to hip-hop/rap
☐ Use Facebook/Twitter

---

[1] £10k = £10,000

D2 **Think-Pair-Share:** Study the descriptions of the seven classes and arrange them in an order from highest to lowest.

D3 Compare your order with the actual one. Find possible reasons for the ranking.
Consider reasons that are related to:
- the people's financial/economic status
- the social contacts
- free-time/cultural activities

Tip
Check text B on page 66 for the correct answer

New affluent workers
Percentage of population: 15%
Average age: 44
- economically secure, but not well off
- have high scores for emerging culture (e.g. watching sport, using social media)
- less interested in highbrow culture (e.g. classical music, theatre)
- often have working class background
- many live in old manufacturing centres of UK

Traditional working class
Percentage of population: 14%
Average age: 66
- many own their own home
- tend to mix socially with people like themselves
- less interested in emerging culture (e.g. going to gym, using social media)
- this group has oldest average age
- jobs in this group include lorry drivers and electricians

Established middle class
Percentage of population: 25%
Average age: 46
- enjoy a diverse range of cultural activities
- socialize with a broad range of people
- many work in management or the traditional professions
- most have middle class backgrounds
- many live outside urban areas

Emergent service workers
Percentage of population: 19%
Average age: 34
- youngest of all class groups
- have highest scores for emerging culture (e.g. watching sport, using social media)
- socialize with a broad range of people
- jobs include chefs, nursing auxiliaries and production assistants
- many live in inexpensive locations in cities like Liverpool and Newcastle

Precariat
Percentage of population: 15%
Average age: 50
- tend to mix socially with people like themselves
- tend not to have a broad range of cultural interests
- jobs in this group include cleaner, van driver and care worker
- more than 80% rent their home
- many live in old industrial areas away from urban centres

Elite
Percentage of population: 6%
Average age: 57
- UK's biggest earners
- score highest for social, cultural and economic factors
- many went to private school and elite universities
- this group is exclusive and very hard to join
- many live in London and the home counties

Technical middle class
Percentage of population: 6%
Average age: 52
- tend to mix socially with people like themselves
- work in research, science and technical occupations
- more interested in emerging culture, (e.g. using social media) than in highbrow culture (e.g. classical music)
- often have mainly middle class backgrounds
- many live in suburban locations

Them and us: Class matters in Britain

D4 a) Divide the class into two groups. Choose one character profile each, study it and decide which social class the profile belongs to.

b) **Pair work:** Present your character to someone from the group that worked on the other character and explain which social class he is in.

Lee Armstrong
- 23, grew up in Gateshead and went to state school
- Rejected university to get a job, works in digital marketing and earns £24,000 a year
- Owns a three-bedroom semi in central Gateshead
- Likes computer games, social networking, watching sport, playing sport, going to the pub, listening to pop music and eating in nice restaurants
- Doesn't go to the theatre, art galleries, museums or listen to classical music
- Friends from secondary school and work

Kevin Henderson
- 23, grew up in Dagenham and went to state school
- Went to university, now works with adults with learning disabilities and earns £18,000 a year
- Still lives with parents in Dagenham
- Likes socializing with friends, going to see all types of live music, art galleries, the theatre and museums
- Not interested in computer games or watching TV
- Wide network of friends from school, university and work

D5 a) **Group work (4):** Each member concentrates on one of the four comments from an Internet discussion board dealing with the Great British Class Survey. Read your comment and identify the person's point of view.

b) Present the message of your statement to the others in your group.

Useful phrases:
… is very critical of the decision to use … as criteria for class
… rather sees the need to define class with the help of …
… is convinced that the survey leaves out important factors, namely that …
… shares the view that class is still a relevant issue, but …
… rejects the notion that …
… questions the kind of data the study is based on as …
… would like other factors to be included in a study of class, namely …
… cannot understand why he/she is supposed to be a member of … because …

We all know young single people are more likely to go out and have a social life – it's not a matter of class. When you get older you know more people, have been to the same museums, stately homes etc so many times you don't go anymore. If you are not a townie* you are also less likely to know the range of people or have a social and cultural life of someone in a city because these things are not available where you are. When you work hard, you could be any class but it would limit your time for other activities that might be relevant to your social contacts and cultural activities.

Sarah, 42

3
Them and us: Class matters in Britain

> Somehow connecting on Facebook counts as culture, whereas volunteering in a local hospital/school/etc doesn't. Watching all kinds of TV programmes counts as culture, but running a local Scouts* group, history project or sports club doesn't.
> Hence, the survey is surprisingly limited in the range of activities it takes into consideration. One would expect a media company like the BBC to insist that a wider range of options were presented, reflecting the current approach to media.
> *David, 35*

> Funnily enough, when I first took the test, I came out as elite. I then remembered one of our friends is a nurse and another works on a farm. I corrected these answers and became middle class again. Clearly, then, to regain my place amongst the elite, all I need to do is contact them and tell them I never want to see them again.
> *Emma, 32*

> The class calculator is obviously pretty basic, and doesn't take into account how old you are. Listening to hip-hop or classical music, or owning a house, are related to how old you are as well as class.
> However, these categories are still quite revealing when it comes to how class really works, how advantages flow down the generations: whether your parents can support you through your studies, internships, can help you start a business or buy your first flat; whether they took you to places like museums and restaurants so you'd feel comfortable in different surroundings; whether their friends and their jobs gave you a wider perspective on jobs that would seem a realistic future. I'm either an emergent service worker, or established middle class, depending on if I put in that I own my flat or rent it. However, I don't really think that's something people would consider to see me as a representative of a certain class.
> *Jack, 22*

Language support
If you want to find out which class someone belongs to according to the Great British Class Survey, you need to take … into account.
As far as I can see, … belongs to the … class
The profile suggests that …
If you consider …'s profession/education/income/…, he/she can be categorised as …
Although … fits into the … class based on his/her circle of friends/freetime activities/…, … rather seems to belong to the … class
…'s cultural activities/educational background/… make him/her seem like a typical representative of the … class
… reminds me of the definition of the … class
Although … make … appear …, all in all, I think that …

c) Compare the different points of view expressed in the statements.

Useful phrases:
What these statements have in common is …
…'s statement resembles that of … as they both …
…'s statement stands out from the rest as it …
All statements share the view that …
In contrast to …, … expresses his/her opinion that …

D6 a) Study one of the three articles about the Great British Class Survey on pages 66–67:
- Note down the most important points in preparation for a presentation of the author's point of view.
- Present the view expressed in the article in your own words. Consider facts, arguments and conclusions.

b) **Pair work:** Find a partner who has worked on the same article. Outline the main points of the article to each other. Give each other feedback on
- whether all the relevant information was included,
- to what extent you managed to express the points in your own words,
- whether you used some of the useful phrases acquired in this section.

c) **Group work (3):** Get together in groups of three – one expert on each text. Present the point of view expressed in your article.

d) **Group work (3):** Discuss whose point of view you find most convincing.

Skills
How to prepare for an oral exam
p. 168

Them and us: Class matters in Britain

A) Paul Routledge, No such thing as the British class system any more? That's rich
(The Mirror, 5 April 2013)

Tony Blair* famously ended the British class system, proclaiming: "We're all middle class now."

Unfortunately, nobody told the employers who carried on hiring and sacking working class people as if the great man had never spoken.

And the nation's ruling elite behaved as before, sending their children to private schools, hogging[1] the best universities and dominating the well-paid professions and government.

Under New Labour*, social mobility virtually seized up, so the haves continued to lord[2] it over the chavs.

Like the IRA*, the class system never went away. It just morphed into something different, less easily defined but there all the same. Sociologists (who else?) have now discovered that there are not three classes – upper, middle and lower – but seven (...).

Such are the findings of the Great British Class Survey, conducted among 160,000 people for the BBC (...).

Class is not just about your job, where you live and how much you earn. It's about who you are.

You can be on the dole[3] and vote Tory*. You can go to Eton* and be left-wing[4] Labour (...). Class is as much about attitudes as it is about circumstances.

Take me, for example. What am I? On the BBC scale, I probably score as established middle class.

I live in my own house surrounded by books and I don't watch soaps.

But my friends in the pub are drawn largely from working class occupations, those who are still working, that is.

I enjoy their company and I hope they enjoy mine. (...)

I'm a devout trade unionist (...).

I'm also a member of the Labour Party but I don't want to be an MP* or run the country.

I don't care how I'm classified by academic pointy-heads[5]. I'm me. Just like you are you. Most of us, I bet, are a bundle of seeming contradictions.

But we get by[6], because we're people, living humankind, not data in a sociologist's statistical tables.

And hurrah for that.

Class divide exists, I grant you that.

The rich and powerful, and employers with the ability to sack you, are in a different league.

They're on the other side: always have been, always will be. They want to control, and exploit.

That's the real class issue, not your music tastes or TV viewing habits.

---

[1] **to hog sth.** = to take or use sth. a lot in a way that stops other people using it
[2] **to lord it over so.** = to behave as though one is superior to so.
[3] **to be on the dole** = to be receiving unemployment benefit
[4] **left-wing** = on the left politically speaking
[5] **academic pointy-heads** = (Am.E. derogatory): intellectual
[6] **to get by** = to cope

B) Mona Chalabi and Ami Sedghi, Classing Britain: why defining social status is so difficult
(The Guardian, 3 April 2013)

(...) The Great British Class Survey results published by the BBC today claims to brush away the traditional upper, middle and working class categorisation and, based on the responses of over 161,000 people, attempts to replace it with the (less catchy?) Elite, Established Middle Class, Technical Middle Class, New Affluent Workers, Traditional Working Class, Emergent Service Workers and the Precarious Proletariat.

Changes in definition aren't just about changes in the socio-economic make up of Britain. They're as much about changes in the way we perceive what constitutes difference and similarity between ourselves.

So, where once riding a bike and having only one pair of shoes may have been an indicator of meagre earnings and weak social status, they might now suggest the ethical choices of a highly skilled professional. This is partly because the architecture of British social hierarchy has undergone huge shifts as a result of broader changes in social, economic and cultural life.

The fact that there are so many components that make up class – and that they are based on perceptions and belief as well as fact – makes social class extremely difficult to measure. The Great British Class Survey has nevertheless had a go. Here, we consider some of the merits and limitations of their research.

Class room
Education was one of the topics omitted from the online class calculator launched today. Despite the huge success of a handful of uneducated entrepreneurs, level of education completed as well as the type of school attended remain huge determinants of social mobility in Britain. (…)
And parents remain a powerful predictor of what class you're in and the class you're capable of moving to. (…) In 2010, the link between individual and parental earnings was found to be the strongest in the UK than any other OECD country*. Many argue that the British educational system can reproduce and reinforce these trends. A 2012 report, also from the OECD found that British schools were more socially segregated than in any other developed country.
As well as education, questions about spending habits were omitted from the online class calculator. (…) questions about where someone goes on holiday and where they do their supermarket shop might provide clues about their socio-economic status. What's more, asking about savings, annual earnings and home ownership (included in the class calculator) might not provide the full picture of wealth as they omit to ask about debt. (…)

Mark Steel, What did I learn from this class survey? Watch out for the postman if he's humming Mozart
(The Independent, 4 April 2013)

They've done another one of those surveys about class. And they've followed the rule of these surveys, that each one has to be more stupid than the last. The results have been on every news channel and in every newspaper, that there are seven classes now apparently. And one of the ways they worked out which one people might be in, is to ask whether or not they listen to jazz, which makes you "established middle class". (…)
Listening to classical music also makes you established middle class. So if you hear the postman humming a bit of Mozart off a car advert, it's probably Stephen Fry* roughing it[7] for the morning. (…)
The survey might show that Roman Abramovich*, on the other hand, would come out as traditional working class as he likes football, sitting on his £500m yacht muttering to Frank Lampard*: "The thing is, Frank, with my background I never stood a chance[8]."
One question the survey didn't seem to bother asking was what job you did, although it does ask for the jobs of your friends. So if you're a cleaner who knows some teachers, that makes you middle class for having teacher friends, but those teachers will be working class for having a friend who's a cleaner. (…)
Going to museums is middle class, using Facebook makes you an emergent service worker, and so on. So the survey doesn't so much measure class, as measure things people like doing.
(…)
Some people have dismissed this survey on the grounds that it proves class no longer exists at all. Jill Kirby, a Conservative adviser from the Centre For Policy Studies*, says that "class has eroded almost completely". That's why it's just coincidence that the Prime Minister*, Chancellor* and Mayor of London are sons of millionaires who went to public schools, two of them to the same one, and it's just as likely that soon half the Cabinet will all have gone to the same comprehensive in Ipswich*.
But for class to have any meaning, it must represent more than which music you listen to, or even whether you went to Eton. It only makes sense if it refers to your relationship with the way society is owned and controlled, and have a common interest.
(…) if you're on the board of a bank, your relationship to society is different to the person who works in a call centre for the bank (…). For most people, that dividing line, as to whether you have any real control over society is still clear. (…)

---

[7] **to rough it** = to go without the luxuries that one is used to
[8] **to stand a chance** = to have a chance to be able to do something

4 Britain is Great

Getting started

Pre-reading

Tip
* means this term is explained in the Names and terms section on pages 182-190

A1 a) Complete the following sentence to define your idea of culture.
Culture is …

b) Now talk about these two definitions of culture and compare them with your own ideas:

> Culture is the widening of the mind and of the spirit. *(Jawaharial Nehru, 1889–1964)*

> Culture is roughly anything we do and the monkeys don't. *(Lord Raglan, 1885–1964)*

A2 a) These words and expressions can be used to describe cultural trends e.g. in fashion, music, art etc. Decide which of them have a positive and which have a negative connotation. Use your dictionaries if necessary.

> trendy • old-fashioned • creative • state-of-the-art • trendsetting •
> ultra-modern • stylish • innovative • forward-looking • with-it • chic •
> behind the times • fashionable • dated • way-out • avant-garde •
> conservative • tasteful • progressive • passé • modern • traditional •
> futuristic • cutting edge • cosmopolitan • oriental • ethnic

b) Choose the three most appropiate adjectives for each of the following:
- fashion
- music
- film
- literature
- theatre
- food
- art
- architecture

A3 a) Here are some statements about culture made by contemporary British trendsetters. Read through them and then look at the posters. Say what image they present of the British music and fashion scenes.

①
Jim Warboy
This country has so much reputation for being creative. We've got so many creative people here who can't get the support to help make their things happen without going abroad. If more money was put into these things it would A) give people a lot more hope in their future, especially younger people. And B) it would generate a lot more new ideas which could then be turned into something that can be sold around the world. It is here it's seen as something like somehow you would lose your money. I would like to see the figures on how much money the Beatles brought into this country. Or the Sex Pistols*, or Boy George* or Mary Quant* or all these people.

Britain is Great: The culture of Great Britain

4

② **Stavros Karelis – Machine-A**
If you walk down a street or if you go out at night in a club you are going to see such amazing people dressed up amazingly well and they just love to dress up, go out and have fun. And this is what London is about, have fun, don't think about it too seriously, don't take it too seriously.

③ For hundreds of years London has been the centre of a diverse and proud music universe which grows stronger with each passing year. The Los Angeles of the United Kingdom (but with more soul), London has seen the rise of the rock and roll, pub rock, punk and britpop movements and will live to see several more genres emerge. Filled with up-and-coming artists, musical celebrities and haloed live music venues and night clubs, London is a must-visit attraction for any music lover.
http://capinterns.com/index.php/en/london-life/lmscene

A4 To coincide with the Olympic Games 2012, the Foreign and Commonwealth Office* launched "The GREAT campaign" to promote the reputation of Britain abroad.
- Get into groups of three.
- Each of you should concentrate on one of the three video clips you are going to watch.
- Note down what is said in your video clip about what makes Britain great in these fields.
- Talk about the information in your groups.
- Discuss to what extent the video clips convince YOU that Britain is great.

1) Victoria Beckham* on British fashion and music

2) Different artists on British music

3) Actor Alistair McGowan* talks about UK creativity (art and film)

DVD

4

Britain is Great: The culture of Great Britain

A5 a) The pictures below illustrate significant cultural icons in Britain. Identify these people, buildings and events and say which cultural areas they belong to.

b) **Group work:** Choose one of the cultural icons illustrated above and research it on the Internet. Present your information on a poster.

c) Hang up the posters in class and do a gallery walk. What do you find most interesting, most impressive and most surprising about the cultural icons? In groups of 4–5, talk about your impressions.

Tip
Cultural icons are people or things which represent an important aspect of a culture, e.g. red double-decker buses in London and the Beatles are cultured icons in Britain.

What's so great about Britain

In September 2011 the British Prime Minister, David Cameron*, launched a campaign to promote GREAT Britain and attract tourists. This campaign had much to do with the Olympic Games that were due to be held in London in 2012, but in particular it aimed to show why Britain is a GREAT place to visit. In doing so the campaign highlighted British culture both past and present.

Music

Most people immediately associate British music with rock and pop, with the Beatles, the Rolling Stones, David Bowie, Queen or with more contemporary singers and bands such as Adele, Robbie Williams, Arctic Monkeys and Coldplay. The UK has remained one of the leading countries in the international music scene for decades and British artists represent many genres of popular music, not only rock and pop and all their different variations but also punk, heavy metal, garage, trip hop and dub step to name but a few.

Less well known to many are British classical composers of the past and present. The works of Henry Purcell, Ralph Vaughan Williams, Benjamin Britten, William Byrd, Edward Elgar, Gustav Holst and the contemporary John Rutter are regularly performed in Great Britain and internationally. More famous is the German-born composer George Frideric Handel, who chose to live in London and became a British subject in 1727. He is particularly famous for his choral work, *The Messiah*. Regular listeners to the *Last Night of the Proms* at the Royal Albert Hall, the final concert in an eight-week summer season of daily classical concerts, will also be familiar with a number of British patriotic songs such as Elgar's *Land of Hope and Glory*, accompanied by a jubilant, singing and flag-waving audience.

In the last few decades Britain has also become famous for its musicals. Andrew Lloyd Webber is probably one of the most successful composers of the 20th century. His musicals include *Cats*, *Evita*, *The Phantom of the Opera*, *Jesus Christ Superstar* and *Starlight Express* and are still performed regularly around the globe.

Architecture

Visitors to Britain will be impressed by the wide variety of old buildings that can be visited. There are a few prehistoric monuments, such as Stonehenge* and also many Roman remains. Not many Anglo-Saxon remains can be found but since the Norman Conquest* in 1066 a remarkable range of architecture has survived. Many historic buildings date back to the Middle Ages. These are castles and manor houses, churches, cathedrals and monasteries scattered over differ-

Britain is Great: The culture of Great Britain

ent parts of the country. They were built to last and, in many cases, they have done. The Normans introduced the Romanesque style of architecture to Britain. This type of architecture is usually called Norman. The predominant medieval style of architecture is however Gothic*.

Speke Hall: a Tudor half-timbered¹ house

More domestic architecture has survived from the 16th and 17th centuries. Houses were built to display status and wealth and many of these palaces and stately homes have survived. In the Tudor period (1485–1603) those who could afford it built houses of brick or stone, Hampton Court is a fine example, whereas others built so-called half-timbered houses. Many of these black and white buildings can still be seen. Two famous architects of this period are Inigo Jones (1573–1652) whose Banqueting Hall is in Whitehall, and Christopher Wren (1632–1723), who designed the new St Paul's cathedral, built after the Great Fire of London in 1666. In fact he was responsible for rebuilding more than 50 churches destroyed in the fire.

Royal Crescent Bath

Some of the most popular architecture in England is 18th century Georgian*. There were many elegant town developments during this period and most of the squares and crescents have remained. There are fine examples of these in the city of Bath*. This was also a period when great country houses were built surrounded by parks and lakes.

The 19th century was characterized by the Industrial Revolution and technical developments such as the production of cast iron and steel. Victorian engineers and architects such as William Paxton and Isambard Kingdom Brunel created buildings and bridges made of cast iron. In contrast to the technical revolution there was also a revival of classical styles during this period. For example, the neo-Gothic* Houses of Parliament were rebuilt by Charles Barry after a fire destroyed parts of the old Parliament buildings in 1834. One of the most important architects and designers of the later 19th and early 20th centuries was the Scotsman Charles Rennie Mackintosh. He was more concerned with the present and the future than with history and tradition and wanted to create buildings for individual needs rather than for the masses. He was inspired by Art Nouveau* and Japanese designs and created many exterior and interior designs in his hometown Glasgow.

Mackintosh Building: the Glasgow School of Art

After the Second World War there was a need for modern cheap housing and this dominated the face of towns and cities all over Britain. This was a period of endless semi-detached housing estates and high-rise developments, particularly in London. Many people were worried that London's panorama, centred on St Paul's Cathedral would be destroyed forever. However, after a decade of unpopularity height is now back in fashion and London has acquired some very tall futuristic buildings in the 21st century including the Gherkin, designed by world-famous British architect Norman Foster and the Shard, designed by the Italian architect, Renzo Piano.

---

¹ **half-timbered house** = a house half built with a visible wooden frame and half with another material, such as stone or brick

Literature

William Shakespeare is probably Britain's most famous writer, but Britains's literary history is much older than that. The most famous piece of old English writing is *Beowulf*, an anonymous epic poem dating from the 8th to the 11th centuries, while Geoffrey Chaucer's *Canterbury Tales*, written in the 14th century is a collection of stories. Most of the literature that was written before the novel evolved as a literary form in the early 17th century was intended to be seen and heard but not necessarily read. Shakespeare wrote plays like *Hamlet* and *Romeo and Juliet* to be performed on stage and he, Christopher Marlowe and other playwrights of the time understood how to entertain their audiences. Unlike the works of his contemporaries and his immediate successors in the 17th century, Shakespeare's plays are still extremely popular worldwide and are performed in many languages. Shakespeare also wrote lyric poetry – another form popular in the 16th century.

Jane Austen   *Charles Dickens*

It was the development of prose fiction and the novel, however, which enabled some of the greatest British writers to emerge, including Henry Fielding, Sir Walter Scott and Jane Austen. The novels of Jane Austen remain very popular and have reached a wider audience due to the adaptation of books such as *Pride and Prejudice* and *Emma* for film and television. The introduction of state education in the 19th century increased adult literacy rates. Novels, which were often published in weekly parts, became an increasingly popular form of entertainment. Charles Dickens is one of the greatest novelists of this period and works such as *Oliver Twist* were widely read in both Britain and America. Other notable authors of the time are the Brontë sisters, Thomas Hardy and George Eliot. The 19th century also brought forth a number of Britain's renowned Romantic poets, including William Blake, William Wordsworth, Percy Bysshe Shelley and John Keats as well as Robert Burns, Scotland's most famous poet, who wrote in the dialect of lowland Scots*. The anniversary of Burns' birthday (25th January) is traditionally celebrated in Scotland with a supper of haggis* and whisky.

The novel has remained the most popular literary form. 20th century novelists such as Virginia Woolf and D.H. Lawrence often use experimental and innovative narrative techniques and structures. However the public appetite for entertainment remains. The range of titles available in genres like science fiction, thrillers, detective stories and fantasy seems to be wider than ever. Fantasy stories such as J.K. Rowling's *Harry Potter* series and J.R.Tolkien's *Lord of the Rings* and *The Hobbit*, have gained enormous popularity, particularly among younger readers. This popularity has certainly been increased by the production of Hollywood films based on them, which again attracts people to read the books.

This is also true of Britain's tradition of crime fiction. The protagonist of Arthur Conan Doyle's Sherlock Holmes stories, which were written in the 19th and early 20th centuries, is now the hero of extremely popular TV and film interpretations. The 'Queen of Crime', Agatha Christie, created Miss Marple and Hercule Poirot in the early 20th century and since then endless film versions have been made of their adventures.

Britain's strong literary tradition continues today, with acclaimed authors from a variety of different cultures (e.g. A.S. Byatt, Salman Rushdie, Ian McEwan, Kazuo Ishiguro, Zadie Smith) producing works which reflect their own background and presenting an outlook on their country and the wider world.

Task:
Choose your top five British cultural icons from the names mentioned in this fact file. Include at least one from each category. Explain your choice to a partner.

Britain is Great: The culture of Great Britain

Practice section

Pre-reading

B1 a) **Group work:** In Julian Barnes' novel *England, England* a group of people is planning to open a Britain-Theme-Park. How would you design the park so that the visitors can experience British culture? In groups, draw a sketch of your theme park and label the attractions.

b) Present your sketch to another group and explain what to expect from each attraction.

c) Point out differences in your concepts.

Comprehension

B2 In Barnes' novel Sir Jack, the tycoon who is the mastermind behind the project, is trying to find a suitable place to realize his vision.

a) Read the text and find the places on the map on the inside of the front cover of this book that are mentioned at the meeting.

b) Name the place Sir Jack has chosen for the theme park and and state the reasons he gives to convince his team.

> Julian Barnes was born in Leicester, England in 1946. He has written numerous novels, short stories and essays and has received several awards for his writing. His writing has earned him much respect as an author who deals with the themes of history, reality, truth and love.

A map of the British Isles had been laid out on the Battle Table, and Sir Jack's Co-ordinating Committee stared at the jigsaw of counties, wondering if it were better to be completely wrong or completely right. Probably neither. Sir Jack, now perambulating[1] behind their backs, gave them a hint.

'England, as the mighty William* and many others have observed, is an island. Therefore, if we
5 are serious, if we are seeking to offer the thing itself, we in turn must go in search of a precious whatsit[2] set in a silver doodah[3].'

They peered at the map as if cartography was a dubious new invention. There seemed either too much choice or too little.

Perhaps some daredevil[4] conceptual leap was called for. 'You're not, by any chance, thinking …
10 Scotland, are you?' A heavily bronchial sigh indicated that, No, dunderhead[5], Sir Jack was not thinking Scotland.

'The Scillies*?'
'Too far.'
'The Channel Islands*?'
15 'Too French.'
'Lundy Island*?'
'Refresh my memory.'
'Famous for its puffins*.'
'Oh, fuck the puffins, for God's sake, Paul. And no boring mud-flats[6] in the Thames estuary,
20 either.'

What could he be thinking? Anglesey* was out. The Isle of Man*? Perhaps Sir Jack's idea was to construct his own purpose-built offshore island. That would not be untypical. Mind you, the thing about Sir Jack was that nothing, in a way, was untypical except what he didn't want to do.

---

[1] **to perambulate** = *formal:* to walk around slowly
[2] **whatsit** = a word you use to refer to sth. that you can't remember the name of
[3] **doodah** = see whatsit. The sentence is an ironic reference to "This precious stone set in the silver sea," from Shakespeare's *Richard II*, Act 2, Part One
[4] **daredevil** = *here:* very daring
[5] **dunderhead** = *dated, mildly derogatory:* so. silly, stupid or foolish
[6] **mud-flat** = areas of wetland covered by the sea at high-tide

'There,' he said, and his curled fist came down like a passport stamp. 'There.'

'The Isle of Wight*,' they answered in straggly[7] unison.

'*Exactly*. Look at her, snuggling into the soft underbelly of England. The little cutie[8]. The little beauty. Look at the shape of her. Pure diamond, that's what struck me straight away. A pure diamond. Little jewel. Little cutie.'

'What's it like, Sir Jack?' asked Mark.

'What's it like? It's perfect on the map, that's what it's like. You been there?'

'No.'

'Anyone?'

No; no; no; no and no. Sir Jack came round to the other side of the map, parked his palms on the Scottish Highlands and faced his inner circle. 'And what do you know of it?' They looked at one another. Sir Jack pressed on. 'Let me help clarify such ignorance, in that case. Name five famous historical events connected with the Isle of Wight?' Silence. 'Name one. Dr Max?' Silence. 'Not your period, no doubt, ho, ho. Good. Name five famous listed buildings[9] on the island whose renovation might cause ructions[10] at Heritage*.' 'Osborne House*,' replied Dr Max in quiz-show mode. 'Very good. Dr Max wins the hair-drier. Name another four.' Silence. 'Good. Name five famous and endangered species of plant, bird or animal whose habitat might be disturbed by our saintly bulldozers?' Silence.

'Good.'

'Cowes Regatta*,' a sudden voice suggested.

'Ah, the phagocytes stir. Very good, Jeff. But not, I think, a bird, plant, listed building or historical event. Any more offers?'

A longer silence. 'Good. Indeed, perfect.'

'But Sir Jack … isn't it, well, presumably, full of inhabitants?'

'No, Mark, it is not full of inhabitants. What it is full of is grateful future employees. (…)

[7] **straggly** = here: untidy
[8] **cutie** = usually s.o. who is attractive or endearing, particularly a woman or girl
[9] **listed building** = a building considered to be of historic or architectural importance and which is protected by law
[10] **ructions** = here: noisy protests

Analysis

Identifying narrative perspective

B3 There are different ways to tell a story. The author has a choice of different narrative perspectives depending on the intended effect.

a) Read the info box to find out about the different kinds of narrative perspective.

b) Determine what kind of narrator tells the story in Julian Barnes' novel.

Britain is Great: The culture of Great Britain

> **Info: Narrative Perspective**
>
> **1. First person narration**
> A first person narrator refers to I and me and is usually the novel's central character but may also be a minor character who merely observes the action.
>
> **2. Third person narration**
> A third person narrator is not part of the story, so the characters in the story are referred to as he, she, they. The third person narrator can be either omniscient or limited:
>
> a) omniscient narrator
>
> The omniscient narrator knows everything about his characters. He can look inside their minds and knows their thoughts and feelings. He may comment on events and/or the behaviour of his characters or he may choose to merely report without an explicit comment. He also knows how the plot will develop and can switch between places and times referring to past events or foreshadowing future developments in the plot.
>
> The omniscient narrator may be
> **intrusive:** he comments directly on events and the behaviour of his characters, often providing a moral judgement or highlighting the general importance of the story.
> **unintrusive:** even though the narrator has insight into the thoughts and feelings of his characters he merely reports them without an explicit comment.
>
> b) limited narrator:
>
> The limited narrator's insight into thoughts and feelings is restricted to one of the characters. He sees and judges the development of the story through the eyes of that particular character only.
>
> **3. Multiple narrators**
> The story is told by different characters in the novel so that the events are seen from different perspectives. Thus the reader is presented with different views of an event and the reasons behind it, as each narrator contributes new aspects. This perspective is frequently chosen in modern novels.

B4 a) Read the extract again and decide whether the narrator is omniscient or limited.

b) In order to prove your point you need to find examples in the text. Some quotations have already been highlighted for you. Match the quotations to the devices in the first column in the grid, which describe the narrative perspective. Explain their effect in the third column. Some of the effects have been explained for you.

device	quotation	explanation of effect
The narrator explicitly describes how the characters feel or what they think, assume, wonder about	Sir Jack's Co-ordinating Committee stared at the jigsaw of counties, wondering if it were better to be completely wrong or completely right.	The narrator reveals that members of the team are not sure how to react to Sir Jack's idea. His plans seem like an unsolvable puzzle.

Britain is Great: The culture of Great Britain

device	quotation	explanation of effect
Interpretation of facts/people		The narrator interprets Sir Jack's reaction as exasperation with members of his team, each of whom Sir Jack views as idiotic.
	They peered at the map as if cartography was a dubious new invention	
Comment		The narrator's description of the response of the team reveals how intimidated they are
	in quiz-show mode	
Reported thought	What could he be thinking?	
Directly addressing the reader	Mind you,	

B5 Choose the persona of either Sir Jack or one of the other members of his committee and rewrite the narration from their perspective. Write in the first person.

Remember that as a first-person narrator you only present your own view.
Think about what kind of person you are. In order to identify with your role consider the following questions:

Member of the team:
- how does Sir Jack make you feel?
- how do you think the other members feel?
- which role does he give you?
- what is your real opinion of the project?

Sir Jack:
- how do you feel about your project and your team?
- why do you treat them like you do?
- what were your expectations?

Comprehension

B6 a) Use your sketch of the theme park from B1 and make a list of all the features you have included.

b) Read the second extract from "England, England" in B7 about the tourist mecca Sir Jack has created and tick the aspects of British culture on your list which are the same as Sir Jack's.

c) Note down any additional features Sir Jack has included and discuss how important they are in reflecting British culture.

B7 Placemat

a) Read the second extract again and note down your ideas about the author's attitude towards the theme park "England, England" in your corner of the placemat.

b) Read your group members' ideas and discuss them.

c) Agree on a common answer and present your conclusion to the class. Give reasons for your decision.

A TOURIST MECCA SET IN A SILVER SEA

It is a classic springtime day outside Buckingham Palace. The clouds are high and fleecy, William Wordsworth's daffodils* are blowin' in the wind, and guardsmen in their traditional
5 'busbies' (bearskin hats) are standing to attention in front of their sentry boxes. Eager crowds press their noses to the railings for a glimpse of the British Royal Family.

Promptly, at 11 o'clock the tall double win-
10 dows behind the balcony open. The ever-popular King and Queen appear, waving and smiling. A ten-gun salute[1] splits the air. The guardsmen present arms and cameras click like old-fashioned turnstiles. A quarter of an hour later,
15 promptly at 11.15, the tall windows close again until the following day.

All, however, is not as it seems. The crowds and the cameras are for real; so are the clouds. But the guardsmen are actors, Buckingham Pal-
20 ace is a half-size replica, and the gun salute electronically produced. Gossip has it that the King and Queen themselves are not real, and that the contract they signed two years ago with Sir Jack Pitman's Pitco Group excuses
25 them from this daily ritual. Insiders confirm that an opt-out clause[2] does exist in the royal contract, but that Their Majesties appreciate the cash fee that accompanies each balcony appearance.

30 This is showtime, but it's also big business. Along with the first Visitors (as they call tourists hereabouts) came the World Bank and the IMF*. Their approval – coupled with the enthusiastic endorsement of the Portland Third Mil-
35 lennium Think Tank – means that this groundbreaking enterprise is likely to be much copied in years and decades to come.

(…)

Once upon a time this used to be the Isle of
40 Wight*, but its current inhabitants prefer a simpler and grander title: they call it The Island. Its official address since declaring independence two years ago is typical of Sir Jack Pitnan's roguish, buccaneering[3] style. He named it Eng-
45 land, England. Cue for song. It was also his original stroke of lateral thinking[4] which brought together in a single hundred-and-fifty-five square mile zone everything the Visitor might want to see of what we used to think of
50 as England. In our time-strapped age, surely it makes sense to be able to visit Stonehenge and Anne Hathaway's Cottage* in the same morning, take in a 'ploughman's lunch'* atop the White Cliffs of Dover, before passing a leisurely
55 afternoon at the Harrods* emporium inside the Tower of London (Beefeaters push your shopping trolley for you!). As for transport between sites: those gas-guzzling[5] tourist buses have been replaced by the eco-friendly pony-and-
60 cart. While if the weather turns showery, you can take a famous black London taxi or even a big red double-decker bus. Both are environmentally clean, being fuelled by solar power.

(…)

65 The project could not have had a more spectacular vindication. Both airports – Tennyson* One and Tennyson Two – are approaching capacity. Visitor thruput[6] has outperformed the most optimistic expectations. The Island itself
70 is packed yet calmly efficient. There is always a friendly 'bobby' (policeman) or 'Beefeater' (Tower of London guard) from whom to ask the way; while the 'cabbies' (taxi-drivers) are all fluent in at least one of the major tourist lan-
75 guages. Most speak English too! Maisie Bransford, of Franklin Tn[7], vacationing with her family, told the Journal, 'We'd heard that England was kind of dowdy[8] and old-fashioned, and not really up with the cutting edge of the
80 modern world. But we've been mighty surprised. It's a real home from home.'

---

[1] **ten-gun salute** = a formal mark of respect performed by intentionally firing ten loaded guns into the air
[2] **opt-out clause** = a sentence in a contract which allows s.o. to get out of that contract if they want to
[3] **buccaneering** = adventurous, bold and risk-taking
[4] **stroke of lateral thinking** = a clever thought
[5] **gas-guzzling** = describes sth., usually a vehicle, which uses a lot of fuel
[6] **thruput** = or throughput; here the number of units put through the system
[7] **Franklin Tn** = Franklin, Tennessee, US
[8] **dowdy** = usually of a woman's clothes: dated, plain, unfashionable

Britain is Great: The culture of Great Britain

Analysis

Analyzing tone

B8 a) The tone of a text reflects the narrator's attitude towards the topic he is dealing with. If the author disapproves of something his tone is likely to be critical. Find the adjectives from the list that can be used if the author wants to
- express a strong dislike of something
- make fun of his subject
- refrain from showing any emotional involvement
- present just the facts
- trigger a contrary response from the reader
- stress the importance of a subject

> playful • serious • matter-of-fact • ironic • aggressive •
> sarcastic • detached • humorous • provocative • witty •
> light-hearted • disapproving • critical • neutral • mocking •
> grave • indifferent • angry • emotional • objective • satirical

b) Choose appropriate adjectives from the list to describe the tone of the extract. Discuss your choice with a partner and give examples from the text to support your view.

B9 In his novel Julian Barnes uses a satirical tone to underline his attitude towards Sir Jack's project.
Satire is a literary form in which wit and humour are used to expose and criticize flaws or negative tendencies in our society, in institutions or in people. Its aim is to make people laugh, only to then make them realize that they themselves have been unmasked.
To create a humorous effect satirical texts often make use of stylistic devices, such as
- irony
- exaggeration
- sarcasm
- paradox

a) Study the highlighted passages and decide which stylistic device is used.

b) Now analyze how Julian Barnes uses satirical elements to ridicule and criticize the glorification and the commercialization of traditional aspects of British culture and traditions.

Checklist:
Text analysis
p. 146

Creative writing

B10 Imagine you are a tourist who has visited Sir Jack's theme park *England, England*. After your visit you write a report for a travel journal. Describe your experience and either recommend the park or warn people about this tourist attraction. Make sure you express a positive or a negative overall attitude towards the project or at least towards different aspects of it.

Checklist:
Creative writing
p. 150

4 Britain is Great: The culture of Great Britain

Getting to the point

Pre-reading

C1 Think-Pair-Share:
a) How can music affect your mood? Write down your thoughts.

b) Exchange your ideas with a partner.

c) Share your ideas with another pair and present them to the class.

Comprehension

C2 Summarize the following extract from the novel "High Fidelity" by Nick Hornby.

Analysis

C3 Characterize the protagonist, Rob, taking into account the narrative perspective and the effect this has on the reader's impression of him.
Think about the following:
- the type of narrator
- what information we get/don't get about him and why.

C4 Analyze Rob's description of the gig in the Lauder and explain how his use of language (tone) reveals his attitude.

Skills Checklist: Summary p. 145

Nick Hornby was born in Redhill, Surrey, in England in 1957. His best-known books are the internationally bestselling novels High Fidelity, About A Boy, How To Be Good and A Long Way Down, some of which have been made into successful films.

Skills Checklist: Text analysis p. 146

Skills Checklist: Creative writing p. 150

[1] **tatty** = showing wear, in poor condition
[2] **surly** = unfriendly and untalkative
[3] **bitter** = a type of dark British beer which is not fizzy and is usually served at slightly cooler than room temperature
[4] **run-of-the-mill** = ordinary, average
[5] **second-division** = from football; second-rate, not as good as first division
[6] **office outing** = a fun trip in which everyone who works in an office or business takes part

---

Rob owns a record shop called Championship Vinyl in London. He employs two young men, Dick and Barry. When they find out that Rob's girlfriend, Laura, has just ended her relationship with him,
5 *they take him for a night out to cheer him up.*

It's an enormous pub, the Lauder, with ceilings so high that the cigarette smoke gathers above your head like a cartoon cloud. It's tatty[1], and draughty, and the benches have had the
10 stuffing slashed out of them, and the staff are surly[2], and the regular clientele are either terrifying or unconscious, and the toilets are wet and smelly, and there's nothing to eat in the evening, and the wine is hilariously bad, and
15 the bitter[3] is fizzy and much too cold; in other words, it's a run-of-the-mill[4] north London pub. We don't come here that often, because the bands that usually play here are the kind of abysmal second-division[5] punk group you'd
20 pay half your wages not to listen to. Occasionally though, like tonight, they stick on some obscure American folk/country artist [...]

The woman we have come to see is called Marie LaSalle; she's got a couple of solo records
25 out on an independent label, and once had one of her songs covered by Nanci Griffith*. Dick says she lives here now; he read somewhere that she finds England more open to the kind of music she makes, which means, presumably,
30 that we're cheerfully indifferent rather than actively hostile. There are a lot of single men here – not single as in unmarried, but single as in no friends. In this sort of company the three of us – me morose and monosyllabic, Dick
35 nervy and shy, Barry solicitously self-censoring – constitute a wild and massive office outing[6]. [...]

Marie LaSalle comes on stage (as it were – there is a little platform and a couple of micro-
40 phones a few yards in front of us) at nine; by five past nine, to my intense irritation and

embarrassment, I'm in tears, and the feel-nothing world that I've been living in for the last few days has vanished.

There are many songs that I've been trying to avoid since Laura went, but the song that Marie LaSalle opens with, the song that makes me cry, is not one of them. The song that makes me cry has never made me cry before; in fact, the song that makes me cry used to make me puke. [...] The song that makes me cry is Marie LaSalle's version of Peter Frampton's* 'Baby I Love Your Way'.

Imagine standing with Barry, and Dick, in his Lemonheads* T- shirt, and listening to a cover version of a Peter Frampton song, and blubbing[7]. [...] I understand that I was in dire need[8] of symptoms to help me understand that I have been deeply traumatized by recent events, but did they have to be this extreme? Couldn't God have settled for something just mildly awful – like an old Diana Ross* hit, say, or an Elton John* original?

And it doesn't stop there. As a result of Marie LaSalle's cover version of 'Baby I Love Your Way' ('I know I'm not supposed to like that song, but I do,' she says with a cheeky smile when she has finished), I find myself in two apparently contradictory states: a) I suddenly miss Laura with a passion that has been entirely absent for the last four days, and b) I fall in love with Marie LaSalle.

These things happen. They happen to men at any rate. Or to this particular man. Sometimes.

It's difficult to explain why or how you can find yourself pulled in two different directions at once, and obviously a certain amount of dreamy irrationality is a pre-requisite. And there's a logic to it, too. Marie is pretty, in that nearly cross-eyed American way [...] All my life I have wanted to go to bed with – no, have a relationship with – a musician: I'd want her to write songs at home. And ask me what I thought of them, and maybe include one of our private jokes in the lyrics, and thank me in the sleeve notes[9], maybe even include a picture of me on the inside cover, in the background somewhere, and I could watch her play live from the back, in the wings. [...]

The Marie bit is easy to understand, then. The Laura thing takes a bit more explaining, but what it is, I think is this: this sentimental music has a great way of taking you back somewhere at the same time that it takes you forward, so you feel nostalgic and hopeful at the same time. Marie's the hopeful, forward part of it – maybe not her necessarily but someone like her, somebody who can turn things around for me. (Exactly that: I always think that women are going to save me, lead me through to a better life, that they can change and redeem me.) And Laura's the backward part, the last person I loved, and when I hear those sweet sticky acoustic guitar chords I reinvent our time together. [...] This is why I shouldn't be listening to pop music at the moment.

[7] **to blub** = to cry
[8] **to be in dire need** = to need very badly
[9] **sleeve notes** = text on the paper sheets inside a CD case

Creative writing

C5 Later Dick and Barry talk about their evening in the pub with Rob. Write a dialogue making it clear how they see Rob as a person.

Britain is Great: The culture of Great Britain

Speaking

Pre-reading

D1 Television is an important part of the culture of a country.
a) Collect words and phrases that can be used to talk about television in a mindmap.

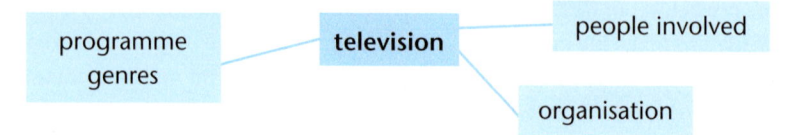

- programme genres
- television
- people involved
- organisation

b) **Buzz group:** Walk around and talk about your viewing habits, which programmes you enjoy most and what role talent shows play.

Preparation for individual speaking task (monologue)

D2 In his novel "Chart Throb" published in 2006 Ben Elton looks behind the scenes of a casting show scripted and produced by Calvin Simms and his team.
Form groups of three or four in which each member works on one of the five following texts only. The assignment is identical for all of you.

a) Read the extract of the novel carefully and take notes on the following aspects:
- who the characters are
- what role they play in the big media game
- what the author criticizes

b) Use your notes to choose an adequate heading for the extract you have read and explain your choice.

Shortlived success
A revelation of true character
Royalty hooked
Young stardom undone

The seduction of fame
High hopes
Plotters and players
A fateful failure

> Ben Elton, born in London in 1959, is an English comedian, author and actor. He first became famous as a stand-up comedian in the 1980s. Since then he has published 13 novels and written two musicals.

Millicent and Graham

'I'll leave you two to it then,' said Graham's mum as she closed the bedroom door behind her. It was the bedroom of a music-mad lad: piles of CDs were stacked along the walls, while on the desk an iPod stood in its dock, connected to two enormous speakers on either side of the bed. There was a vinyl deck[1] too and a decent-sized collection of old-fashioned LPs[2] all lovingly catalogued. There were electric guitars, bongo drums, tuning forks, an iMac and the usual Pro Tools[3] paraphernalia. The only difference between this bedroom and that of the majority of other music-mad young men who dreamed of pop superstardom was that there was absolutely no mess. This room was perfectly ordered, with everything in its proper place, where it could be located instantly. And there was nothing on the walls. No posters, no pictures, no framed drumskins signed by members of heavy metal bands, in fact nothing at all.

Millicent sat down beside Graham on the bed. Graham had his acoustic guitar on his lap but Millicent reached out to take it from him.

'Come on,' she said firmly. 'We have to sing unaccompanied, you know that.'

---

[1] **vinyl deck** = a turntable for playing records, of the type often used by DJs
[2] **LPs** = a vinyl music record
[3] **Pro Tools** = a computer program for recording and editing which is widely used in the music industry

'But it's so stupid,' Graham replied. 'We're so much better with the guitar.'

'It's the same rules for everyone, Graham. You know how much you hate special treatment.'

'I only hate it when it's an excuse for denying me normal treatment,' he replied. 'I don't mind cheating.'

'I wrote and asked them. They said we can use instruments later, if we get through the opening rounds.'

'Of course we'll get through. I mean how good are we?' Graham posed the question in the modern, rhetorical sense, meaning that he was quite certain in his own mind that they were very good indeed.

Millicent took hold of the guitar and as she did so her hand touched his and for a moment each of them exerted a tiny pressure.

'We shouldn't really be skiving off[4] college, you know,' she said.

'You don't get an audition for *Chart Throb* every day of the week, Milly, and anyway we won't need qualifications when we're stars.' Graham replied.

'Don't get your hopes up[5] too high, Graham.'

'We're good, Milly. Everybody says so.'

'Yes, and everybody who goes on that show says that everybody says they're good. Come on, I thought we were going to rehearse.'

[4] **to skive off** = to not go somewhere, such as work or school, although one should go
[5] **to get one's hopes up** = to start thinking that sth. one wants is actually going to happen

Peroxide: Rise and Fall

Peroxide, two near-naked blonde teenagers, had been selected and had thereafter done a surprisingly good audition before the three judges. It turned out that their embarrassingly inept attempts at sexuality were not their only promising feature. They could actually sing and suddenly everybody had got rather excited about them.

Emma could still remember the production meeting that had taken place the previous year when Calvin had announced his plan for them.

'We'll chuck them out after the next round,' he explained, to everyone's surprise. 'You have to play the long game.'

'I thought you might put them in the final,' Beryl remarked. 'Thought they were just your type. They can sing at least as well as half the other finalists, they're cute and they're absolutely fucking desperate. What could be better? I mean, did you see the way they cried when we put them through?'

'Exactly, these are Alpha[1] Clingers, particularly the younger one,' Calvin agreed. 'They can cry even better than they sing. If they cry like that when they win, *imagine* what's going to happen when they lose.'

'Why not give them a bit of a run then, so they can lose big time?' Beryl had persisted.

'They're lovely-looking girls and quite frankly we're way over[2] our quota on Fatties[3] and Dogs[4].'

'The long game, darling, the long game. You have to ask yourself, what's the story?'

'And what is it?'

'Well, we could certainly give these birds[5] a run, as you say, and I've no doubt they'd be good TV.'

'Plus all the cunty[6] ex-boyfriends crawling out of the woodwork to talk about the girls' insatiable man-hungry needs and eight-times-a-night marathon sex sessions,' Beryl chipped in.

'That's right,' Calvin replied. 'It's there for the taking[7] and I'm sure you all think we should grab it with both hands. But how about *this*? We build them up[8] on the first round, big stuff, give them the whole "You are the best thing to come through that door all day" and "Thank God for some real talent" bit. *Then*, shockingly, we dump them almost immediately, straight after round two. You're horrified, Beryl, the girls weep, you hug them, shout at me, throw water over Rodney, but I am immovable and of course Rodney votes with me because he does what he's fucking told. Just kidding, Rodney.'

[1] **Alpha** = *here*: the best, masters of a skill
[2] **way over** = a long way over
[3] **Fatty** = *derogatory*: name for a fat person
[4] **Dog** = *derogatory*: an ugly woman
[5] **bird** = *informal*: a woman
[6] **cunty** = *vulgar slang, here*: stupid, badly-behaving, unpleasant
[7] **to be there for the taking** = to be easy to get if you want it
[8] **to build so. up** = to praise so. a lot

Prince Charles

'The monarchy is in crisis, sir!' Calvin stood up now, his teacup rattling in his hand. 'Destroyed by the very people it represents! It is time to reach out to those people, sir! Reach out to them and save their treasured national institutions from the ridicule they have allowed them to descend into!'

'By appearing on a nationwide talent show?'

'Yes! By appearing on the single most influential, ubiquitous and powerful cultural institution in the country. You, sir, with the help of your passionate commitment to organic farming, high-fibre diets and full youth employment, and your pleasant light baritone, can save the monarchy as surely as Queen Bess* did at Tilbury. This, sir, is your duty!'

'My duty?'

'Yes! your duty!'

'To appear on *Chart Throb*?'

'Yes, sir! Your country needs you.'

His Royal Highness did not reply. For a time he sipped his tea in silence, seemingly trying to come to terms with[1] the enormity of what was being suggested.

'Sir,' Calvin said with heavy significance, 'we are living in a *post-modern world*.' This was a phrase which Calvin used regularly and with great effect, despite having no idea what it meant.

Still the Prince remained silent.

'*Plus*,' Calvin urged, laying his trump card[2] down on the table, 'people will love you again.'

His Royal Highness looked up.

'Do you … Do you really think so?'

It seemed to Calvin that there was a wealth of weariness in his sad eyes.

'Of course,' Calvin said quietly. 'Everyone loves the winner of *Chart Throb*.'

'Winner?'

Calvin had almost revealed too much of his hand.

'Well, perhaps not *winner*, sir, that of course will be up to the public to decide, but as the country's foremost judge of talent and personality I am convinced that you could go a very long way. At least far enough for people to have the opportunity to see the *real you*.'

Once more the Prince fell silent for the time it took to nibble a biscuit. When he spoke again Calvin knew he had his man.

---

[1] **to come to terms with sth.** = to accept a situation because it cannot be changed

[2] **trump card** = *here:* a piece of information which allows one to win an argument

---

Georgie

Georgie was the younger of the two members of Peroxide, a pop duo which she and her friend 'Chelle had formed while attending Saturday morning drama classes and which the previous year had triumphantly sailed through the first round of *Chart Throb* only to be sensationally dumped in the second. Georgie had been just seventeen at the time, too young, in her father's opinion, to be appearing half-naked on television.

'If it's a singing competition why can't you wear some clothes?' he asked.

'The show's all about having what it takes, Dad,' Georgia would reply, standing on the living-room carpet in little more than her underwear. 'Calvin's always saying it … do you have what it takes? Well, thus is what it takes.'

The skimpy costumes had been 'Chelle's idea. At nineteen, she was very much the senior partner in the act.

Georgia's parents were firmly of the opinion that their daughter's eating disorders had begun with those costumes. 'Chelle was a natural exhibitionist who would happily have worn her hotpants and bra top to the pub, but Georgia had what her school counsellor called 'body issues'. She was a slim girl who, when she stood before the mirror, saw a fat girl staring back. Despite being generally acknowledged as very pretty, Georgia could never quite convince herself that her body was good enough to be displayed alongside the confident 'Chelle's and so she began to punish it for its inadequacy.

After Peroxide's sudden and brutal ejection from *Chart Throb* Georgia had become convinced that they had failed because she hadn't been thin enough. The more people expressed surprise that she and 'Chelle had failed to advance to the Pop School stage of the competition, the more she believed that it was her fault.

In the weeks following the ejection Georgia's parents had watched in despair as their beautiful daughter had gone to war with her own body.

Chris

'Yes, Christian, it's true. We won't be renewing,' Calvin was saying. 'Of course I was going to call you myself, I've no idea how the *Sun** got hold of it ... Christian, please, keep it together. It's an album deal, nobody died.'

But of course somebody had died. Christian Appleyard, pop star, had departed this earth and what was left was a pathetic creature indeed. Christian Appleyard, sad act[1], loser, joke. The distance between fame and notoriety, between adulation and derision, cannot be measured in feet and inches; the tipping point[2] is merely a moment, a moment when suddenly the consciousness of the public changes. Crowds are fickle in a way that individuals can never be. An individual had a conscience, while a crowd can afford to follow its rawest, basest instincts and its instincts were clearly that Christian's fifteen minutes were well and truly up.

'Screw 'em[3],' Calvin was saying. 'So some builders laughed at you. So what? Did they ever get a number-one album? You did, mate. Nobody can take that away from you.'

It was true, nobody could ever take that away, not even Christian himself, although he would come to wish he could.

'Look, Christian mate,' Calvin continued. 'You've had a lot of fun, we've all had fun but, you know, parties come to an end ... Brad's still selling albums, Christian, you're not, that's why he still has a deal, that's the reality of the business.'

Bradley Vine, runner-up to Christian's winner on the first ever *Chart Throb* two years before. Apparently he still had it, Christian did not.

'The mums like him, mate, what can I tell you?' Calvin explained. 'You had the kids and that's life.'

Calvin looked at his watch. He should not be having this conversation. He should never have given that lad his number, but it had all been so exciting that first time around. They had all felt like a team, judges and contestants together. Even Calvin had got carried away a little. For a moment even he had half believed that what was being created was real.

'Look, I have to go, Christian. We'll talk again, OK ... I don't know when, but we'll talk.' Calvin pressed red and put his phone down.

'Wants to know why you've dumped[4] him?' Rodney enquired.

'I didn't dump him, the public did,' Calvin replied.

[1] **sad act** = *informal:* so. who behaves in a way that does not deserve respect
[2] **tipping point** = the time when important things start happening in a situation, in particular things that can't be changed
[3] **screw 'em** = *here:* don't think or worry about them
[4] **to dump so.** = *here:* to end so.'s contract with a record label

4 Britain is Great: The culture of Great Britain

Presentation

Skills
How to prepare for an oral exam p. 168

D3 Use your notes to sum up the extract from the novel in your own words and outline the author's criticism.
- Think of a comprehensive introductory sentence.

- To conclude your presentation state your own view on the author's intention.
- Practice your presentation, then give your talk.

Language support

My extract from the novel "…" by …
  deals with …
  is set in …
  focuses on the topic/problem/situation of …
In the extract I dealt with/I read we learn about …
  the characters presented are …

– In my view …
– As far as I can see …
– Evidently it is the author's intention to …
– Judging by the tone/style of the extract, I would say that the author …
– The author depicts the situation in quite a humorous/drastic/exaggerated way so I would conclude …/consequently I think/ would say/assume that …

Checklist
Since all group members rely on you for the follow-up task you must present the information clearly.
In order to use the information in the following discussion it is really important that your group members give you feedback

- **on the content:**
  ✓ present the situation clearly
  ✓ use formulations that are not taken from the original text
  ✓ use your own words not those of the text

- **on your language performance:**
  ✓ use a varied and complex vocabulary
  ✓ pronounce the words correctly
  ✓ vary the sentence structure

Britain is Great: The culture of Great Britain

Discussion (dialogue)

D4 Compare your impressions of the author's presentation of the casting show and the people involved and discuss if Ben Elton's view can be applied to German TV productions. The following phrases may be helpful:

In your discussion you should react to what has been said before:

- You might agree or disagree. You already know a lot of phrases some of which are fairly formal.
  Here are some more conversational ways to voice a different opinion.

Language support

… is very/somewhat similar in that it also shows …
… is slightly/definitely different since/as …
… focuses on a different aspect/highlights a different angle

– That's an interesting observation
– That's a good point/valid argument
– That is certainly a different way of looking at it
– Well, my experience is somewhat different
– There seems to be some truth in it, but many people …
– Oh, I didn't think about …

– Well, that's one way of looking at it, but …
– That may be true in some respects/cases/ for some people but …
– The way I see it …
– I'm not sure that this is true
– Fair enough

– I wouldn't say so
– I sometimes wonder
– It makes me wonder

Skills
How to prepare for an oral exam
p. 168

5 Awkward partners and a special relationship

Getting started

A1 a) **Pair work:** Work with a partner and write down your ideas about these relationships:
- "Britain and the European Union" and
- "Britain and the United States".

Use cards of two different colours for the two relationships.

b) **Cluster** your cards on the board and compare the relationships.

A2 Britain and Europe
a) Study all the headlines and say what they express about the relationship between Britain and the EU.

Daily Mail
THE DAY HE PUT BRITAIN FIRST
Defiant Cameron stands up to Euro bullies – but French plot revenge for historic veto

The Independent
The EU leaves Britain
- Eurozone nations agree 'fiscal compact' to boost stability
- Six others join new pact, with three more expected to do so
- UK isolated after Cameron blocks EU-wide treaty change

The Telegraph

William Hague on the EU membership vote: We won't leave Europe, but it won't rule us

Negotiation is the key to Britain's relationship with Europe, not turning our backs on it.

EuropeanVoice.com

UK

Awkward partners … but still married
By Kirsty Hughes – 26.07.2007

Awkward partners and a special relationship: Britain and the EU/Britain and the USA

A3 Britain and the United States of America
a) Look at the two pictures and describe your immediate impressions of the relationship between Britain and the USA.

b) Describe the pictures in detail and identify the (common) elements that gave you this impression.

How to describe pictures p. 172

A4 Read the following texts and collect words and phrases which can be used to describe the relationships between countries.

"And that is the key to our relationship. Yes, it is founded on a deep emotional connection, by sentiment and ties of people and culture. But the reason it thrives, the reason why this is such a natural partnership, is because it advances our common interests and shared values. It is a perfect alignment of what we both need and what we both believe. And the reason it remains strong is because it delivers[1] time and again[2]. Ours is not just a special relationship, it is an essential relationship – for us and for the world."
David Cameron/Barrack Obama, 23 May 2011

Neither the sure prevention of war, nor the continuous rise of world organization will be gained without what I have called the fraternal association of the English-speaking peoples … a special relationship between the British Commonwealth* and Empire and the United States.
Churchill, Fulton, Missouri, on 5 March 1946*

"I've come here today to reaffirm one of the oldest, one of the strongest alliances the world has ever known. It has long been said that the United States and the United Kingdom share a special relationship. […]
The reason for this close friendship doesn't just have to do with our shared history, our shared heritage; our ties of language and culture; or even the strong partnership between our governments. Our relationship is special because of the values and beliefs that have united our people through the ages[3]."
Obama's speech to UK Parliament, BBC, 25 May 2011

[1] **to deliver** = *here:* to do sth. successfully as promised
[2] **time and again** = repeatedly
[3] **through the ages** = over the centuries

5 Awkward partners and a special relationship: Britain and the EU/Britain and the USA

Tip
* means this term is explained in the Names and terms section on pages 182-190

Britain: Europe's Awkward Partner – And Proud Of It
31 May 2006

Posted by David in Europe. trackback

Ever since the early concept of the European Union after the Second World War, the United Kingdom has been an awkward partner. "We are with Europe but not of it," said Churchill, and the Labour administrations of Attlee shared this sentiment. Britain felt closer to her historic partners – the Commonwealth and the United States of America – where Churchill had fostered a close and strong special relationship. Churchill's belief in an "alliance of the English speaking world" was far closer to the government and public opinion than any ideas of European unity.

http://chameleonsonbicycles.wordpress.com

A5 Freeze frames

a) **Group work:** Create a freeze frame illustrating the relationships between Britain and the USA on the one hand and Britain and the European Union on the other hand. Imagine the following people are at a G8* summit meeting: The president of the USA, the British prime minister and the German chancellor or any other European head of state.
- Form groups of 4.
- Each group member takes on the role of one of the leaders. Only the British prime minister is impersonated by two students in your group.
- Discuss within your group how you could best visualize the relations between Britain and the European Union (Prime Minister No. 1) and between Britain and the US (Prime Minister No. 2) in one single freeze frame.
- Devise a statement for each politician in the frame which underlines the relationships expressed. Use the vocabulary from A2 and A4.

b) First present your freeze frames to the class without speaking. Your classmates should identify the characters in your frames.

c) Now make your statements.

d) Discuss the interpretations of the freeze frames and compare them with your own intentions.

Britain and the United States of America

Relations between Britain and what later became the United States of America began in the seventeenth century. Under James I (1603–1625) and Charles I (1625–1649), English settlers established a number of colonies along the eastern coast of North America. To begin with, the home government didn't take very much notice of them. However, by 1750 France and Spain had also colonised large parts of North America and this led to rivalry and conflict between the three European powers. In 1763, Britain defeated France in the Seven Years' War* and the British government saw its American colonies as a useful source of income to pay off its debts from the war. Tensions between the mother country[1] and the American colonies gradually increased as more and more taxes were levied on them.

The colonists demanded representation in parliament in return for taxes, but this was refused. So in 1773 a group of colonists openly rebelled with the "Boston Tea Party" and threw the cargoes of three tea ships into Boston harbour in protest against a tax on tea. One year later delegates of the 13 colonies decided to suspend trade with Britain, which led to the American War of Independence (1775–1783). The Declaration of Independence on July 4, 1776 marked the birth of the new republic.

The Boston Tea Party

Relations between the two powers did not improve at the beginning of the 19th century. The British still had an important colony in Canada and were thus strategically a threat to the young American Republic. In 1812 the Americans declared war on the British in order to protect American trading rights and preserve the freedom of the seas[2] for American ships. The British raided Washington and set fire to the presidential palace, later known as the White House. However, the countries negotiated a peace settlement in 1815.

The British later supported the US government in the Monroe Doctrine of 1823, which aimed to prevent further European colonial ambitions in the West of America. Britain backed the Monroe Doctrine as good for both its imperial defence of Canada and trade. By then, the United States and Britain had embarked on a mutually beneficial trade system.

In the American Civil War (1861–65) the southern Confederate states* assumed that the British would support them against the government in Washington. But although there was some sympathy with the idea in Britain, the government did not support slavery and thus decided to remain neutral. Moreover, the British economy was quite dependent on trade with the United States by this time and did not want to risk losing cheap imports of grain.

At the beginning of the First World War (1914–18), both the United Kingdom and Germany carried out propaganda campaigns to gain the support of the United States, which by this time had built up a large fleet of ships. The US government was intent on pursuing a policy of neutrality and was willing to export goods to any country. After the sinking of the British luxury ship, the Lusitania, killing 128 Americans, there was, however, a strong swing of public opinion against the Germans in the United States and in 1917 it declared war on Germany. US troops played an important role in defeating Germany on the Western Front and bringing the Great War to an end.

During the 1920s and 1930s the United States pursued a policy of isolationism[3] and was rarely active in foreign affairs[4]. This was mainly because they were absorbed with internal and economic affairs during this period. They refused to join the League of Nations* although this idea had been put forward by the US president, Woodrow Wilson. However, the UK and the United States remained on friendly terms bilaterally[5] and the British appeasement policy towards Nazi Germany was generally supported in the US.

Despite their sympathy towards France and Britain during the conflict with Germany, the US government continued to maintain its neutral-

---

[1] **mother country** = the country where the colonists originally came from
[2] **freedom of the seas** = a legal principle allowing ships to go anywhere on the ocean, other than the water along other countries' coastlines.
[3] **policy of isolationism** = a country's policy of not having political relationships with other countries
[4] **foreign affairs** = matters that involve other countries
[5] **bilaterally** = *here:* on both sides; mutually agreed between two parties

Awkward partners and a special relationship: Britain and the EU/Britain and the USA

ity in World War II until the Japanese attack on the American fleet in Pearl Harbour* in December 1941. The United States and Britain then cooperated in the invasions of France, Germany and Italy and at the end of the war they shared the occupation of Germany with France and the Soviet Union.

After World War II, relations between the two countries became closer and closer. They were both charter members[6] of the United Nations. Furthermore, both countries were central to the overall cold war policy of containment[7] of communism and played a leading role in the creation of the North Atlantic Treaty Organization* (NATO), to fight Communist aggression in Europe. In 1958, the US-Great Britain Mutual Defence Act was signed, allowing the United States to transfer nuclear secrets and material to Britain. It also allowed Britain to conduct underground atomic tests in the United States, which began in 1962.

As a result of these strong diplomatic and military ties Britain remained a loyal partner of various US governments in their foreign policy. British soldiers were sent to fight alongside Americans in the Korean War, 1950–53. Although Britain was not militarily involved in the Vietnam War (1956–75), it supported the United States in the conflict. British troops saw action in the 1991 Gulf War and, following the 9/11 attacks, Tony Blair sent British soldiers to Afghanistan and Iraq in the war against terror. However, in August 2013 parliament rejected supporting the United States in a possible military intervention in Syria.

Britain and the EU

Twenty-two years after the EEC* (European Economic Community) was formed, Britain finally became a member at the third attempt on January 1st 1973. How and why did Britain join the so-called "Common Market"?

Immediately after the Second World War Britain held on to her strategic roles as the main ally of the United States of America and head of the British Empire or Commonwealth*. So, although in 1946 Winston Churchill* urged France and Germany to take a lead in creating a European union, he also made it clear that it was not Britain's ambition to be part of it. The special relationship to the United States was essentially a political barrier to any British participation in European unity. Furthermore, the leadership of the Commonwealth had considerable economic and political importance for Britain, so that they saw no need for closer links with Europe. Thus, both the Conservative Party and the Labour party rejected membership of the European Coal and Steel Community* in 1951, the first step towards a common European economic policy. The Atlantic Axis* and the Commonwealth seemed at the time more important for the British economy than trade links with Europe.

However, the post-war recovery period put a huge strain on the British economy. At the same time Britain was reluctantly being forced to abandon her role as a leading world power. The post-war independence of India in 1947 and the defeat by Egypt in the Suez Crisis* in 1956 revealed her financial and military weakness. Relationships with the United States were also strained after the United States refused to support Britain and France during the Suez Crisis. Britain was now internationally overshadowed by the United States and the Soviet Union and the Cold War* dominated international relations. These developments led the British government to rethink its attitude to Europe.

In 1959 Great Britain and six other countries outside the EEC created the EFTA* (European Free Trade Association) for European states who were unwilling or unable to join the EEC. The EFTA countries were, however, not the most important countries for British imports and exports, so that in 1961 Britain applied to join the EEC. Their bid was not successful because

---

[6] **charter member** = an original or founder member
[7] **policy of containment** = US policy intended to stop the spread of communism

Awkward partners and a special relationship: Britain and the EU/Britain and the USA

Charles de Gaulle, the French president, believed that Britain was still too strongly involved with the United States and the Commonwealth, and vetoed it. He was afraid of American influence in Europe. A second bid in 1964 was also vetoed by France on similar grounds.

It was not until de Gaulle's resignation in 1969 that Britain was given the chance to join the club. Under the new French president, Pompidou, a good working relationship between the two countries was set up and the Conservative prime minister, Edward Heath, successfully reapplied for membership in 1971. In 1975 a referendum endorsed British membership of the European Community with 67 % of the British people voting in favour of it. It was backed by both the Labour government and the Conservative opposition.

Although Britain had fought hard to join the European club she remained one of its most critical members. The common agricultural policy[8] was criticised by the Conservative government under Margaret Thatcher. It was seen as favouring other European countries more than Britain because Britain had fewer farms and Thatcher therefore demanded special concessions for the UK. After Britain threatened to stop payments, these concessions were granted to it in 1984. Britain's motives for being part of the EEC continued to be purely economic.

Later, another Conservative prime minister, John Major, received considerable criticism from his own back-benchers after he signed the Maastricht Treaty* in 1992, which introduced European cooperation on foreign policy and security although he refused to endorse both the plans for a single European currency as well as the Social Chapter*, both important elements of the Maastricht Treaty. While other European countries moved towards a single currency and giving greater powers to Brussels, many people in Britain continued to oppose any concessions to Europe, which might involve any loss of national sovereignty.

Under Tony Blair, who became prime minister in 1997, the Labour Party promoted a pro-European policy and Blair immediately signed the Social Chapter when he came to power. He declared it his aim to give Britain a central role in Europe. He and his successor Gordon Brown certainly succeeded in giving Britain a more positive European image than their predecessors. However, the special relationship to the United States was strongly reaffirmed after 9/11 and Britain supported the United States in Afghanistan, estranging her European partners. As chancellor of the exchequer*, Gordon Brown also blocked Tony Blair's attempts to join the Euro.

David Cameron committed his Conservative party to loosening Britain's ties to Europe once more. He pledged a referendum before the end of 2017, and, if re-elected, promised to renegotiate Britain's membership. It is not clear how the majority of Britons will vote in such a referendum. Growing support of the United Kingdom Independence Party (Ukip), which campaigns to leave the EU, is certainly a reflection of euroscepticism in the UK. Their success in by-elections in 2014, however, was also the result of dissatisfaction with the government's handling of the economy, immigration and crime. Ukip's right-wing nationalist policies on such issues have also attracted many supporters . It is therefore not clear how the majority of British people will vote in the referendum.

[8] **common agricultural policy** = a system of agricultural subsidies and other programmes agreed by EU member countries

Optional tasks

1. Draw a time-line illustrating the development of Anglo-American relations from the 17th to the 20th century.

2. Choose one of the pictures. Describe it and explain its historical context.

Practice section

Comprehension

B1 a) Read the following excerpts from former British Prime Minister Gordon Brown's speech to US Congress* and write a "breaking news" ticker message of no more than three abbreviated sentences that summarize the content of his speech.

b) Compare your ticker message with a partner's.

c) State Gordon Brown's attitude towards (a) America and (b) Anglo-American relations. Quote from the text to support your answer.

Gordon Brown's speech to US Congress

guardian.co.uk, Wednesday 4 March 2009 16.34 GMT

Madam Speaker, Mr Vice-President, distinguished members of Congress, I come to this great capital of this great nation, an America renewed under a new president to say that
5 America's faith in the future has been, is and always will be an inspiration to the whole world.
[…]
Madam Speaker, Mr Vice-President, I come in friendship to renew, for new times, our special
10 relationship founded upon our shared history, our shared values and, I believe, our shared futures. I grew up in the 1960s as America, led by President Kennedy*, looked to the heavens and saw not the endless void of the unknown,
15 but a new frontier to dare to discover and explore. People said it couldn't be done – but America did it.

And 20 years later, in the 1980s, America led by President Reagan* refused to accept the fate
20 of millions trapped behind an iron curtain, and insisted instead that the people of eastern Europe be allowed to join the ranks of nations which live safe, strong and free. People said it would never happen in our lifetime but it did,
25 and the Berlin Wall was torn down brick by brick.

So early in my life I came to understand that America is not just the indispensable nation, it is the irrepressible nation. Throughout your
30 history Americans have led insurrections in the human imagination, have summoned revolutionary times through your belief that there is no such thing as an impossible endeavour. It is never possible to come here without having
35 your faith in the future renewed.

Throughout a whole century the American people stood liberty's ground not just in one world war but in two.

And I want you to know that we will never
40 forget the sacrifice and service of the American soldiers who gave their lives for people whose names they never knew, and whose faces they never saw, and yet people who have lived in freedom thanks to the bravery and valour of
45 the Americans who gave the "last full measure of devotion".
[…]
In the hardest days of the last century, faith in the future kept America alive and I tell you
50 that America kept faith in the future alive for all the world.

Almost every family in Britain has a tie that binds them to America. So I want you to know that whenever a young American soldier or
55 marine, sailor or airman is killed in conflict anywhere in the world, we, the people of Britain, grieve with you. Know that your loss is our loss, your families' sorrow is our families' sorrow and your nation's determination is our
60 nation's determination that they shall not have died in vain.

And let me pay tribute to the soldiers, yours and ours, who again fight side by side in the plains of Afghanistan and the streets of Iraq,

Awkward partners and a special relationship: Britain and the EU/Britain and the USA

just as their forefathers fought side by side in the sands of Tunisia, on the beaches of Normandy and then on the bridges over the Rhine. And after that terrible September morning when your homeland was attacked, the Coldstream guards* at Buckingham Palace played the Star Spangled Banner*. Our own British tribute as we wept for our friends in the land of the free and the home of the brave.

And let me promise you our continued support to ensure there is no hiding place for terrorists, no safe haven for terrorism. You should be proud that in the hard years since 2001 you have shown that while terrorists may destroy buildings and even, tragically, lives, they have not, and will not ever, destroy the American spirit.

So let it be said of the friendship between our two countries; that it is in times of trial – true, in the face of fear – faithful and amidst the storms of change – constant.

And let it be said of our friendship – formed and forged over two tumultuous centuries, a friendship tested in war and strengthened in peace – that it has not just endured but is renewed in each generation to better serve our shared values and fulfil the hopes and dreams of the day. Not an alliance of convenience, but a partnership of purpose.

Alliances can wither or be destroyed, but partnerships of purpose are indestructible. Friendships can be shaken, but our friendship is unshakeable. Treaties can be broken but our partnership is unbreakable.

And I know there is no power on earth that can drive us apart.

[…]

And let me say that you now have the most pro-American European leadership in living memory. A leadership that wants to cooperate more closely together, in order to cooperate more closely with you. There is no old Europe, no new Europe, there is only your friend Europe.

So once again I say we should seize the moment – because never before have I seen a world so willing to come together. Never before has that been more needed. And never before have the benefits of cooperation been so far-reaching.

So when people here and in other countries ask what more can we do now to bring an end to this downturn, let me say this – we can achieve more working together. And just think of what we can do if we combine not just in a partnership for security but in a new partnership for prosperity too.

Analysis

B2 Analyze the rhetorical devices Gordon Brown uses and explain their effects on the audience. In order to do this you should first

- study the rhetorical devices in the info-box on page 96
- identify and name the rhetorical devices used in the speech
- explain why he uses them and to what effect

Then look at these examples which could appear in the main body of your analysis.

1. Gordon Brown uses the rhetorical device repetition – here in a group of three – to emphasize the common history and ideology of Britain and the USA: "I come in friendship to renew, for new times, our special relationship founded upon **our shared history, our shared values** and, I believe, **our shared futures**," (ll. 9–13). The effect is to address and involve the audience in his speech and persuade them of their mutual interests.
2. Gordon Brown also employs antithesis/contrast in order to underline and here even idealize the strength of their relationship: "Friendships can be **shaken**, but our friendship is **unshakeable**. Treaties can be **broken** but our partnership is **unbreakable**," (ll. 97–99). He thus also flatters the members of Congress and the United States as a nation.

Checklist: Text analysis p. 146

Language support: expressing intention and effect

to convince someone of something
to persuade someone to do something
to underline a point of view
to illustrate a point
to gloss over the facts
to flatter someone
to evoke a feeling of something
to suggest something
to call to one's mind
to imply something
to advocate an idea
to convey a message
to hint at something

Checklist
✓ State the topic dealt with in the political speech (introduction).
✓ Identify the most obvious and most effectively used rhetorical devices.
✓ Explain their effects.
✓ Explain the interplay of the speaker's message and the means used to convince the audience.
✓ Use appropriate vocabulary (see language support).

Info: Rhetorical devices, definitions and their effects

rhetorical device	definitions and effects
alliteration	emphasis that occurs through the repetition of initial consonant letters of two or more neighbouring words; e.g. "bigger box", "red rose"
allusion	a reference to sth. which is common knowledge to the speaker and the audience, e.g. a famous historical or literary figure or event: "a King who took us to the mountain-top and pointed the way to the Promised Land" (Obama refers to Martin Luther King, who explained his vision of America's future in his "I have a dream" speech)
anaphora	the repetition of identical words or phrases at the beginning of a sentence to put emphasis on sth., e.g. "as long as apartheid exists we will march; as long as detention without trial exists we will march; as long as our leaders are in jail we will march ..." (Allan Boesack)
antithesis/ contrast	a contrast between two things; denotes the opposing of ideas by means of grammatically parallel arrangements of words, clauses or sentences so as to produce an effective contrast, e.g: "It used to be hot, it becomes cool. It used to be strong, it becomes weak." (Malcolm X)
exaggeration	representing (sth.) as being larger, greater, better, or worse than it really is, e.g. "We've heard this complaint a thousand times."
group of three	a group of three related ideas, e.g. "our openness, hospitality and generosity"
inversion	the reversal of the normal word order, typically for rhetorical effect: "No longer can we believe in the truth of his words."
metaphor	a word or phrase used to describe so./sth. else which creates an image in the reader's mind and makes the description more powerful, e.g. "they blazed a trail toward freedom through the darkest of nights". (Barack Obama)
parallelism	the same or similar grammatical structure; e.g. "pay any price, bear any burden, support any friend". Parallel structures are usually used for more emphasis.
pathos	a quality in a situation that causes feelings of sadness and pity in an audience, e.g. "Even worse than this is the fact that pass laws keep husband and wife apart and lead to the breakdown of family life."
receiver-including words or pronouns	including the audience by using personal pronouns to create a sense of unity "we", "my friends", "fellow countrymen", "our"
repetition	repeating certain words or phrases for the purpose of emphasis, e.g. "Different people, different beliefs, different yearnings, different hopes, different dreams" (Jimmy Carter)
rhetorical question	an assertion in the form of a question which strongly suggests a particular response or whose answer has the obvious intention of including the audience, e.g."Don't we all want to become rich and famous?"

Awkward partners and a special relationship: Britain and the EU/Britain and the USA

B3 a) Practise reading and delivering Gordon Brown's speech. Take into account body language and facial expressions to emphasize his message.

b) Deliver Brown's speech to a partner.

c) Your partner should give you detailed feedback on your performance taking into account articulation, fluency, volume, pauses, eye contact and body language.

B4 Read the excerpts from former Prime Minister Tony Blair's speech delivered in Ghent in 2000 and note down key aspects under the following three headings:
- the history and achievements of the European Union
- Britain's relations with the EU in the past
- Blair's vision of Britain in Europe in the future

B5 a) Identify the rhetorical devices used in Blair's speech.

b) Compare the effect created by the devices Blair used with that of Brown's speech and consider which of the two speeches might have the greater impact on the audience.

Skills
How to give feedback
p. 164

Language support: giving feedback
verbal performance
articulation: to speak clearly, to mumble, to speak with a full voice, to swallow words
volume: appropriate, too loud, too quiet
rate: to accelerate, to include pauses, to speak fluently, to stumble over words, to get stuck
non-verbal performance:
to keep eye contact, to use natural gestures, to use your hands, to react to the audience, to use facial expressions, to pace around

Skills
Checklist: Text analysis
p. 146

Tony Blair's Ghent Speech, 2000

guardian.co.uk, Wednesday 23 February

At a time when the European Union is embarking on radical expansion and internal reform, I would like to take a moment to put the challenges facing Europe in context.

5 My starting point is this: the European Union has been one of the outstanding political achievements of the twentieth century.
[…]
The project that began with the European Coal
10 and Steel Community had one over-arching objective: to end the feud between France and Germany that had been at the heart of one European and two world wars in less than a century.
15 The project has succeeded brilliantly. It has turned the age-old rivalry between France and Germany into friendship and partnership, so much so that France and Germany have been the driving force behind the European project
20 for 50 years.
But the European Union has done more than that, much more.
It has provided a framework for law and institutions which respects the rights of Europe's
25 democracies, large and small, which allows competition but prevents dominance.
It has provided the framework for Europe's prosperity, not just free trade in Europe, but a single market and, increasingly, a single econ-
30 omy.
And it has provided a clear path forward for countries emerging from political dictatorship and centrally planned economics.
It was the European Union more than any
35 other institution that helped Greece, Spain and Portugal turn their back on dictatorship. Not by force of arms, but by force of example.
It was the European Union and with it the vision of a prosperous, democratic, European
40 Germany that helped bring down the Berlin Wall, so setting off the chain reaction that ended the Cold War.
And it is the hope and promise of European Union membership that is now driving politi-
45 cal and economic reform across eastern Europe and the Balkans, from Latvia to Bulgaria, from Poland to Croatia.
That is strengthening the hand of those who believe in democracy and free enterprise,
50 against those who would exploit the fear of change to play the card of nationalism and protectionism.

5 Awkward partners and a special relationship: Britain and the EU/Britain and the USA

The European Union is on the threshold of achieving the dreams of its founders. Of reuniting the continent in peace, democracy and prosperity. But Britain could have played and can play a larger part in it.

Britain's relations with Europe have too often been ambivalent or indifferent. Indeed, I believe Britain's hesitation over Europe was one of my country's greatest miscalculations of the post-war years.

We opted out of the European Coal and Steel Community. We opted out of the European Economic Community. We opted out of the Social Chapter. And we played little part in the debate over the single currency. When we finally decided to join many of these institutions, we found unsurprisingly that they did not reflect British interests or British experience as much as we would have wished. Yet, as our history shows, Britain's place has always been at the centre of Europe. England was a European power long before it became an imperial one.

[…]

Of course, Britain could survive outside the European Union. But it would be a poorer, weaker Britain. We could probably get access to the Single Market, as Norway and Switzerland do. But the price would be applying Europe's laws without having the chance to shape them. That is why I am determined that Britain should play its full part in Europe – for the same reason that Belgium or France play their full part in Europe: because that is what is best for my country.

A few miles from here, in Bruges, another British Prime Minister made a speech. From it stemmed the isolationist and hostile view of the European Union. My disagreement with Mrs Thatcher's speech in Bruges is not that its criticisms were all unjustified. Some were justified. Some indeed were and are shared by others in the European Union. My disagreement is that the response to those criticisms was for Britain to withdraw into its shell[1], to opt-out, to see the European Union as Britain vs[2] Europe. The result was not that Europe stopped moving, but that Britain stopped shaping the form and direction of that movement. The very lesson that the development of the Single Market taught us where Britain was heavily engaged was abandoned.

The idea of Britain vs Europe also infected the debate in Britain and encouraged the perception that Europe was something done to Britain, over which we had little say.

And as we lost influence in Europe, it did not help us in America. Britain has close ties with America. They will remain close, no more so than under this Government. But America wants Britain to be a strong ally in a strong Europe. The stronger we are in Europe, the stronger our American relationship.

I hold to my view that Britain's destiny is to be a leading partner in Europe. It is right for Britain, and it is right for Europe. It is a central ambition for the New Labour* Government.

The change in our relations in Europe since May 1997 has been fundamental. Britain has fully participated in every new initiative: economic reform; defence and foreign policy; institutional change and enlargement; immigration and crime. To each we have made a substantive and clear contribution. Without it, the nature of the changes would have been very different.

[…]

[1] to withdraw into its shell = to avoid contact with others
[2] vs = versus

Comment

B6 Choose one of the assignments:

a) Write a comparison with the title: Awkward partners and special relations: Britain and her relationship with Europe and the United States. Use your findings from B1 and B4.

or

b) "Awkward partners and special friends?" – Comment on Britain's relationship to the EU on the one hand and the United States on the other.

Checklist: Comment p. 148

Awkward partners and a special relationship: Britain and the EU/Britain and the USA

Creative writing

B7 The European Youth Parliament (EYP) has invited you – as a delegate of the German National Committee – to attend a meeting to debate the following resolution: "Turning awkward partners into special friends – improving relations between Britain and the European Union".

a) Group work: collect ideas for concrete steps that could improve the relationship.

b) Write a speech in which you present and defend your ideas. Use the rhetorical devices on page 96.

c) Deliver your speech to the class.

d) Give feedback on your classmates' speeches.

Checklist:
Speech
p. 155

5 Awkward partners and a special relationship: Britain and the EU/Britain and the USA

Getting to the point

Comprehension

C1 Read David Cameron's speech on foreign policy and national security which he gave at the British American Project on 11th September 2006. Summarize his view on the Atlantic Alliance*.

Checklist: Summary p. 145

Analysis

C2 a) Examine Cameron's reasons for wanting "a rebalanced special relationship" (l. 110).

b) Identify the rhetorical devices Cameron uses in his speech and explain their effect on the audience.

Checklist: Text analysis p. 146

Comment

C3 On the basis of what you have learned in this theme, comment on Cameron's attitude to the United States as reflected in this speech.

Checklist: Comment p. 148

David Cameron's speech

Monday, 11 September 2006

Conservative party leader's speech on foreign policy and national security

"It is an honour to be speaking to the British American Project today, on this sombre anniversary. Your organisation is one of the most illustrious of the countless ties that connect our
5 two countries. Today we remember the almost 3,000 dead, killed in the most callous and indiscriminate act of terrorism in modern history.

There is much we owe to their memories. To
10 find and defeat those responsible for planning international terror. To do everything we can to stop further outrages. And, above all, to make the world safer for the future. Fighting terrorism is the most consuming concern for modern
15 government.

I know that if my party wins the next election, the moment I walk through the front door of Downing Street I will have the huge responsibility of protecting the British public
20 from this threat. It will involve action to support and enhance our security response. It will involve action to make our society stronger at home. And it will require firm action on the international front. It is the international
25 dimension that I'd like to focus on today.
[…]
I find it extremely troubling how many people – not just in countries affected by war and instability, but here in the west, here in Britain
30 regard America not as a beacon of freedom and a pro-democracy superpower, but as the world's worst power. Anti-Americanism represents an intellectual and moral surrender. It is a complacent cowardice born of resentment of success
35 and a desire for the world's problems simply to go away.

I and my party are instinctive friends of America, and passionate supporters of the Atlantic Alliance. We believe in the alliance for
40 both emotional and rational reasons. Emotional – because we share so much. A set of values and beliefs about the world – a common language, common institutions, and our common belief in individual liberty. Profound
45 memories too – our soldiers fighting together to liberate Europe; our joint effort to withstand and defeat the Soviet empire.

But there are rational reasons for the Atlantic Alliance as well. The fact is that Britain just cannot achieve the things we want to achieve in the world unless we work with the world's superpower. So when it comes to the special relationship with America, Conservatives feel it, understand it and believe in it. All Conservatives share this attitude.

[…]

Britain does not need to establish her identity by recklessly poking the United States in the eye[1], as some like to do. But we will serve neither our own, nor America's, nor the world's interests if we are seen as America's unconditional associate in every endeavour. Our duty is to our own citizens, and to our own conception of what is right for the world. We should be solid but not slavish in our friendship with America. It all comes down to a sense of confidence. Your long-standing friend will tell you the truth, confident that the friendship will survive. Your newest friend will tell you what you want to hear, eager to please so as not to put the friendship at risk.

We have never, until recently, been uncritical allies of America. We have for more than half a century acted as a junior partner to the United States. Churchill, though he found it difficult, was junior partner to Roosevelt; Margaret Thatcher to Ronald Reagan, John Major to George Bush Senior in the first Gulf war. It is not an easy part to play, but these three prime ministers learned to carry it through with skill and success. I worry that we have recently lost the art. I fear that if we continue as at present we may combine the maximum of exposure with the minimum of real influence over decisions. The sooner we rediscover the right balance the better for Britain and our alliance. This is not anti-American. This is what America wants.

[…]

I am a liberal conservative, rather than a neo-conservative. Liberal – because I support the aim of spreading freedom and democracy, and support humanitarian intervention. Conservative – because I recognize the complexities of human nature, and am sceptical of grand schemes to remake the world. A liberal conservative approach to foreign policy today is based on five propositions. First, that we should understand fully the threat we face. Second, that democracy cannot quickly be imposed from outside. Third, that our strategy needs to go far beyond military action. Fourth, that we need a new multilateralism[2] to tackle the new global challenges we face. And fifth, that we must strive to act with moral authority.

[…]

I have set out today the principles according to which I would conduct that struggle:
Passionate support for the Atlantic Alliance within a rebalanced special relationship.
Retaining the strengths of the neo-conservative approach while learning from its failures.
And basing our actions on a new approach to foreign affairs – liberal conservatism, which I believe is right for our times and right for the struggle we face."

[1] **to poke so. in the eye** = *here:* to attack so.
[2] **multilateralism** = agreement between three or more parties

6 God save the Queen

Getting started

A1 a) Watch an excerpt from the 1975 film *Monty Python and the Holy Grail** about the British system of government. Take notes on the following aspects:
- how Arthur became king.
- how the peasant thinks the country should be ruled.

b) Compare your findings in class.

c) The extract is taken from a comedy. Point out what this scene is trying to make fun of.

d) **Card survey:** note down questions that arise from the film excerpt about the current system of government in the UK and group them on the board.

e) Check the "Knowing your facts" section on pages 104–105 or the Internet to find the answers and present them in class.

A2 In 2012, Queen Elizabeth II celebrated her Diamond Jubilee. Among other events taking place on June 3, 2012, a flotilla[1] of 1,000 ships – including a barge with the Queen – sailed down the River Thames in London to celebrate her 60 years on the throne.

a) Look at the photo and the headline below and find out what two friends, Joan Smith and Rosie Boycott, discussed on that occasion.

b) Listen to their conversation and collect their arguments for and against the monarchy.

c) Add more arguments to your lists. Use the Internet to help you.

d) Divide the class into two sides – a republican and a royalist one.
On each side, form small groups of four people. Compare your arguments and prepare counterarguments so that you are prepared for a debate and can defend your position.

e) **American Debate:** Debate the motion "The end of Queen Elizabeth II's reign should mean the end of the British monarchy in general and Britain should become a republic."

Tip
* means this term is explained in the Names and terms section on pages 182-190

Peter Tatchell (b.1952) – Australian-born British political campaigner, especially for gay equality

The Queen's diamond jubilee: royalist or republican?

What will you be doing for the jubilee? Rosie Boycott is looking forward to joining the celebratory flotilla, while Joan Smith will be rallying[2] the republican troops. As final preparations for the jubilee celebration get under way, old friends Rosie Boycott and Joan Smith discuss their plans for the holiday weekend – and thrash out[3] their differences about the monarchy.

Interview by Oliver Laughland

'David Beckham for president' … republican Joan Smith and her old friend and Queen defender, Rosie Boycott. Photograph: Linda Nylind for the Guardian

[1] **flotilla** = a group of small boats or ships
[2] **to rally the troops** = to bring a group of soldiers back together to continue fighting despite previous defeat or disadvantage
[3] **to thrash out the difference** = to debate a point of disagreement

God save the Queen: Political system in GB

A3 a) Choose one of the cartoons below, then follow these steps to work on it:
1. Describe the cartoon in detail.
2. Interpret the cartoon and explain its overall message. Consider both visual and text elements.
3. Present your cartoon to the class.

b) Compare the messages of the cartoons and relate them to the arguments for and against the monarchy in A2.

c) Based on what you have learnt about the British system of government, discuss if you would prefer Germany to have a monarch instead of a president.

Skills
How to work with cartoons
p. 174

"God bless the Royal Family...what would we do without them?"

God save the Queen: Political system in GB

Monarchy and the political system

Britain may be one of the few countries in Europe that still has a monarchy, but at the same time it is the oldest democracy in the world. However, Britain has never had a written constitution in its history. Instead the political system is based on a number of documents that are linked to important events in British history and may be considered as essential steps on the way to democracy.

The Magna Carta (Great Charter) 1215

As the earls and barons in the Middle Ages were often dissatisfied with the way their kings governed the country, they frequently rebelled against decisions they did not agree with. In 1215 they made King John sign a document that limited the king's power and protected their own privileges.

It was agreed that there should be a council of barons and church dignitaries, and that no free man should be imprisoned, prosecuted or banished without the lawful judgement of his peers. As a result, the Magna Carta diminished the absolute power of the king and aimed to protect the individual baron against any arbitrary authoritarian[1] acts of the ruler. Although this charter was originally designed for the nobility only, the rules that granted the barons more rights would later come to apply to everyone.

The term "parliament" was coined[2] to refer to meetings the king held with his barons and high-ranking representatives of the church in order to seek their advice. It first "met" in 1236 but at the time "parliament" was not a regular institution as the king would call those he wanted to talk to at any time that suited him.

In 1258, the barons wanted regular meetings of parliament three times a year and demanded that parliament should not only include the barons and earls, but also 12 non-noble representatives chosen from the counties.

Since 1327 the representatives of the counties and of the towns had met as a permanent part of parliament, and from 1332 on they met separately in their own chamber. This became known as the House of Commons.

The Bill of Rights 1689

As parliament had gradually limited the power of the crown over the centuries, the restoration of the monarchy after the Civil War* (1642–1651) and the rule of The Lord Protector Oliver Cromwell* (1653–1658) meant that all English and later British kings or queens would merely play the role of **constitutional monarchs**.

The Bill of Rights of 1689, was yet another constitutional document that limited the powers of the crown while reinforcing the rights of parliament: it contained rules for freedom of speech in parliament, required the king to convene meetings with parliament at regular intervals and established immunity for members of parliament so that they did not have to fear retributions from the king if they voiced their criticism or made controversial claims.

Later developments

Up to the end of the 19th century the people entitled to vote in parliamentary elections were a small group of men who were mainly rich landowners. Their main concern was to protect their own interests, i.e. to protect their property against taxation and the interference of the state as well as against the consequences of social unrest.

But the industrial revolution brought about many changes. People moved from the country, where agriculture was in decline, to the big cities where factories needed large workforces. Yet, the growth of the urban population was not immediately reflected in parliament: small villages of historic importance might still have two representatives in parliament, while urban areas like Manchester or Birmingham were not represented at all. The growing importance of the big cities and their population called for a change in the distribution of seats in the Commons and reforms concerning the right to vote were essential achievements in the development of parliamentary democracy in the 19th century.

Women, however, were still not allowed to vote at the beginning of the 20th century. As they had the same duties as male citizens concerning taxation and the law, they felt entitled to the same political rights as men.

---

[1] **authoritarian** = forcing people to obey strict rules and laws
[2] **to coin a term** = to invent a new way of saying something

God save the Queen: Political system in GB

The women who fought for their right to vote in the early 20th century were called suffragettes. Apart from peaceful demonstrations they also resorted to militant methods of campaigning until most women over 30 were granted the right to vote in 1918. Still, it took another ten years before all women gained the right to vote at the age of 21.

Today **parliament** is an essential part of UK politics. Its main roles are:
- examining and challenging the work of the government (scrutiny)
- debating and passing all laws (legislation)
- enabling the government to raise taxes

There are two Houses: the **House of Commons** and the **House of Lords.**

The House of Commons
Currently the UK is divided into 650 parliamentary constituencies, each of which is represented by one member of parliament (MP) in the House of Commons. Each constituency has roughly the same number of voters (approximately 68,175) even if the area of the constituencies may vary considerably. The boundaries of the constituencies are examined every five years to see if changes need to be made to reflect fluctuations in population.

The House of Lords
The House of Lords is the second chamber of the UK parliament, often referred to as the Upper House. Currently, it has about 760 members. In contrast to the House of Commons they are not elected, but are either high-ranking members of the Church of England*, life peers* who are appointed by the Queen following the recommendation of the leaders of political parties, or hereditary peers, who have inherited the title. Since parliamentary reform in 1999 only 92 hereditary peers at the most are permitted to sit in the Lords. The House of Lords is independent from the elected House of Commons. Its main function is to examine and revise the work of the government thereby sharing the task of shaping laws and checking the government's legislation. Not all members (peers) have a political background, but, since they represent a wide range of professions they bring extensive expertise to political debate.

General elections
General elections are held every five years. Voters elect the members of parliament for their constituency who represent their interests and concerns in the House of Commons. The political party that wins a majority of seats normally forms the government.

First-past-the-post voting
MPs are elected in a first-past-the-post voting system. Voters put a cross (X) next to their favoured candidate on the ballot paper. The candidate with the most votes in a constituency is elected to represent it, while all the other votes in that constituency count for nothing (winner-takes-all). This system is considered by many people to be unfair because voters who did not vote for the winning candidate are not represented in parliament and the number of seats smaller parties get nationally does not reflect their full share of the national vote.

In the media you will find different phrases to refer to central government such as **Downing Street** or simply **Number 10**, the official home and the office of the Prime Minister; **Westminster** which stands for Parliament; and **Whitehall**, the road in central London where many government buildings are located and which is used to refer to British governmental administration.

God save the Queen: Political system in GB

Practice section

Constitutional Monarchy

Pre-viewing

B1 Study the chart and explain the role of the prime minister and the monarch

The UK system of government

Judiciary
The UK Courts of Law
- 12 professional judges
- it upholds the law
- it represents the rule of law
- it designs, amends and approves bills*

The Crown
The Monarch
- ceremonial head of state/ represents UK internationally
- upholds traditions
- gives Royal Assent* to Acts* of Parliament

appoints justices

appoints life peers

appoints prime minister

can dissolve

Appointed legislature
The House of Lords
- approx. 760 members (life peers, Anglican bishops, 92 hereditary peers)
- life peers can be recommended by the prime minister, leaders of opposition parties or a commission and are appointed by the crown
- it represents the unwritten Constitution

The Executive
The Government
- the leader of the party with most MPs in the Commons becomes **prime minister** (head of the government)
- the prime minister appoints approx. 20 ministers/heads of government departments to the **cabinet**
- it puts forward laws and runs the government
- it represents the will of the majority

Elected legislature
The House of Commons
- MPs are elected from 650 constituencies (in first-past-the-post electoral system every five years)
- the party with the most MPs forms the government
- it designs, amends and approves bills
- it represents the will of the people

elects

Electorate
(all men and women over the age of 18)

God save the Queen: Political system in GB

6

Labour Party
- founded in 1900
- political position: centre-left party (social democratic)
- main objectives: multiculturalism, extended welfare state*, redistribution of wealth*, increased rights for workers

Conservative Party
- officially named the Conservative and Unionist Party but commonly known as the Conservative Party
- colloquially referred to as the Tory Party or simply the Tories
- party originally founded in 1834
- political position: centre-right (conservative)
- main objectives: British Unionism, free-market policies and creation of wealth*, preventing state multiculturalism, Euroscepticism*, retaining sterling as the UK currency in preference to the euro

Liberal Democratic Party
- formed in 1988 when the Liberal and Social Democratic Parties merged to form a new single party
- main objectives: constitutional and electoral reform*, progressive taxation*, environmentalism*, human rights laws

UK Independence Party
- Eurosceptic right-wing populist party founded in 1993
- main objective: withdrawal of UK from EU
- first major electoral success in 2004 European Election with 12 MEPs elected
- currently overtaking Liberal Democrats as third force

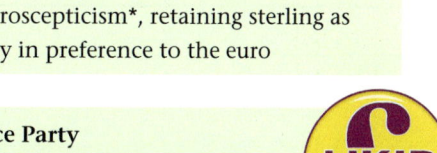

Comprehension

The film *The Queen* covers a time span in 1997 when 43-year-old Labour candidate Tony Blair had just won the election and become prime minister. Soon after his election the death of Princess Diana brings about a serious crisis for the British monarchy.
In the film original news footage is combined with fictitious film scenes.

B2 Watch excerpt 1 from the film *The Queen* (3.37–9.26)

DVD

a) Describe the first meeting between Prime Minister Tony Blair and the Queen. Outline what is said during Blair's visit to the palace
- between Blair and the Queen
- Cherie and Tony Blair
- the Queen and her advisor

b) Observe the body language of the Queen, Blair and his wife. Discuss what it reveals about their feelings and attitudes.

Language support	
body language	feeling/attitude
raising an eyebrow • shrugging shoulders • extending a hand • bowing • curtseying • smiling • frowning • grinning • gesticulating • standing to attention	nervous • disdainful • superior, cocky • reassuring • condescending • over-zealous • self-confident • full of anticipation • insecure • in awe • indifferent • defiant • sheepish • arrogant • self-assured

c) Compare the PM and the Queen's constitutional roles (see chart) to the way their relationship is depicted in the scene.

6 God save the Queen: Political system in GB

Analysis

B3 In films cinematic devices such as camera position, camera movement and editing are used to influence our understanding of the characters, their relationships and their problems.

a) Look at the stills and note down what emotions are conveyed. Consider the situation and the emotional state of the respective persons as well as their relationships.

Picture	a) emotions conveyed	b) identification of cinematic device	c) explanation of effect

Language support: perception of characters and their relationship			
The still The position of the people The facial expression The stance	conveys suggests indicates reveals seems to reveal illustrates highlights intensifies	an impression of/a feeling of • distance • proximity • inferiority • superiority mutual understanding a certain indifference a conflict	• isolation • dominance • community • joy/pride/respect

God save the Queen: Political system in GB

b) Read the definitions of the different cinematic devices and match them with the stills. Be careful! Not all the definitions have a corresponding still. At the same time some stills may be labelled with two terms.

device	definition
field size (distance between the camera and the object filmed)	
long shot	provides a view of the situation or setting from a distance. It is often used as an introduction.
medium long shot	shows a person or people in interaction with their surroundings
full shot	gives a view of the entire figure of a person to show action or to give an impression of a constellation of characters
medium shot	shows a person down to the waist, often used to present two people in conversation
close-up	a full-screen shot of a person's face to show emotions revealed by their facial expression; it can also be used to draw attention to an object that is of particular interest to the plot or has a symbolic function
establishing shot	to give an impression of the location at the beginning of a scene
camera angle	
high angle shot	the camera looks down on the object so that it seems smaller, less important or inferior
low angle shot	the camera looks up at the object so that it seems more important or intimidating as it is shown in a superior position
eye-level shot or straight-on angle	the camera looks straight at the person: this may suggest a neutral view, however, it can also mean that two people who are not on the same level for some reason (wealth, age, academic standing, social class) are presented as equal to each other
point-of-view	
point-of-view shot	assumes the perspective of one of the characters so that we seem to look through his/her eyes
over-the-shoulder shot	often used to present two people in conversation: you are looking straight at one person from behind the second person when it is important to reveal the reaction to what is being said
reverse angle shot	a sequence of point-of-view shots in which the perspective changes from one speaker to the other or from a character to what he/she perceives
camera movement	
panning shot	the camera moves horizontally, i.e. to the left or to the right
tilting shot	the camera moves vertically, i.e. upwards or downwards
tracking shot	the camera follows a person or an object
zooming in/ zooming out	a stationary camera seems to move closer to or further away from the object, thus focussing on it or showing it in its surroundings.

c) Explain to what extent the camera work has affected your first impressions of the respective situations presented in the stills.

6 God save the Queen: Political system in GB

B4 After Diana's death the Queen, who is staying at Balmoral in Scotland with her family, does not address the public in a statement or go to London where Princess Diana's coffin is kept at Buckingham Palace before the funeral. The Queen has decided this death is a family matter rather than a state affair, since, after her divorce from Prince Charles, Diana is no longer a member of the royal family. Besides, the Queen has been brought up not to show her emotions in public. This behaviour, however, is not understood by the public and consequently seems to threaten the monarchy. Tony Blair spends almost a week trying to convince the Queen of the necessity to come to London and acknowledge Diana's achievements. Eventually the Queen agrees. Her speech is sent to Downing Street, but before it is broadcast live, one of Blair's spin doctors changes some of the wording.

In order to analyze the sequence of excerpt 2 (1.15.59–1.19.55) work with a partner. The viewing log may help you.

a) Watch the excerpt and note down what happens in the scenes.

b) Note down what cinematic devices are used and explain their function in the context of the scene. Give special consideration to possible metaphorical meanings of objects or shots. Of course you cannot document every single detail of the camera work but certain devices stand out and produce a special effect.

Viewing log

scene	action	cinematic device and picture content	function/effect/meaning
arrival of the motorcade in front of Buckingham Palace		• establishing shot of crowds and approaching cars • medium shot of Queen and Prince Phillip in car, shown from outside	• to show extreme interest of the people and situation the Queen will be confronted with • to show reaction to crowd/ symbolism of car as protection from crowd but also isolation/imprisonment in the role
in the spin doctor's office		• tilting shot from … • close-up of	
in the Prime Minister's office			
in front of Buckingham Palace			

God save the Queen: Political system in GB

scene	action	cinematic device and picture content	function/effect/meaning
in the Prime Minister's office			
in front of Buckingham Palace		• close-up of Queen's face and reverse angle shots of letters to Diana	

c) Compare and discuss your results

B5 Study the information on editing and explain the function in this sequence.

Editing: the way shots are arranged in a structural sequence
Every film is made up of a sequence of shots. The way shots are linked is called editing or montage. This can be used to slow down or speed up the film and thus create suspense, to focus on important details or to provide additional meaning

cut	the change from one shot to another
cross-cutting/ parallel action	alternating between different shots to present action that is taking place at the same time
match cut	connecting two different scenes by a visual or acoustic parallelism, e.g. zooming in on a letter a character is writing in one scene, opening of a letter by a different character in the next scene

B6 Music is rarely used in this film, but it accompanies the second scene in front of Buckingham Palace. Describe the music and explain why it is used in this particular scene.

Language support: music	
rhythm and pace	mood
fast, slow, frantic, monotonous	playful • cheerful • boisterous sad • solemn • sorrowful • mysterious • hesitant • yearning • sentimental scary • threatening • eerie • aggressive

B7 Analyze to what extent the use of cinematic devices supports the message the director wants to convey about the monarch's predicament. Use your results from B4.

Comment

B8 "Ever since Diana people want glamour and tears … the grand performance … and I'm not very good at that. I prefer to keep my feelings to myself … foolishly I believed that's what the people wanted from their Queen … duty first, self second. It's how I was brought up." Use the quotation from the film as a starting point to discuss what you consider important in the role of a modern monarch.

Skills
Checklist:
Comment
p. 148

6 God save the Queen: Political system in GB

Getting to the point

Pre-viewing

C1 In 1997, the Labour leader Tony Blair became British prime minister. By that time Bill Clinton had already won a second term as US president. The 2010 film *The Special Relationship* shows how the two politicians developed a special relationship not only between the two countries, but also on a personal level.

a) Watch the first two minutes (02:02–4:03) of the film showing Tony Blair as he travels to Washington to visit the Democratic Party's campaign advisers shortly after they helped Bill Clinton to win the US presidential election on November 3, 1992. Describe your first impression of Tony Blair and refer to:
- camera work,
- the plot and
- aspects of the acting (gestures, facial expressions, body language) to support your view.

b) Compare your findings in class.

c) Watch the scene again and note down how Clinton's campaign adviser explains their victory in the presidential election.

d) Discuss what this meeting tells you about campaigning and say how you feel about it.

Comprehension

C2 Having in the meantime become leader of the Labour Party and the Leader of the Opposition in the House of Commons, Tony Blair started to visit various political leaders abroad in the build-up to the 1997 UK general election, which he went on to win. Right after his victory on May 1, 1997, Blair was congratulated on his success by other world leaders such as French president Jacques Chirac and US president Bill Clinton.

a) Watch the next part of the film (4:04–5:44). Point out how Blair's status as a politician and the way he presents himself differ from the scene you watched in C1.

b) Watch the scene showing Blair after his election victory (12:22–15:30). Describe how similar or different Blair's relationship to Chirac and Clinton is in comparison to the scene in a).

Checklist: Summary p. 145

C3 Summarize how Tony Blair experiences his victory in the 1997 general election and his behaviour towards the people congratulating him.
In order to do this, watch the scene following Blair's election victory again (12:22–15:30) and take notes.

Analysis

C4 Analyze how elements of plot, camera work, acting and other devices are used to present Blair's relationship to Chirac and Clinton in this scene (12:22–15:30).

Checklist:
Text analysis
p. 146

Comment

C5 In reviews, the film *The Special Relationship* was criticized for placing too much emphasis on historical accuracy as opposed to telling an exciting story.
Discuss whether recent historical events can be adequately presented in feature films like *The Special Relationship*.
Consider the options of presenting the event as a documentary or as a more highly dramatized feature film.

Checklist:
Comment
p. 148

7 In or out

Getting started

A1 Watch this video and explain in a graphic organiser how the following terms relate to each other.

www.diesterweg.de/cta/74003/links

Queen	Prime Minister	parliament	government
state	nation	England	Scotland
Wales	Northern Ireland	Great Britain	United Kingdom

A2 Many people know at least some facts about England. But what about Scotland, Wales and Northern Ireland?

a) Get into groups of three. Each member does some research on one of the three nations. Make notes on the following aspects: culture, language, customs, geographical characteristics.

b) In your group, give a short talk on your topic. The others note down the most important facts.

c) Discuss in your group to what extent these nations differ from each other and from England in particular.

d) Share your findings with the group, concentrating on the most important information.

Skills: How to describe pictures p. 172

A3 **Four corners:** Describe the pictures below and then interpret them. State their central message.

In or out: Devolution

7

A4 a) Read this definition of devolution. Use a dictionary if necessary.

> Devolution involves the transfer of powers from a superior to an inferior political authority. More precisely, devolution may be defined as consisting of three elements: the transfer to a subordinate elected body, on a geographical basis, of functions at present exercised by ministers and Parliament. These functions may be either legislative, the power to make laws, or executive – within a primary legal framework still determined at Westminster.
> (Vernon Bogdanor: Devolution in the United Kingdom (1999) Oxford University Press)

b) Imagine you worked for a British children's TV channel and had to explain devolution to young viewers.
Write a script for a short TV clip that explains devolution to children. Then perform it.

A5 a) Watch the video and say what it is about.

www.diesterweg.de/cta/74003/links

b) Watch it again and complete the grid.

c) Compare your results with your partner and add missing information.

	Scotland	Wales	Northern Ireland
Name of "parliament"		• The National Assembly	
Issues decided by national "parliament"	• education		• reduction of rates (communal taxes)
Issues decided by state parliament in Westminster		• defence	• subsidies for public spending

d) Discuss why Westminster does not devolve major powers such as defence or public spending.

e) Compare devolution in the UK with German federalism.

A6 Supporters of devolution say democracy is improved by devolution as people gain more control of their local affairs, but critics say it is costly and divisive[1].

[1] **divisive** = likely to cause conflicts between people

a) Listen to the podcast and note down the central arguments in favour of devolution.

DVD

b) Listen again and explain the following terms and phrases in the context they are used:

> Devomax • sovereignty of the people • Unionist • dependent on the umbilical cord • Big Brother • to bypass Westminster • devolution coming to fruition

115

7 In or out: Devolution

a) Study the timeline and write down five quiz questions on separate slips of paper.

b) **Group work:** Put your questions face down in the middle and take turns to pick a question. The first one to answer wins a point.

A timeline of devolution

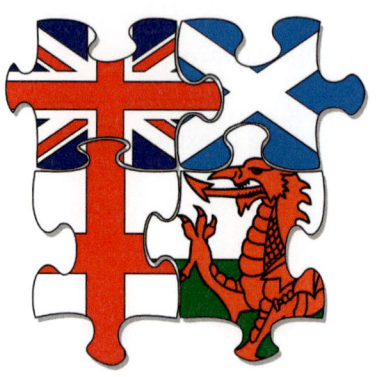

Ireland
Wales
Scotland
Westminster

16th century
English Protestant rulers take control of Ireland and give Catholic Irish land in the province of Ulster to Protestant settlers from England and Scotland.

1536
An Act of Union effectively makes Wales a region of England.

1707
The Act of Union establishes Great Britain by uniting Scotland and England, but devolves legal powers to Scotland.

1790–1914
Irish Catholic nationalists try to win back their independence (Home Rule) but Irish Protestants fight to keep Ireland and Britain united. The Home Rule decision is delayed because of World War I.

1885
The office of Secretary of State for Scotland is re-established for the first time since 1746.

1920
Because the Irish cannot agree on the Home Rule Question, Westminster passes the Government of Ireland Act, which partitions Ireland into *Northern Ireland* or *Ulster* (six north-eastern counties) and the southern counties (Republic of Ireland). The latter become the Republic of Ireland in 1921 under the Partition Treaty.

1921–1971
The real power in Northern Ireland lies with the Stormont government in Belfast which is dominated by the Protestant majority.

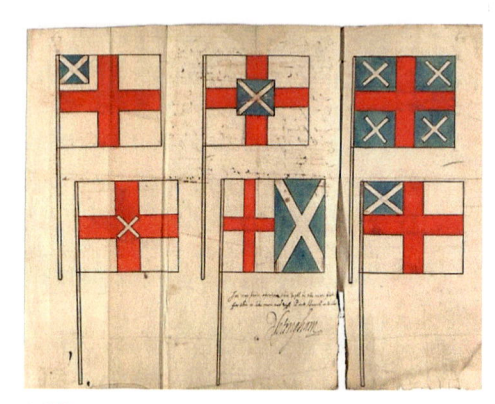

In or out: Devolution

1925
Plaid Cymru[1], the Welsh nationalist party, is founded.

1920s
David Lloyd George leads the *Cymru Fydd* (Young Wales) faction within the Liberal Party.

1950s
Conservative government appoints Ministers for Welsh Affairs following a surge in support for *Plaid Cymru*.

Late 1960s
The discovery of North Sea oil off the Scottish coast leads to considerable resentment of London's exploitation of a "Scottish" asset. Support for the SNP grows.

1972
On the 24th March the British government suspends the Stormont parliament and begins to govern Northern Ireland directly from London due to political instability in the province after "the Troubles" (the conflict between Protestants and Catholics) began in the late 1960s.

March 1979
Scottish and Welsh voters both reject devolution in the referendums; more than 40 per cent of Scots do not bother to vote. Shortly afterwards, the incoming Conservative government repeals both acts. Devolution is declared "dead for a generation".

1998
Scotland Act 1998 and the Government of Wales Bill are introduced. They pave[2] the way for devolution in Scotland and Wales.

April 1998
The Belfast Agreement, or Good Friday Agreement, is signed by the British and Irish governments and supported by most political parties in Northern Ireland: powers are to be devolved at some point in the future with the approval of the political parties.

1928
The Scottish Office, a government department dealing with Scottish affairs, is established. It lasted until the process of devolution began in 1999.

1934
John MacCormack founds the Scottish National Party (SNP), a political party which campaigns for Scottish independence.

1964
Labour government establishes the Welsh Office with a seat in the Cabinet.

1969
A Royal Commission on the Constitution is set up to report on nationalism and the possibility of local and regional government in Wales and Scotland.

1973
The Royal Commission recommends legislation and executive devolution for Scotland and Wales. The proposals are rejected as unworkable.

1978
Revised recommendations from the Royal Commission lead to the Scotland Act and the Wales Act, both subject to referendums.

July 1997
A White Paper (official government report) on devolution is published by the new Labour government.

September 1997
Referendums are held in Scotland and Wales. Both endorse proposals for an assembly in their country, the Welsh by a very small majority.

6 May 1999
Elections to the Welsh and Scottish Assemblies are held.

---

[1] **Plaid Cymru** /ˌplaɪd ˈkʌmri/

[2] **to pave the way for sth** = to create a situation that makes it possible for sth to happen

7 In or out: Devolution

26 May 1999
The opening ceremony of the National Assembly for Wales takes place in Cardiff Bay and is attended by the Queen.

2000–2006
Disagreements remain in Northern Ireland over major issues including decommissioning (disarming weapons and explosives by paramilitary groups). Devolution is restored and suspended on a number of occasions. A breakthrough is finally achieved in August 2001 when a procedure for decommissioning is agreed.

13 October 2006
A roadmap[3] to restore devolution to Northern Ireland is unveiled by the British and Irish governments.

1 December 2009
A bill paving the way for the devolution of policing and justice in the future passes its final stage in the Northern Ireland Assembly.

March 2011
In a referendum the majority of the Welsh people vote in favour of more legislative powers being transferred from the UK parliament in Westminster to the Welsh Assembly. The number of areas the Assembly can make laws on is not increased – but the Welsh gain more independence from Westminster in the process of law-making.

12 May 1999
First meeting of the Scottish Parliament at Holyrood in Edinburgh.

1 July 1999
Devolution Day. The Scottish Parliament assumes its full powers in the presence of the Queen.

The National Assembly for Wales comes into effect. The powers of the Secretary of State for Wales in Westminster are transferred to the National Assembly.

4 February 2010
The Democratic Unionist Party, traditionally in favour of a Union with the UK, and *Sinn Fein*, an Irish Republican Party, reach an agreement on devolution. Policing and justice powers are transferred from Westminster to Northern Ireland.

18 September 2014
The Scottish Government holds a referendum to decide whether Scotland should become an independent state. A majority of Scots (ca 55%) vote in favour of Scotland remaining part of the United Kingdom.

---

[3] **road map** = a plan that makes it easier to do sth

In or out: Devolution

7

Practice section

Pre-reading

B1 a) Watch the video clip and note down what event it shows.

www.diesterweg.de/cta/74003/links

b) Watch it again and note down what hopes and expectations David Cameron and Alex Salmond have for Britain.

Comprehension: Editorial

B2 Think, Pair, Share
The newspaper editorial expresses the point of view of a newspaper on a popular topic.
a) Read the editorial "Scottish independence: the other One Nation debate" and use the language switchboard below to sum up its theme.

b) Compare your suggestion with your partner's and agree on the version you think is most apt.

c) Explain your decision to another pair.

The Guardian editorial of Monday 15 October 2012	comments on addresses focuses on tackles deals with is concerned with	the issue of the controversy about the question of the topic of the debate on	David Cameron and Alex Salmond's agreement on the compromise between David Cameron and Alex Salmond on David Cameron's decision to accept England and Scotland's deal over	the Scottish independence referendum

---

The Guardian, Monday 15 October 2012

Scottish independence: the other One Nation debate

In Edinburgh the question was not the division between the rich and the poor, but the division between Scotland and the United Kingdom

5 Do we live as one nation or two? That question has dominated the party conference season. It returned with a vengeance[1] on Monday, but not in a form that Benjamin Disraeli would have expected. In Edinburgh on Monday the
10 question was not the division between the two nations of the rich and the poor, but the division between Scotland and the United Kingdom.

[1] with a vengeance = way of emphasizing that something happens in an extreme way or with a lot of force

119

7 In or out: Devolution

Tip
* means this term is explained in the Names and terms section on pages 182-190

The signing of an agreement between the UK and the Scottish governments on the terms of the independence referendum is a milestone. Both sides appear ready to accept the outcome. It would feel more historic if the vote were going to happen any time soon, rather than in 2014. But the vote will be the first time that Scotland has voted on its national status in the democratic era. It may lead to the further splintering of the UK. It would change the lives of everyone in these islands. There is no doubt that the Scottish people voted for this process to begin. By handing the Scottish Nationalists a majority of seats at Holyrood* last year, they put[2] the future of the union unequivocally in the arena. (...)

The UK government deserves[3] credit for this approach. It is the democratic path. But it may look like reckless overconfidence if Scotland votes yes. Don't underestimate this moment. Monday's agreement between David Cameron and Alex Salmond is not the end of the phoney war[4], however. There will be plenty more phoney war between now and autumn 2014. But the terms of combat for the future of Britain have now been set. They are, broadly speaking, the right ones. Both sides deserve some credit for the readiness to compromise. A few weeks ago, it looked as if a deal might not be done, with Mr Salmond in particular posing as a leader who could ignore the UK and the law.

The deal means that the referendum will have a firm legal basis. It will be crafted in Scotland with British authority. This was essential. Without such a basis, the possibility of legal challenge to both the referendum and the result was very real. The constitution has been followed, but in a politically practical way.

Both sides have won something in the trading between the Scottish secretary, Michael Moore, and the deputy first minister, Nicola Sturgeon. But it is Mr Moore, and behind him Mr Cameron, who have come[5] off best. Restricting the referendum to a single question – an independent Scotland or not? – removes the possibility that independence might win by a wafer-thin[6] majority while further devolution – which may actually be what most Scots want – was overwhelmingly endorsed. That would have been a recipe for political confusion. Having a single question deals with that.

All the current polling shows that the single question – whatever its eventual form and whatever the franchise terms – will go the way of the status quo. That is why Mr Cameron signed[7] on the dotted line. But the result is certainly not a done deal[8]. The mood will change over the next two years. And the current polling also shows that the Scottish Nationalists remain Scotland's dominant party, at least in the Holyrood context. Mr Salmond signed off partly because he is a gambler and partly because he thinks he will be returned as first minister in 2016, whatever the result in 2014. Two years is too long to wait. But the deal is done. There is a rich debate to conduct now, not just in Scotland, about the best constitutional arrangements for these islands – and not least about the rights of 16- and 17-year-olds in the process. On Wednesday, the Liberal Democrats will make some proposals. At the weekend Mr Salmond addresses his party conference. Let us not prejudge the unfolding argument, but let the guiding star of it always be the best way of securing the good of all.

[2] **to put sth in the arena** = to make sth an important topic of national debate
[3] **to deserve credit for sth** = to deserve praise for sth
[4] **phoney war** = a phase at the beginning of World War II when war had been declared but there was no real military action
[5] **to come off best** = to achieve the best result in an activity
[6] **wafer-thin** = extremely thin
[7] **to sign on the dotted line** = to sign a contract or other legal agreement
[8] **a done deal** = something that has already been decided and cannot be changed

---

B3 Find words and phrases in the article, which have similar meanings to the following:

important event • breaking up • unmistakably • fake • extremely small • supported by a great number of people • something has been settled

B4 a) Note down the answers to these standard journalistic questions:

who? • what? • where? • when? • why?

In or out: Devolution

b) Use your sentence from B2 and your answers in B4a to summarize the main arguments put forward by the author of this article.

Checklist:
Summary p. 145

Checklist
Summary writing
- ✓ Use the simple past tense.
- ✓ Don't quote from the text.
- ✓ Use your own words.
- ✓ Don't give your personal opinion.
- ✓ Use connectives to link your sentences.

Analysis: Point of view of an editorial

B5 a) Identify the author's point of view in this editorial. In order to do this:
- find expressions, like the ones highlighted in the editorial, which reveal his point of view towards the British government's policy.
- categorize them as positive, negative or neutral.
- come to a conclusion about the author's point of view.

positive +	neutral	negative –
UK government deserves credit (l. 30)	Both sides deserve some credit (l. 41)	may look like reckless overconfidence (l. 32)

b) Explain your conclusion to a partner.

c) Write a short paragraph explaining the point of view expressed by the author of this editorial.

Language support
The author:
- *is in favour of …*
- *opposes …*
- *makes a case for/against …*
- *does not come to a clear-cut conclusion about …*
- *remains neutral in his approach towards …*

7

In or out: Devolution

Analysis: Letter to the editor

You will sometimes be asked to write a letter to the editor commenting on the point of view expressed in an editorial. In order to do so, you must understand both the structure and the type of language used in such letters.

B6 Look at this letter to the editor. The colour coding shows the typical structure for such a letter.

1. Begin the letter with a simple salutation, Sir or Madam.	Sir,
2. Refer to the editorial you wish to comment on.	In your editorial (The other One Nation debate, 15 October), like many other commentators, you opine[1] that the omission of the third choice – "devolution max" – from the Scottish referendum question was a defeat for Alex Salmond and the SNP. I am not so sure. Indeed, I think his support for that option was a "Brer Rabbit*, don't throw me in the briar patch" move: giving David Cameron an easy win and removing the biggest danger to Scottish independence: devolution max.
3. Say why you are writing the letter in the opening sentence.	
4. Voice your own opinion clearly and tell the reader your key point at the beginning.	
5. Give evidence to support your opinion.	Opinion polls consistently show that this option is favoured by the majority of Scots, so the question is: which way will these people move? Cameron, and indeed all the anti-independence camp, are gambling that they will vote no, buoyed[2] up by vague talk of increased devolution after a no vote. However, many Scots remember the first devolution vote, when similar promises were made, and subsequently ignored. With two years of the SNP banging[3] on about this, and a "Westminster can't be trusted" agenda, I believe that the SNP are gambling that they will attract many of the devolution max supporters.
	Perhaps, even so, they cannot win. But support in excess of around 35–40% of the voters could – and would – be seen as a good result for the SNP, paving the way for another push for independence.
6. Write your name and your place of residence only at the end of the letter.	**Mark Austin** *London*

[1] **to opine** = to state an opinion
[2] **to be buoyed up by sth** = to be supported by sth
[3] **to bang on about sth** = to not stop talking about sth

B7 Look closely at the structure of Mark Austin's letter and match the paragraphs to these descriptions. There are more descriptions than you need.

1. This paragraph provides arguments/evidence to back up the author's point of view.
2. This paragraph states why Mark Austin is writing the letter and his point of view.
3. This paragraph summarizes the arguments put forward in the editorial.
4. This paragraph reconfirms the author's point of view.

B8 Now read Mark Austin's letter again and note down what he disagrees with in the editorial and why.

In or out: Devolution

B9 The author of the letter to the editor uses rhetorical devices and strategies to make his letter more convincing. Find examples of:

a) rhetorical questions
b) alliteration
c) metaphor
d) allusion
e) facts and figures

> **Tip**
> For more information see page 96

Creative writing: Letter to the editor

B10 Write a letter to the editor supporting Cameron's agreement with Salmond on a referendum. In order to do so, study the tips and the colour-coding in B6 and use at least two rhetorical devices.

Checklist: Letter to the editor p. 154

7 In or out: Devolution

Getting to the point

Pre-reading

C1 Before working on the editorial below you should refer back to what you found out about Wales in Section A and "Knowing Your Facts". More information on Welsh devolution can be found under the following link:

www.diesterweg.de/cta/74003/links

Comprehension

C2 Read the editorial below. State its theme in one sentence and then summarize the main arguments the editor uses to support his opening sentence "Do not take Wales for granted" (l.1).

Analysis

C3 Analyze the language used by the editor to support his point of view. Consider both the stylistic devices and the rhetorical strategies he uses.

Creative writing

Checklist:
Letter to the editor
p. 154

C4 Write a letter to the editor in which you disagree with the view the author puts forward in this editorial. Argue that Welsh people do not want to change their relationship with England.
Remember to:
- note down your arguments
- plan the structure of your letter
- support your arguments using rhetorical devices and strategies.
- write clearly and concisely

The Guardian   1 March 2012

Wales: drumbeat of devolution

Do not take Wales for granted. That is the very clear message coming from the St David's Day* opinion poll conducted for BBC Wales by ICM* this week. At first glance, David Cameron may
5 nevertheless be tempted to dismiss the new poll. Only 7% of the Welsh voters surveyed by ICM say they want Wales to be an independent country – though admittedly the figure rises to 12% if Scotland were to vote for separation in
10 2014. Either way, these are not figures to send a chill through London politicians' hearts.

It would be a mistake, though, to assume that the persistent recent failure of Plaid Cymru* to match the surge of support for the Scottish
15 National party means that Welsh national feeling is a phenomenon of little political account[1]. The BBC/ICM poll figures, which should concentrate minds, are those, which concern the Welsh assembly's powers. Only one in three
20 Welsh voters (32%) agree with the status quo in which the assembly has no tax-varying powers[2] at all. The other two-thirds are split between

[1] **to be of little account** = to be not very important
[2] **tax-varying powers** = powers that a government has to tax people and businesses

wanting the assembly to have power over some taxes (36%) and all taxes (28%). Either of these changes would represent a major change in the political geometry of the UK.

The old assumption that Wales would always back away from radical change in its relationship with London is in steady and fascinating decline. Independence may not be on the agenda, but further Welsh self-government certainly is. The nation which voted by a ratio of 4:1 against devolution in 1979, then in favour of devolution by a whisker[3] in 1997, last year voted by nearly 2:1 for devolved legislative powers and is now, according to the new poll, in favour of some form of taxation powers by a similar margin. This is a large shift of sentiment with big political implications.

Devolution in Wales has not thrown up the kind of full-frontal[4] challenge to the United Kingdom that has been generated in Scotland. But the movements of opinion in Wales pose unavoidable questions about political relationships nevertheless, even if Scotland votes to stay in the union. The UK government has established a commission on Welsh fiscal[5] devolution which has now been given a significant push by the new poll. There is talk of devolving policing to Wales (it has happened in Scotland and Northern Ireland), and Wales's first minister Carwyn Jones favours some sort of distinctive Welsh legal system. Mr Jones spoke yesterday of the future prospect of a looser UK with multiple centres of accountability.

All these ideas push in the same direction towards the need to address Welsh feeling afresh and towards a more imaginative approach to the possibilities, not least for England, of a more federal UK. Generations have been brought up to think of "England & Wales" as one. But those days are ebbing[6] away. Today there is England. And there is Wales.

[3] **by a whisker** = by a very small amount
[4] **full-frontal** = direct and extreme
[5] **fiscal devolution** = devolving the power to raise taxes from a national government to a regional government
[6] **ebb away** = to gradually become smaller or less; disappear

http://www.guardian.co.uk/commentisfree/2012/mar/01/wales-drumbeat-devolution

In or out: Devolution

Mediation

The term 'mediation' was originally a legal one. It means an attempt to come to a peaceful agreement between two disputing parties. However, in language learning the main goal of mediation as a skill is transposing content from one language to another.
You must not translate literally! The text has to provide the required information in neutral language. It is important keep in mind the purpose and addressee as outlined in the task.

Ihre Schule arbeitet an einem Europa-Projekt mit. Sie haben folgenden Text gefunden. Verfassen Sie auf dessen Basis einen englischsprachigen Artikel, in dem Sie Trends zur Regionalisierung in Europa vorstellen und deutlich machen, welche Probleme das zur Folge hätte. Ihr Text soll etwa 250 Wörter umfassen.

In order to do this, follow these steps:

D1 a) Skim read the text and find out what it is about.

b) Read the text carefully, identify relevant passages, key sentences and key words you need to complete the mediation task.

c) Note down the relevant information in English.

d) Write the article.

How to improve your mediation skills p. 170

Checklist
✓ Do not translate literally!
✓ Leave out unimportant details that are not relevant for the reader.
✓ You don't have to recreate the original text. Feel free to restructure it according to your purpose.
✓ Do not add information which is not given in the text.
✓ Leave out your own opinion.
✓ Transfer direct speech into indirect speech where necessary, using verbs like *say, claim, believe, suggest,* etc.
✓ If you don't know the exact translation of a word or phrase, just paraphrase it (say it in a different way).

D2 **Peer-editing:** Check your partner's text bearing in mind the checklist and the following questions.
- Is the essential information included?
- Are facts and terms the addressee might not be familiar with explained?
- Has a word for word translation been avoided at all times?
- Has direct speech been transferred into indirect speech?
- Are there any personal statements or comments?
- Is the style of writing neutral?
- Are there any false friends that need correction?

In or out: Devolution

ZEIT ONLINE 5. Dezember 2007

Das neue Heilige Römische Reich

Flamen, Schotten, Katalanen – gehört die Zukunft einem zersplitterten Europa der Regionen?
Eine Kolumne.

Von Joachim Fritz-Vannahme

Noch gibt es Belgien. Wenngleich das Land schon seit einem halben Jahr ohne nationale Regierung auskommen muss. Flamen und Wallonen konnten sich dieser Tage beim erneuten Anlauf nur darauf einigen, weiter gänzlich uneins zu sein. (...)
Es geht um den Fortbestand Belgiens. Das Land mit seinen zehn Millionen Einwohnern geht weiter seinen Weg vom einstigen Zentralismus über den Föderalismus zum Konföderalismus zum – tja, wohin eigentlich?
Womöglich in die Aufspaltung in ein zusehends selbstbewusstes und starkes Flandern, ein krisengeschütteltes Wallonien und eine Hauptstadt Brüssel, die sich schon heute vorsichtshalber mit dem Titel „Hauptstadt Europas" schmückt. Ein Zerfall in Frieden, da wird kein Schuss fallen, wenigstens das.
Sollte es so weit kommen, wird das Beispiel wohl Schule machen. Das Vereinigte Königreich gliedert sich, pünktlich zum 300. Geburtstag der Act of Union, bereits in ein selbstbewusstes Schottland, ein kesses Wales und ein zergrübeltes England, das nicht recht weiß, was ihm allein zu Haus denn noch bleibt, und das bei der National(!)elf. Die Devolution hat sich in den zehn Jahren von Tony Blair jedenfalls prächtig entwickelt, auf Kosten des Britischen.
In Spanien wird die Figur des Königs (nicht die Person Juan Carlos) zum Debattenthema. Viele Katalanen, die Basken allemal, Galizier und Andalusier empfinden die konstitutionelle Monarchie als einschnürende Nationalklammer. Die italienische Lega Nord sitzt zwar derzeit auf römischen Oppositionsbänken und hat ihren Ruf nach Abspaltung gedämpft zur Forderung nach Devolution nach britischem Vorbild, blickt aber fasziniert auf das belgische Patt.

Machen wir an dieser Stelle ruhig eine Denkpause auf unserer Reise durch die Europäische Union.
Schon jetzt wären wir, den Erfolg jener Unabhängigkeitsbestrebungen einmal ganz hypothetisch vorausgesetzt, bei einer Union mit acht neuen Mitgliedern. Droht da die friedliche Balkanisierung der EU, und das just in dem Augenblick, da der halbwegs befriedete Balkan um Aufnahme bittet? Wird auf Dauer das Europa der Nationen verwandelt zu einem Europa der Regionen? Und wie soll das eigentlich gehen, wo doch alle Verträge zur Gründung und Neubegründung der Union ausgehandelt, unterschrieben und gutgeheißen wurden von den Nationen? Und wo soll das alles enden – in Zersplitterung und Zerfall?
Das Heilige Römische Reich zählte nach dem Westfälischen Frieden 1648 mehr als 300 regionale Herrscher(....). Und obendrein noch einen Kaiser. Alle waren stolz auf ihre Region. Zu Machterweiterung, Eroberung, Krieg war das Gebilde irgendwann nicht mehr in der Lage, der Friedenssicherung galt das Trachten des Reiches.
Historiker entdecken da in jüngster Zeit eine Menge Lernstoff für die Gegenwart und die eine oder andere entfernte Ähnlichkeit mit der Europäischen Union. Weshalb die Antwort auf die eben gestellten, bänglichen Fragen leicht fällt: Gerade weil das Europa der Nationen so erfolgreich war, muss niemand ein Europa der Regionen fürchten. So lange, wie bisher die Regionalisten und Sezessionisten nur nach Europa streben.

*http://www.zeit.de/online/2007/49/
europa-regionen*

8 The legacy of empire

Getting started

A1 Talk about the different ethnic and migrant groups that are part of German society. Think about the following aspects:
- countries of origin
- reasons for coming to Germany
- their contributions to the German way of life.

A2 Multiculturalism means different things to different people.
a) Think about what it means to you and write a short definition.

b) Compare your definition with two of your classmates' and point out differences and similarities.

c) Read the two definitions below and compare them with your own.

The pros and cons of multiculturalism. But what exactly is it?
Does anybody actually agree on what multiculturalism means – and is it a good or bad thing? BBC News Online asked a range of thinkers for a short definition.

PROFESSOR SIR BERNARD CRICK – Chair of the 'Life in the UK' report which led to the new citizenship tests

I see no incompatibility between multiculturalism and Britishness. Britishness must be part of multiculturalism.
For a long time the UK has been a multicultural state composed of England, Northern Ireland, Scotland and Wales, and also a multicultural society … made up of a diverse range of cultures and identities, and one that emphasises the need for a continuous process of mutual engagement and learning about each other with respect, understanding and tolerance.
In other words, dual identities have been common, even before large-scale immigration.
[…] To be British means that we respect the laws, the parliamentary and democratic political structures, traditional values of mutual tolerance, respect for equal rights …
But Britishness does not mean a single culture. Integration is the co-existence of communities and unimpeded movement between them, it is not assimilation.
Britishness is a strong concept but not all embracing.

RUTH LEA – Director of the Centre for Policy Studies, a centre-right think tank

There are two ways in which people interpret multiculturalism.
The first one is the more common way and that is every culture has the right to exist and there is no over-arching thread that holds them together.
That is the multiculturalism we think is so destructive because there's no thread to hold society together.
There is another way to define multiculturalism which I would call diversity where people have their own cultural beliefs and they happily coexist – but there is a common thread of Britishness or whatever you want to call it to hold society together.
And that is clearly what I would support because you do accept that people have different cultures and you accept them.
It is a positive acceptance not a negative tolerance.

The legacy of empire: Commonwealth and multiculturalism

8

A3 **In pairs:** Describe the two photos and talk about what they imply about multiculturalism and/or integration in Britain.

Skills
How to describe pictures
p. 172

A4 a) Watch the video (0:00 to minute 1:47) and note down who came to Britain when.

www.diesterweg.de/cta/74003/links

b) Speculate why people from those particular countries came to Britain.

A5 a) Study the map of the British Empire in 1914 on the inside of the back cover of this book and watch the two BBC video clips presented by Jeremy Paxman. Compare the information with your speculations from A4b.

www.diesterweg.de/cta/74003/links

b) **Vocabulary:** Watch the two video clips again. Copy and complete the list of words and phrases in the table.

Clip 1	Clip 2
blood, tears, …	a nation of many …
cruel, unjust, …	ties: family, …, …
looks, sports, …, …	the Empire on which the …
genetic … of Britain	greed, lust of …
pride, shame, …	moral mission to …
	the sheer e…
	a sense of …

A6 Today one legacy of the British Empire is the Commonwealth of Nations.

a) The word "commonwealth" combines common and wealth. Look up the different meanings of these two words.

b) **Think-pair-share:** Collect factors that in your opinion contribute to the common wealth of people.

A7 a) Study the information on the Commonwealth on the *Knowing your facts* page. Compare the facts with your ideas from A6b: Which factors that you thought of are mentioned and an integral part of the Commonwealth?

b) Talk to your partner about what you did not anticipate and what you find astonishing.

c) **Group work (4):** Visualize the information on the Commonwealth in a mind map. Think of categories first, e.g. leaders, aims, …

8 The legacy of empire: Commonwealth and multiculturalism

A8 a) Read the comments below about the Commonwealth and decide whether the authors approve or disapprove of the institution.

b) Collect words and phrases used to characterize the Commonwealth in a positive and in a negative way in a T-chart.

positive	negative
	sign of a primitive culture

c) Use the information and the vocabulary from this section to explain what is meant by the "legacy of empire".

Comments

Editors' Picks

16. the_Sluiceterer
13TH MARCH 2012 – 13:11
It's like a club of the 18th century. A queen/king is a sign of a primitive culture which is yet to embrace itself on equal terms for all.

14. John Stevens
13TH MARCH 2012 – 9:28
I think the commonwealth is extremely important to share diverse cultures and ideas. Closing the doors to countries who have different human rights laws such as gay rights would not help to bring the advanced thinking from countries such as ours into the more slowly developing countries. After all when the commonwealth was begun it was also illegal in the UK to be gay and we had the death penalty.

7. Simon Morgan
12TH MARCH 2012 – 22:12
So nice to see the Commonwealth flourishing! The critics will always slam it as a legacy of our wicked colonial past. The fact that it is actually growing in popularity is answer enough to them. The sporting and cultural links it provides are unprecedented. And it does of course promote democracy and freedom.

6. Cariboo
12TH MARCH 2012 – 20:01
The Commonwealth is a shambolic talking shop and a waste of time. We certainly do not need an alternative to the UN. On the contrary, we should strengthen the UN rather than support an alternative institution.

2. coastwalker
12TH MARCH 2012 – 13:07
Like any club it should confer on the members a sense of community and purpose. The nations in the Commonwealth are so diverse that it must be a good thing for them to talk. It would be a bad day for global democracy if we were to give up on the concept.

http://www.bbc.com/news/world-17283505

The legacy of empire: Commonwealth and multiculturalism

1. The growth and decline of the British Empire:
   Watch the animated map on Wikipedia that shows the development of the British Empire from 1492 to 2007: *http://en.wikipedia.org/wiki/Territorial_evolution_of_the_British_Empire*

1. The Commonwealth today

The Commonwealth is an association of 54 member countries founded in 1931. Membership stretches across the world's continents and oceans. It includes 30% of the world's population, that's around 1.8 billion people, over half of whom are (aged) 25 or under.

The modern Commonwealth originates from a time in the late 19th and early 20th centuries, when a number of colonies within the British Empire started to acquire greater autonomy. It took on its current shape after India and Pakistan became independent countries in 1947. After that the Commonwealth dropped the 'British' from the title, no longer pledged allegiance to the crown in its statute and became an association for decolonised nations.

Many of the members also have similar judicial, educational and public administration systems.

The British monarch is the head of the Commonwealth and is recognised as a "symbol of their free association". The monarch's duties as leader are attending the Commonwealth Summits and the Commonwealth Games, which take place every four years. In addition, the monarch broadcasts a message to all Commonwealth nations on Commonwealth Day every year, which is on the second Monday in March.

Next in the leader hierarchy is the secretary-general, who acts as chief executive of the Commonwealth. The secretary-general is elected from a pool of Commonwealth diplomats and foreign ministers by the heads of government.

The Commonwealth today is a myriad of different countries. Members include Canada, the world's largest territory, some of the poorest nations in the world such as Mozambique and Tanzania, and small, isolated island states and landlocked nations as well as some of today's most rapidly industrialising countries like India and Malaysia. Despite this range of diversity, all members are united by common values and principles: a common language and heritage.

Each secretary-general serves a four year term and can only serve a maximum of two terms. The role currently belongs to Kamalesh Sharma, who originally assumed office on the 1st April 2008 and was re-elected in 2011.
The secretary-general is head of the Secretariat in London, which serves as the headquarters and executive arm of the Commonwealth. Commonwealth Heads Of Government Meetings (CHOGM) take place every two years to discuss the issues of common interest and concern.

The legacy of empire: Commonwealth and multiculturalism

The Secretariat then takes on the responsibility of carrying out programmes agreed upon during these and other miscellaneous meetings between the Commonwealth leaders and the heads of government.

Since the nations are all voluntary members of the Commonwealth, there is no official constitution, charter or contractual obligations between members as with the UN. All members work together in a spirit of cooperation and understanding and commit themselves to the statements of beliefs set out by the heads of government. Such topics include racial equality, the alleviation of poverty and the promotion of social and economic development. This is chiefly achieved through CFTC – the Commonwealth Fund for Technical Cooperation.

Should a member nation violate the common principles, beliefs or moral authority of the Commonwealth, they will have to answer to the Commonwealth Ministerial Action Group (CMAG). The group was established in 1995 and its function is to deal with governments which persistently violate principles of the Commonwealth. It has the authority to impose economic sanctions or even suspend memberships. For example, Zimbabwe's membership was suspended in March 2002 after elections there were blighted by violence and intimidation. This suspension was extended indefinitely in December 2003 by the CMAG.

The Commonwealth Games were first held in 1930 and are now the third largest international, multi-sport event in the world. They involve athletes from the Commonwealth of Nations competing for medals.

2. Multiculturalism

During the last 200 years, various groups of immigrants have arrived in Britain for many different reasons. Some fled from persecution, as the Jewish people did from Russia and Poland in the 19th century. Others came to Britain to escape poverty or to seek employment. In 1948 492 Jamaicans, and later on Caribbeans, were encouraged to come to the UK in order to help rebuild post-war Britain. In the 1950s and 60s Indian, Pakistani and Bangladeshi people settled in the UK, followed by Vietnamese people and East African Asians in the 1970s. From the 1980s until 2000, refugees began arriving from Eastern Europe in growing numbers. In 2004 the European Union granted citizens from 10 more countries the right to live and work in Britain, which led to a significant increase in immigrants seeking employment in the UK.

London alone is home to citizens of over 90 countries from all over the world. In fact, one in three of all Londoners belongs to an ethnic minority. 3.2% of Londoners consider themselves as mixed race according to the last census in 2011. This also showed that the population of England as a whole was 87% white British but in London the share of white British was 59.8%.

London openly welcomes people from different cultures and religions since there are 40 Hindu temples, a minimum of 25 Sikh temples and about 150 mosques in the city. When asked in the 2001 census, 58.2% of people said they were Christian, 15.8% answered "No Religion" and 8.7% preferred not to answer the question about which religion they belonged to.

8

The legacy of empire: Commonwealth and multiculturalism

Practice section

Pre-reading

B1 a) Describe the picture.

b) Groups of seven: Each of you choose a different person from the bus queue and write down what they are thinking while they are waiting.

c) In groups of seven re-enact the scene depicted in the photograph and voice your thoughts.

> Skills
> How to describe pictures p. 172

B2 Read the opening paragraph of Shereen Pandit's short story "She Shall Not Be Moved". Discuss the following questions with your partner:
- Who might the narrator be?
- What might the narrator have wanted to do something about?
- Who might the narrator have wanted to give "a piece of my mind"?

"I swear, if it hadn't been so late, I'd have done something about it. Or if the previous two number 201 buses hadn't vanished into thin air[1]. Or if it hadn't been so cold. Or if I didn't have Mariam with me, her almost turning blue with the cold. Yes, I would definitely have done something about it, there and then. I would have given him a piece of my mind. And them."

[1] **to vanish into thin air** = to disappear suddenly in a mysterious way

Comprehension

B3 a) Read the story on pages 134–137 and share your first impressions with a partner.

b) Answer the questions in B2.

c) Look up the meaning of these adjectives in a dictionary. Decide which adjectives best describe the two white women, the bus driver, the Somali woman, and the narrator. Give reasons.

> sensitive • considerate • caring • thick-skinned • ruthless • stand-offish
> impulsive • aggressive • confident • desperate • inferior (to so.) • patient
> selfish • affectionate • bitter • condescending • determined • intolerant
> awkward • bewildered • embarrassed • grumpy • repulsive • bold
> cowardly • obedient • serious • arrogant • compassionate • cruel
> indifferent • sociable • hostile • thoughtless • kind

133

"She Shall Not Be Moved" by Shereen Pandit (2005)

The legacy of empire: Commonwealth and multiculturalism

Shereen Pandit is a British author, lawyer and political activist who was originally born in South Africa. She has won numerous short story prizes, including the Booktrust London Award and regularly tutors creative writing groups in schools and colleges.

Tip
* means this term is explained in the Names and terms section on pages 182-190

I swear, if it hadn't been so late, I'd have done something about it. Or if the previous two number 201 buses hadn't vanished into thin air. Or if it hadn't been so cold. Or if I didn't
5 have Mariam with me, her almost turning blue with the cold. Yes, I would definitely have done something about it, there and then. I would have given him a piece of my mind. And them.

But the thing is, it was late, and the buses
10 hadn't come for more than an hour. And this being London, it was pretty darned cold and there was Mariam, shivering next to me. So I was highly pleased, I tell you, when that bus finally pulled up. I paid. That's another thing,
15 it was the last change I had on me and I couldn't afford to get chucked off, could I? Anyhow, this bus finally comes, I put Mariam up alongside me, while I pay. Then I try to move her along into the bus ahead of me.
20 Only, we can't move. The aisle's blocked by this huge woman, with a pram in the middle of the aisle. She seems to be Somali, from her clothes – long dark dress, hair covered with a veil, like what nuns used to wear, arms covered to the
25 wrists, nothing but face and hands showing. The driver shouts at me to move down the bus, only I can't because of the pram. I'm about to say to him, well get this woman to move out of the way – it's one of those modern buses with a
30 special place for prams – when I see what the problem is.

There are these two women, sitting in those fold up seats in the pram space. White, fifty-ish, wrinkles full of powder and grey roots
35 under the blonde rinse, mouths like dried up prunes, both of them. One of them's wearing a buttoned up cardie[1] like Pauline in *EastEnders**. The other one's wearing a colourless crumpled and none too clean mac[2] of some kind. The
40 bigbreasted, big bottomed type. Both looked strong enough in the arm to lift a good few down the pubs every night.

They're sitting right under that notice which says: "Please allow wheelchair users and those
45 with prams priority in using this space". Which means, these two are supposed to get up so the Somali woman can put her pram in the space left when their seats fold up. Only, they're star-ing hard out of the window, pretending they
50 haven't heard a word of what's going on, and if they did, it's nothing to do with them.

[…] There're two empty seats right opposite the women. They can just move over the aisle. I look hard at them, trying to will them to look
55 around. They finally can't resist looking round to see the havoc they've caused. They're still trying to be nonchalant, but you can see this gleam of satisfaction in their eyes, their mouths growing even thinner as they jam their lips
60 grimly together, as if to say: "That'll show you who's boss!".

I take the chance to point the empty seats out to them. Politely. I'm doing as my mum said when I was young, always show them
65 we're better. So, even though I've got a small kid with me, I'm not scrambling to grab the seat. Usually I let Mariam sit down because buses jerking around can be dangerous for kids, especially kids like Mariam, small for her age
70 and skinny to boot[3]. But do these old so-and-so's[4] take the seat I'm pointing out to them? Not likely[5]. They look at me, then look at the seats as if they're a pile of dogdirt I'm offering. Then they mutter something to each other,
75 turn up their noses and stare out the window again, like it's nothing to do with them.

The Somali woman, meantime, has squashed herself tight up against the side of the aisle, just below the stairs. If anyone really wants to, they
80 can squeeze past and go on upstairs. Her face is tight too. Lips set. Eyes blank. Head held high. She looks like a haughty queen. She's done her best to accommodate other passengers by leaving them what inches she can, and now she
85 just shuts off and looks into space.

Through all this, the driver's been yelling on and off. Finally, his door swings open – the glassed in bit leading into the bus, I mean. Right, I think, here he comes, he's going to
90 make the old witches move. He's not scared of them, big, strapping[6] bloke, he doesn't have to be scared of anyone or anything. Besides, he's got right on his side. They can't even complain amongst themselves, let alone to his employers
95 that he's taking sides with the Somali woman just because they're both black.

---

[1] **cardie** = short for cardigan
[2] **mac** = a coat that stops you from getting wet in the rain (mackintosh)
[3] **to boot** = *here:* as well
[4] **a so-and-so** = *slang:* an unpleasant person
[5] **not likely** = (spoken language) used for saying that you or someone else certainly will not do something
[6] **strapping** = *informal:* tall and strong

But oh no! He comes at this Somali woman and yells at her that either she folds up the pram or she leaves the bus. He's all over[7] her, leaning right into her face and shouting. I reckon he's going to hit her. I hate violence and I turn Mariam's face away. I don't like her seeing ugliness like this. The Somali woman doesn't give an inch. Except to turn aside disdainfully because this bloke's spit is flying in her face. Pulling her wrapper more closely about her, she says scornfully that she's not doing either. And you can see why not. Her baby's asleep in the pram and she's already got another small one hanging onto her. One hand on the pram, another on the toddler.

Her face is full of contempt for this driver, but her voice isn't rude or loud or anything. Just firm. She's paid, she's got these kids, she's staying put. He shouts and storms. Eventually he gives up and goes back and starts the bus so it jerks and she and the kid and the pram nearly go flying[8], except for the pram being stuck. Me, I'm totally shocked at his attitude. I'm really building[9] up a head of steam here. If it wasn't for all the stuff I said before, at this stage I really would have given[10] him a go. But he's gone back and there's nothing I can do about him.

I tell the Somali woman to sit down in the empty seat, thinking she can at least hold the small one on her lap and maybe I could steady the pram while Mariam sits next to her. She shakes her head wordlessly. It's like she's used up all her words on the driver. I reckon maybe, in spite of her looking so proud and firm, she's too timid to give[10] the women a go. Maybe she's worried, being black and a foreigner, probably a refugee and all. Maybe she also doesn't like a scene and is already embarrassed enough by the women. Maybe if she'd said something to them directly, I would have backed her. But how could I go and attack them out of the blue, make them move, if she's not saying anything to them?

The two women, deciding that they aren't having enough fun, start a loud conversation with each other about how they're not getting up, no way. Cardie reckons to Mac that "they" – meaning women with prams, or does she mean black women – just pretend "they" want to park the pram and then snatch the seats. "They" want everything their way. Definitely black people this time. And on and on they go. I'm fuming[11], amongst other things, because Mariam is being subjected to all this racist hogwash. But what's the point in having a go? It'll only lead to a row lasting the whole bus ride and I probably will get chucked off then for stirring. Even if I'm in the right. They can say what they like about anti-racist laws, but I've yet to see them stop people like these two slinging their poison around.

I look at the other passengers in the second half of the bus, past the stairs. All white. No-one's saying anything, no-one's seeing anything, no-one's hearing anything. Not their business. Mariam starts to nudge me and whispers to me to tell the driver to tell the old witches to move. She doesn't call them that, though. Calls them "those two ladies". Ladies my backside[12].

[…] Mariam glares at the women. She glares at me. I know what she's thinking. How many times have I told her to stand up against wrongdoing. How many times have I pushed her into standing up against bullies at school, whether they're bullying her or someone else. And her only such a small kid for her age.

We try to bring her up thinking about right and wrong. Like how many times have I told her that I'm only living in this miserable country because I'd got into trouble back home, fighting for our rights. There are political posters and slogans all over the house. One of them's got Pastor Niemöller's* speech: "First they came for the Jews …" and all that. She knows, all right. She knows that I should be speaking up for this Somali woman.

And here I'm saying nothing, doing nothing. Every once in a while, when people get on and mutter about the aisle being blocked, the driver shouts at the Somali woman. She stands there like a rock. Cardie and Mac have restarted their loud conversation about "them" wanting to take everything over. I laugh in their faces and start agreeing loudly with Mariam, but I don't say anything to them. […]

Then the bus empties a bit. Another middle aged woman gets on, about the same age as the two troublemakers. But this one's sort of frailer

---

[7] **to be all over so.** = *here:* to be confrontative, leaving no space
[8] **to go flying** = to move quickly through the air and fall to the ground
[9] **to build up a head of steam** = *here:* to become really angry
[10] **to give so. a go** = *here:* to shout at so.
[11] **to fume** = to be extremely angry
[12] **my backside** = *slang:* used for saying you do not believe what someone is saying to you

The legacy of empire: Commonwealth and multiculturalism

looking. Now my mum, when we were kids, she'd only have given[13] us what-for if we didn't get up and offer our seats to older people. I've still got the habit drilled into me. I don't like Mariam getting up, like I said, in case she falls, so usually I give up my seat. But this time, I sit tight. Mariam gives me a questioning look, then makes[14] to get up for this new old lady, but I pull her down. Call me a reverse racist if you like, but if those white women won't get up for the Somali woman, then I'm not giving my seat or my kid's to one of their kind. No way. I didn't start this.

Now they start a loud conversation about "their" manners. Meaning me. I glare at them and say nothing. I can feel Mariam wriggling with impatience for me to mouth off at them. But I reckon with the driver on their side, even against this poor woman with her pram and her kids, what chance have I got? He'd probably call the police for me, if I gave them lip[15]. And guess whose side the police would be on! So I glare and sit tight. I stare straight ahead, like this old lady standing is nothing to do with me. I can feel my lips tighten with satisfaction at getting back at the other two. See how they feel when it's one of their kind getting a dose of it.

But I'm feeling right small inside. I feel like a real sod[16]. Not only for not standing up for the Somali woman, but for not giving my seat to the old white woman. Plus Mariam starts hassling about getting up for the old woman. I almost blow my top at Mariam. I mean, can't she see what I'm doing? Standing up to them? I pull her down again and glare at her, whispering "No!" fiercely at her as she struggles to stand up and give her seat to the old woman standing.

Then I feel like a right idiot, getting upset at Mariam. The kid's only doing what she's been taught. I make my excuses to Mariam, but she's not taking any notice of me. [...]

I feel sick at the thought of what she's thinking of me. The thing is, what can I do? You can teach kids to stand up against bullies, but sometimes they've got to learn discretion is the better part of valour[17]. I start to explain, but Mariam isn't taking any notice. She looks again at the old woman swaying about on the bus, trying to hold on to prevent herself falling. Then she gives me a look – like I've chucked away her favourite teddy bear.

At last we get to Wood Green and the troublemakers get off, slinging a last few barbs over their shoulders. At that, the Somali woman finally snaps. She lets go of the pram and leans out the doorway and shouts "racists!" after them. They're still hurling abuse at her, as if they were the injured parties, as they disappear into the crowd, everybody staring. But thank God, it's Wood Green* and the sea of faces staring interestedly at us is as much black as white.

The Somali woman starts to struggle to turn the pram so she can get off too. I offer to help her, muttering to her that she should report the driver. What's the good of that, she says bitterly. But why do you think he's taking their part, I ask her, because I am truly confused. I mean he's a black man. The black woman is clearly in the right, so, as I said before, he can't get into trouble with the company if he tells the white women to get up or get off.

The Somali woman gives me a long look: "Because he's a slave," she says. "He is a slave," she repeats loudly through the still open back door of the bus, at the driver collecting fares from passengers boarding at the front. I realise from her attitude that they probably already played it all out, she and the women and the driver, before I got on the bus.

"But me," she says, looking at me hard again, "I am not a slave. I would rather die than be one." Her voice is like granite, hard and unmovable. Every word falls heavy as a stone between us, cuts into me like a diamond.

I feel my face turn red as I take Mariam's hand. All through Mariam's class, that woman's words go round and round in my head. I reckon it's me she's called a slave too, for not sticking up for her. And the thing is, I'm not even mad at her if that's what she's saying. I'm just upset at myself for not doing anything.

And then there's Mariam. People reckon kids forget things quickly. But I know Mariam. All afternoon I sit there watching her. I want to tell her she still shouldn't let people walk all over her, just because they're white, or stronger, or richer, or anything. I don't want her not to stick up for other people if she sees wrong done

---

[13] **to give so. what-for** = to punish someone or speak to them severely because they have done something wrong
[14] **to make to do sth.** = to start to do sth.
[15] **to give so. lip** = to talk to so. in a way that shows you do not respect them
[16] **sod** = impolite word for someone who you dislike or who annoys you
[17] **discretion is the better part of valour** = used for saying it is better not to take too many risks

to them. But I also want to tell her that you can't always do that – you've got to pick your moments. Then I ask myself what's the good of raking[18] it all up again? What's done is done[19]. [...] So why can't I forget the whole thing? Is it because I imagine a bit of Mariam's look of this afternoon still about her every time she looks at me?

[18] **to rake sth up** = to mention something unpleasant that happened in the past and that someone else does not want to talk about
[19] **What's done is done.** = used for saying that something bad or wrong has already been done and cannot be changed

Characterization

B4 a) Study the info-box.

b) Think of a fictional character from a novel you are familiar with and decide whether he/she is a flat or a round character. Think about his/her *appearance, actions* and *attitude* and describe your character to a partner.

Info: Characters and characterization

The 'people' in a short story or novel are referred to as **characters**. The novelist E. M. Forster, in his critical work *Aspects of the Novel* (1927), made a useful distinction between **flat characters** and **round characters**.

Flat characters are two-dimensional and do not change during the course of a fictional text. They are often described briefly, with one or two vivid details.

Round characters have complex personalities, are characterized in more subtle ways, and develop during the course of a story. Like people in real life, they reveal themselves gradually, they can surprise us, but just like real people we do not expect them to behave erratically, without any motivation.

The characters in literature are usually a mixture of main characters, who tend to be 'round', and minor characters, who tend to be 'flat'.

The narrator can simply **show** us a character in action, and leave the interpretation up to us (**implicit/indirect** characterization), or can also **tell** us about the character – give us background information and make judgements for us (**explicit/direct** characterization). Often a narrative text can contain both elements of showing and moments of telling. When reading fiction we take our ideas about a character from the following indications:

Outward appearance and social background: physical appearance – what the character looks like; social status and/or personal possessions he/she has. This is usually all the information one gets on flat characters.

Actions and traits: Certain significant actions such as falling in love, marrying, resigning from a job, even murder, suicide and so on have dramatic impact, but often it is what builds up to and follows such moments that tells us more about a character. It is the observation of small character traits and everyday behaviour that are used for characterization.

Attitude – conversations and/or thoughts: What a character says reveals a lot. However, a character might say one thing and mean something entirely different, or indeed be thinking something else. In presenting conversation, the author has a wide choice between showing and telling. What a character thinks may reveal more than what is said about the character's attitude, and 'getting inside the head' of a character is crucial for a sound characterization.

Alex Martin and Robert Hill, *The Anatomy of the Novel (1996)*

The legacy of empire: Commonwealth and multiculturalism

B5 In the following grid you can find all the information on the bus driver in Shereen Pandit's short story.
First study the grid and then make your own for the Somali woman or the narrator.

aspect	showing	telling
Outward appearance & social background	big strapping bloke, (l. 91) they're both black (l. 96)	–
Actions & traits	The driver shouts at me to move down the bus. (l. 26) Through all this, the driver's been yelling on and off. (ll. 86–87) He comes at this Somali woman and yells at her that either she folds up the pram or she leaves the bus. He's all over her, leaning right into her face and shouting. I reckon he's going to hit her. (ll. 97–101) this bloke's spit is flying in her face. (ll. 105–106) He shouts and storms. Eventually he gives up and goes back and starts the bus so it jerks. (ll. 115–117)	He's not scared of them. (ll. 90–91) he doesn't have to be scared of anyone or anything. Besides, he's got right on his side. (ll. 91–93) Me, I'm totally shocked at his attitude. (l. 119) But why do you think he's taking their part, I ask her, because I am truly confused. I mean he's a black man. (ll. 264–266) "Because he's a slave," she says. "He is a slave," she repeats loudly. (ll. 271–272)
Attitude, conversations and/or thoughts	–	–

B6 When writing a characterization you need to draw conclusions from your findings. This can best be expressed with the help of precise and suitable adjectives. Here are some examples of what can be concluded about the bus driver from the information in the grid.

> Examples:
> "The driver shouts at me to move down the bus."(l. 26) / "Through all this, the driver's been yelling on and off." (ll. 86–87) → aggressive, hostile
>
> "But why do you think he's taking their part, I ask her, because I am truly confused. I mean he's a black man." (ll. 264–266) → perplexing, inexplicable, incongruous behaviour as he treats the Somali woman in an unfair/unjust and prejudiced/ discriminatory way although she is in the right.
>
> Do the same for the Somali woman or the narrator.

The legacy of empire: Commonwealth and multiculturalism

B7 a) Before you write a characterization of the Somali woman or the narrator, read these parts of a model characterization of the bus driver:

Introduction
The black bus driver in Shereen Pandit's short story "She Shall Not Be Moved", published in 2005, is a flat character who is portrayed as a prejudiced, unjust and aggressive man.

Main part
By asking the Somali woman "But why do you think he's taking their part […] I mean he's a black man" (ll.264–266) the narrator expresses her confusion about his perplexing, incongruous behaviour as he treats the Somali woman in an unfair/unjust and prejudiced/discriminatory way although she is in the right.

…

Conclusion
In conclusion, the bus driver remains an ambivalent character whose actions baffle the narrator because he is not willing to stand up against racist attitudes and is thus called a slave.

b) Now write a characterization of the Somali woman or the narrator.

> **Language support**
>
> *Use the following phrases if appropriate:*
> The main character/protagonist seems/appears to be …
> His behaviour suggests that …
> From the way he/she acts/behaves you can assume that …
> The language the writer uses helps to create …

> **Checklist**
> *characterization*
> ✓ Apply this structure:
>   • introduction,
>   • main part: paragraphs characterizing the three As (appearance, actions, attitude)
>   • conclusion
> ✓ Use precise adjectives
> ✓ Give evidence (quotations/lines)
> ✓ Use the present tense
> ✓ Use formal language
> ✓ Use linking devices/connectives

Peer editing

B8 a) Read your partner's characterization carefully and check whether he/she has considered the criteria listed below. Give your partner feedback on each of these points:

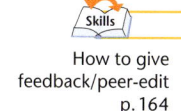

I Content:
  • Facts (name, age, profession, social background etc.)
  • Outward appearance/looks

Skills: How to structure a text p. 156

Skills: Checklist: Text analysis p. 146

Skills: How to give feedback/peer-edit p. 164

The legacy of empire: Commonwealth and multiculturalism

- Actions, behaviour, language, character traits
- Attitudes, feelings, thoughts, opinions, character traits

II Language and style:
- Present tense
- Formal language
- Linking words
- Characterizing adjectives

III Structure:
- Introduction, introductory sentence
- Paragraphs
- Evidence (e.g. page numbers or quotations?)
- Conclusion
- Cohesion

b) Rewrite your own characterization to improve it. Make sure that you follow the guidelines above.

Comment/Creative writing

Checklist: Comment p. 148

B9 Comment on the narrator's statement: "You can teach kids to stand up against bullies, but sometimes they've got to learn discretion is the better part of valour."

The legacy of empire: Commonwealth and multiculturalism

Getting to the point

Pre-reading: meeting the characters

C1 You will meet three main characters in the short story "Loose Change" by Andrea Levy. The first is the narrator. The story begins like this:

"I'm not in the habit of making friends of strangers. I'm a Londoner."

a) Choose one of the following adjectives to describe a person who is "not in the habit of making friends of strangers". Explain your choice.
- insensitive
- unfriendly
- unsympathetic
- reserved
- self-confident
- self-centred
- self-conscious

b) Think of more adjectives to describe this person.

c) Read the rest of the first paragraph. Speculate about how the story might continue.

I AM NOT IN THE HABIT of making friends of strangers. I'm a Londoner. Not even little grey-haired old ladies passing comment on the weather can shame a response from me. I'm a Londoner – aloof sweats from my pores. But I was in a bit of a predicament; my period was two days early and I was caught unprepared.

Comprehension

C2 Read the whole story and summarize it in five sentences only.

Checklist: Summary p. 145

Characterization

C3 Characterize the narrator.
Tip: Use the checklist in B7.

Checklist: Text analysis p. 146

Comment/Creative writing

C4 Comment on the narrator's behaviour at the end of the short story.

Or:
Imagine you are the narrator. Write a diary entry reflecting on what you experienced that day.

Checklist: Comment p. 148

Checklist: Diary entry p. 147

8 The legacy of empire: Commonwealth and multiculturalism

> **Andrea Levy** is a British author who was born in London in 1956. She has won several prizes for her novels – in particular *Small Island*. She has also been a judge for various literary awards.

"Loose Change" by Andrea Levy (2005)

I AM NOT IN THE HABIT of making friends of strangers. I'm a Londoner. Not even little grey-haired old ladies passing comment on the weather can shame a response from me. I'm a Londoner – aloof sweats from my pores. But I was in a bit of a predicament; my period was two days early and I was caught unprepared.

I'd just gone into the National Portrait Gallery to get out of the cold. It had begun to feel, as I'd walked through the bleak streets, like acid was being thrown at my exposed skin. My fingers were numb, searching in my purse for change for the tampon machine; I barely felt the pull of the zip. But I didn't have any coins. I was forced to ask in a loud voice in this small lavatory, 'Has anyone got three twenty-pence pieces?'

Everyone seemed to leave the place at once – all of them Londoners I was sure of it. Only she was left – fixing her hair in the mirror.

'Do you have change?'

She turned round slowly as I held out a ten-pound note. She had the most spectacular eyebrows. I could see the lines of black hair, like magnetised iron filings, tumbling across her eyes and almost joining above her nose. I must have been staring to recall them so clearly. She had wide black eyes and a round face with such a solid jaw line that she looked to have taken a gentle whack from Tom and Jerry's cartoon frying pan. She dug into the pocket of her jacket and pulled out a bulging handful of money. It was coppers[1] mostly. Some of it tinkled on to the floor. But she had change: too much – I didn't want a bag full of the stuff myself.

'Have you a five-pound note as well?' I asked.

She dropped the coins on to the basin area, spreading them out into the soapy puddles of water that were lying there. Then she said, 'You look?' She had an accent but I couldn't tell then where it was from; I thought maybe Spain.

'Is this all you've got?' I asked. She nodded. 'Well, look, let me just take this now …'

I picked three damp coins out of the pile. 'Then I'll get some change in the shop and pay them back to you.' Her gaze was as keen as a cat with string. 'Do you understand? Only I don't want all those coins.'

'Yes,' she said softly.

I was grateful. I took the money. But when I emerged from the cubicle the girl and her handful of change were gone.

I found her again staring at the portrait of Darcy Bussell. Her head was inclining from one side to the other as if the painting were a dress she might soon try on for size. I approached her about the money but she just said, 'This is good picture.'

Was it my explanation left dangling or the fact that she liked the dreadful painting that caused my mouth to gape?

'Really, you like it?' I said.

'She doesn't look real. It looks like …' Her eyelids fluttered sleepily as she searched for the right word, 'a dream.'

That particular picture always reminded me of the doodles girls drew in their rough books at school.

'You don't like?' she asked. I shrugged. 'You show me one you like,' she said.

As I mentioned before, I'm not in the habit of making friends of strangers, but there was something about this girl. Her eyes were encircled with dark shadows so that even when she smiled – introducing herself cheerfully as Laylor – they remained as mournful as a glum kid at a party. I took this fraternisation as defeat but I had to introduce her to a better portrait. Alan Bennett with his mysterious little brown bag didn't impress her at all. She preferred the photograph of Beckham. Germaine Greer made her top lip curl and as for A. S. Byatt, she laughed out loud, 'This is child make this?'

We were almost making a scene. Laylor couldn't keep her voice down and people were beginning to watch us. I wanted to be released from my obligation.

'Look, let me buy us both a cup of tea,' I said. 'Then I can give you back your money.'

She brought out her handful of change again as we sat down at a table – eagerly passing it across to me to take some for the tea.

'No, I'll get this,' I said.

Her money jangled like a win on a slot machine as she tipped it back into her pocket.

---

[1] **coppers** = coins of low value made of copper or bronze (old fashioned)

When I got back with the tea, I pushed over the twenty-pences I owed her. She began playing with them on the tabletop – pushing one around the other two in a figure of eight. Suddenly she leant towards me as if there were a conspiracy between us and said, 'I like art.' With that announcement a light briefly came on in those dull eyes to reveal that she was no more than eighteen. A student perhaps.

'Where are you from?' I asked.

'Uzbekistan,' she said.

Was that the Balkans? I wasn't sure. 'Where is that?'

She licked her finger, then with great concentration drew an outline on to the tabletop. 'This is Uzbekistan,' she said. She licked her finger again to carefully plop a wet dot on to the map saying, 'And I come from here – Tashkent.'

'And where is all this?' I said, indicating the area around the little map with its slowly evaporating borders and town. She screwed up her face as if to say nowhere.

'Are you on holiday?' I asked.

She nodded.

'How long are you here for?'

Leaning her elbows on the table she took a sip of her tea. 'Ehh, it is bitter!' she shouted.

'Put some sugar in it,' I said, pushing the sugar sachets toward her.

She was reluctant, 'Is for free?' she asked.

'Yes, take one.'

The sugar spilled as she clumsily opened the packet. I laughed it off but she, with the focus of a prayer, put her cup up to the edge of the table and swept the sugar into it with the side of her hand. The rest of the detritus[2] that was on the tabletop fell into the tea as well. Some crumbs, a tiny scrap of paper and a curly black hair floated on the surface of her drink. I felt sick as she put the cup back to her mouth.

'Pour that one away, I'll get you another one.'

Just as I said that a young boy arrived at our table and stood, legs astride, before her. He pushed down the hood on his padded coat. His head was curious – flat as a cardboard[3] cut-out – with hair stuck to his sweaty forehead in black curlicues. And his face was as doggedly determined as two fists raised. They began talking in whatever language it was they spoke. Laylor's tone pleading – the boy's aggrieved. Laylor took the money from her pocket and held it up to him. She slapped his hand away when he tried to wrest[4] all the coins from her palm. Then, as abruptly as he had appeared, he left.

Laylor called something after him. Everyone turned to stare at her, except the boy, who just carried on.

'Who was that?'

With the teacup resting on her lip, she said, 'My brother. He want to know where we sleep tonight.'

'Oh, yes, where's that?' I was rummaging through the contents of my bag for a tissue, so it was casually asked.

'It's square we have slept before.'

'Which hotel is it?' I thought of the Russell Hotel, that was on a square with uniformed attendants, bed turning-down facilities, old-world style.

She was picking the curly black hair off her tongue when she said, 'No hotel, just the square.'

It was then I began to notice things I had not seen before: dirt under each of her chipped fingernails, the collar of her blouse crumpled and unironed, a tiny cut on her cheek, a fringe that looked to have been cut with blunt nail-clippers. I found a tissue and used it to wipe my sweating palms.

'How do you mean just in the square?'

'We sleep out in the square,' she said. It was so simple she spread her hands to suggest the lie of her bed.

She nodded. 'Tonight?'

The memory of the bitter cold still tingled at my fingertips as I said, 'Why?' It took her no more than two breaths to tell me the story. She and her brother had had to leave their country, Uzbekistan, when their parents, who were journalists, were arrested. It was arranged very quickly – friends of their parents acquired passports for them and put them on to a plane. They had been in England for three days but they knew no one here. This country was just a safe place. Now all the money they had could be lifted in the palm of a hand to a stranger in a toilet. So they were sleeping rough – in the shelter of a square, covered in blankets, on top of some cardboard.

---

[2] **detritus** = waste that is left after sth has been used

[3] **cardboard cut-out** = *here:* looks like it has been cut out of cardboard and does not seem real

[4] **to wrest** = to take sth. off so. using force

At the next table a woman was complaining loudly that there was too much froth on her coffee. Her companion was relating the miserable tale of her daughter's attempt to get into publishing. What did they think about the strange girl sitting opposite me?

Nothing. Only I knew what a menacing place Laylor's world had become. She'd lost a tooth. I noticed the ugly gap when she smiled at me saying, 'I love London.'

She had sought me out – sifted me from the crowd. This young woman was desperate for help. She'd even cunningly made[5] me obliged to her.

'I have picture of Tower Bridge at home on wall although I have not seen yet.'

But why me? I had my son to think of. Why pick on a single mother with a young son? We haven't got the time. Those two women at the next table, with their matching hand bags and shoes, they did nothing but lunch. Why hadn't she approached them instead?

'From little girl, I always want to see it …' she went on.

I didn't know anything about people in her situation. Didn't they have to go somewhere? Croydon, was it? Couldn't she have gone to the police? Or some charity?

My life was hard enough without this stranger tramping through it. She smelt of mildewed washing. Imagine her dragging that awful stink into my kitchen. Cupping her filthy hands round my bone china. Smearing my white linen. Her big face with its pantomime eyebrows leering over my son. Slumping on to my sofa and kicking off her muddy boots as she yanked me down into her particular hell. How would I ever get rid of her?

'You know where is Tower Bridge?'

Perhaps there was something tender-hearted in my face. When my grandma first came to England from the Caribbean she lived through days as lonely and cold as an open grave. The story she told all her grandchildren was about the stranger who woke her while she was sleeping in a doorway and offered her a warm bed for the night. It was this act of benevolence that kept my grandmother alive. She was convinced of it. Her Good Samaritan.

'Is something wrong?' the girl asked.

Now my grandmother talks with passion about scrounging refugees; those asylum seekers who can't even speak the language, storming the country and making it difficult for her and everyone else.

'Last week …' she began, her voice quivering, 'I was in home.' This was embarrassing. I couldn't turn the other way, the girl was staring straight at me. 'This day, Friday,' she went on, 'I cooked fish for my mother and brother.' The whites of her eyes were becoming soft and pink; she was going to cry. 'This day Friday I am here in London,' she said. 'And I worry I will not see my mother again.'

Only a savage would turn away when it was merely kindness that was needed. I resolved to help her. I had three warm bedrooms, one of them empty. I would make her dinner. Fried chicken or maybe poached fish in wine. I would run her a bath filled with bubbles. Wrap her in thick towels heated on a rail. I would then hunt out some warm clothes and after I had put my son to bed I would make her cocoa. We would sit and talk. I would let her tell me all that she had been through. Wipe her tears and assure her that she was now safe. I would phone a colleague from school and ask him for advice.

Then in the morning I would take Laylor to wherever she needed to go. And before we said goodbye I would press my phone number into her hand.

All Laylor's grandchildren would know my name.

Her nose was running with snot[6]. She pulled down the sleeve of her jacket to drag it across her face and said, 'I must find my brother.'

I didn't have any more tissues. I'll get you something to wipe your nose,' I said.

I got up from the table. She watched me, frowning; the tiny hairs of her eyebrows locking together like Velcro[7]. I walked to the counter where serviettes were lying in a neat pile. I picked up four. Then standing straight I walked on. Not back to Laylor but up the stairs to the exit. I pushed through the revolving doors and threw myself into the cold.

---

[5] **to make so. obliged to so.** = to make so. feel that they have to help so.

[6] **snot** = *impolite*: thick wet substance that is produced in the nose

[7] **Velcro** = two bands of cloth with special surfaces that stick together, used for fastening clothes

Checklist: Summary

A summary is for someone who has not read the text and needs to know the essence of what it is about. The readers of your summary do not expect you to go into detail; instead they want a short version of the text. Therefore, a written summary only gives a general idea of what the text is about and the most important information.

Dos	**Before writing:**
	✓ Read the text carefully and highlight key words and/or key sentences.
	✓ Divide the text up into parts or sub-sections.
	✓ Find an appropriate sentence or keywords to summarize each sub-section.
	Writing an introduction:
	✓ The introductory sentence of your summary should include the author, title, type of text, the place and date of publication, and the main idea. In other words, you need to answer these wh-questions:
	   ✓ **Who** is the author?
	   ✓ **When** was the text published?
	   ✓ **Where** was it published?
	   ✓ **What** type of text is it?
	   ✓ **What** topic does the text deal with? State the underlying problem or conflict, and not simply its content.
	Writing the main part:
	✓ The main part of your summary connects the highlighted passages and the summaries or key words of the sub-sections.
	✓ Focus on the essentials/on basic facts.
	✓ Use the present tense.
	✓ Use your own words.
	✓ Use formal language.
	✓ Use connectives to link your sentences.

Don'ts	✓ Don't include irrelevant details. ✓ Don't use the present progressive. ✓ Don't use quotations or direct speech. ✓ Don't give your personal opinion. ✓ Don't start analyzing the text. ✓ Don't try to create suspense.
Language support	**Introduction:** ✓ The short story/novel/article/poem/film … "[title]" … ✓ The extract from the … "[title]" … by [author] … ✓ … written by [author] in [year] … ✓ … written by [author] and published in [year/source]… ✓ … deals with/is about/shows/illustrates … **Stating the topic/purpose of a text:** ✓ The text/story … is about/shows/presents/depicts/alludes to/refers to/ criticizes/targets/comments on/exposes … the fact that/the problem of … ✓ See page 159 for more language support to connect your sentences. **Main part:** ✓ According to the author, … ✓ The author believes/claims/emphasizes/states/points out … ✓ From the author's point of view, … ✓ The author is of the opinion that …

Checklist: Text analysis

When writing a text analysis, analyzing chronologically often seems easier, but can be problematic if your task is to concentrate on a certain aspect of the text you are analyzing. Plan your text well before you start writing your analysis to find out whether a chronological or an aspect-oriented analysis works better. If you are supposed to analyze a development, for example, a chronological analysis might work better. If you are examining a certain character, you should concentrate on relevant aspects.

Always examine the (stylistic/rhetorical/structural/…) devices the author uses and explain why they are used/what they support and what their effect on the reader is. Like in any other text, your text should follow the structure of **introduction – main part – conclusion** (see pp. 160 ff.).

Dos	
	✓ Begin with a central claim. In order to do that, keep the central message or problem of the text in mind, but also the task you are working on.
	✓ Structure your text logically; analyze the text either chronologically or aspect-oriented.
	✓ Distinguish between types of texts. When you analyze prose, for example, narrative techniques are especially important. When you analyze poetry, pay special attention to rhyme and rhythm. And when you analyze non-fictional texts, the argumentative structure may be the most relevant aspect.
	✓ Give examples for important stylistic devices (direct or indirect quotations), explain them/their meaning and analyze their effect on the reader.
	✓ Always combine findings on language/structure and content/message.
	✓ Use the present tense.
	✓ Use connectives to link your ideas. Look at page 159 for help.
	✓ Use formal and neutral language.
	✓ End with a conclusion that doesn't only sum up your findings, but also refers back to the task and states your results on a more abstract level.
Don'ts	✓ Don't use the past tense.
	✓ Don't only paraphrase the text you are analyzing.
	✓ Don't speculate – you must use evidence from the text to support your findings.
	✓ Don't write about every detail.
Language support	**Writing about language/style:**
	✓ *formal/informal/colloquial/vulgar/academic/clear/objective/vivid/… language*
	✓ *complex/simple sentences*
	✓ *a serious/friendly/humorous/ironic/polite/rude/critical/optimistic/… tone*
	✓ *The style of the text is plain/condensed/vivid/pompous/artificial/…*
	Writing about stylistic/rhetorical devices:
	✓ *The author uses metaphorical language to …*
	✓ *The author employs stylistic devices to …*
	✓ *The author uses figures of speech to …*
	✓ *The stylistic devices underline/enhance the arguments/message of the text.*
	✓ *The stylistic device supports/affirms the author's/the text's message.*
	✓ *The stylistic device/metaphor/… brings out the message …*
	✓ *to describe/depict …*
	✓ *to examine/explain/analyze the stylistic devices*
	✓ *to make a comparison …*
	Writing about characters, atmosphere, situations:
	✓ *to make use of/use … to create a … atmosphere*

Checklist: Diary entry

In a diary entry you write about personal experiences, thoughts and feelings. Write the events in chronological order. This will make your diary entry sound more authentic. Imagine you are having an interior monologue (= talking to yourself) or writing to your best friend (who's called diary). You can exaggerate, especially concerning your feelings.

Dos	**Plan the structure of your diary entry to include the following parts:** **Introduction and salutation:** ✓ Write the date, e.g. *3rd March, 2011* (usually in the top right-hand corner). ✓ Begin with the salutation *Dear Diary*, … ✓ Write an introductory sentence. This could be a description of your general state of mind. **Main part:** Write chronologically about ✓ what happened (to you), what you experienced. ✓ how you felt and feel about it. ✓ include your dreams, hopes and secrets. **Conclusion:** ✓ Close with a concluding sentence, e.g. a reflection on your day or what you have written/how it has helped you. ✓ Write your name at the end – you can also add *Bye* or *Goodnight*, but this is optional.
Don'ts	✓ Don't be formal and complicated. ✓ Don't get lost in detail – your diary should not include things you are not interested in and/or were not involved in. ✓ Don't simply describe but write down your thoughts and opinions about events, people etc.
Language support	**Use informal language:** ✓ Short forms, e.g. *I'll, couldn't, wouldn't*, … ✓ Colloquial language, e.g. *kind of, maybe, like*, … ✓ Incomplete sentences, e.g. *Worked hard today!* ✓ Exclamations, e.g. *Why bother? Brilliant! Awesome! Wicked!* **Use connectives to organize your ideas:** *besides, so, anyway, all the same, all the more so because, (un)fortunately, happily/funnily/strangely enough, suddenly, to my surprise*, … **Ideas for an introductory sentence:** ✓ *Life will never be the same again.* ✓ *Something dreadful/incredible happened today.* ✓ *I still can't believe it really happened.* ✓ *I'm over the moon!* ✓ *Why do those things always happen to me?* **To express your personal hopes and wishes:** ✓ *If only …, I really/sincerely hope that …, Hopefully …, I feel hopeful that …* ✓ *I wish … /It's my one real wish to …* ✓ *Just my luck to …* **Ideas for a concluding sentence:** ✓ *Well, that's all for now! I need to get some sleep.* ✓ *Writing all this down helps me feel better.* ✓ *I really don't know what to do about this, I'm desperate!*

Checklist: Comment

In a comment you are asked to give your opinion and explain it. This could be in response to something that has happened or on the views expressed in a newspaper article, discussion etc. When commenting on an issue, you should not only pay attention to arguments and the correct use of language (grammar, choice of words, etc.), but also to the structure of your text. Like in any other text, your text should follow the structure of **introduction** –

main part – **conclusion** (see pp. 157 f.).
Before you start writing, it is necessary to think about how you can present your ideas most effectively in a sequence of paragraphs. Moreover, you should make the relationship between your points clear by using connectives, e.g. to point out contrasts and contradictions.

Dos	**Plan the structure of your comment to include the following parts.** **Introduction:** ✓ Try to get your reader's attention by starting in an interesting way. ✓ Include the topic/question you will write about as outlined in the task. **Main part:** ✓ Identify and refer to the arguments put forward in the text. ✓ Clearly state your own opinion on the topic. ✓ Weigh up and reply to arguments that do not support your point of view. ✓ Include evidence to support/refute arguments (expert opinions; statistics etc.). ✓ Base your arguments on facts and put them forward coherently and unemotionally – that is more convincing. **Conclusion:** ✓ Sum up your arguments. ✓ Come to a logical conclusion about the topic/question stating your opinion. **Organize your ideas coherently:** ✓ Organize your ideas into paragraphs. ✓ Link your ideas/paragraphs with connectives. Look at page 159 for help. **Use formal language:** ✓ Use connectives (*in addition, finally, moreover, however*, etc.). ✓ Use the passive voice occasionally. ✓ Try to avoid using "I" too frequently. There are many other ways of expressing your opinion.
Don'ts	✓ Don't start writing before you have planned your answer and know what conclusion you will come to. ✓ Don't just state arguments/opinions without supporting them. ✓ Don't use informal language, e.g. short forms (*don't, can't*, etc.), colloquial language (*kids, gonna*, etc.) or slang.

Checklist: Comment

Language support

Introduction:
Referring to the topic/question:
- ✓ This comment/answer will discuss/consider/argue …
- ✓ The problem/issue to be discussed in this comment is …
- ✓ The text/article/story/author … raises the question of/introduces the problem of …, which will be discussed in this comment.
- ✓ … is a topic that has given rise to serious discussions over …
- ✓ … is a hotly-debated topic right now as …
- ✓ … seems important to weigh up the benefits and drawbacks of …

Main part:
Identifying and referring to arguments:
- ✓ The main problem/issue/question that is touched upon in this article is …
- ✓ The author states/argues/claims/maintains/supports the idea/puts forward the argument/denies the fact/contradicts the opinion that …

Presenting your own opinion:
- ✓ It is my belief/opinion that …/In my opinion …/Personally …
- ✓ As far as I can see/am concerned …/As I see it …
- ✓ I (completely) agree/(absolutely) disagree with …
- ✓ As opposed to … I (strongly) believe that …

Weighing up and countering arguments:
- ✓ Taking into account what has been said so far, I …
- ✓ Having considered the different arguments, I …/Considering the fact that …
- ✓ On the one hand …, on the other hand …
- ✓ Whereas girls generally like to use the Internet to …, boys prefer to use it to …
- ✓ In contrast to A, B …
- ✓ Looking at the problem from A's side, you have to admit that …
- ✓ Another important point/factor/argument to consider is …
- ✓ Supporters/Opponents of … argue/might argue that …
- ✓ Others claim/assert that …
- ✓ While there is no doubt/question that …, … must also be considered/mentioned.
- ✓ It must also be taken into consideration that …

Conclusion:
- ✓ All in all, it can be said that …
- ✓ In conclusion, I would like to say that …
- ✓ After weighing up the arguments carefully, I come to the conclusion that …
- ✓ Having looked at the issue from different points of view, I firmly believe that …
- ✓ To conclude, …
- ✓ To sum up, …

Checklist: Creative writing

A. Continuation of a prose text

You may be asked to continue a prose text you have read or write a passage from the point of view of one of the characters in the story. You need to write in a similar way as the author. Pay attention to the author's style and the developments in the story. Decide if your development is plausible and fits in with what has happened before.

Dos	

	Content:
	✓ Stay in line with the plot and atmosphere.
	✓ You are not entirely free as you are expected to show in your text production that you have digested the original text. So you have to use the information from that text as a basis for a plausible sequel.
	✓ Mention certain features (places, details of landscape or weather) that have been introduced.
	✓ Make sure you present the characters in a way that does not contradict their previous behaviour unless this change in character is part of your story.
	✓ If possible refer back to events in the text you have dealt with.
	
	Point of view (narrative perspective):
	✓ Adopt the same narrative perspective:
	  • First person narrator
	  • Third person narrator
	    • Omniscient (knowing and commenting on all the characters' thoughts and feelings, foreshadowing future events) or
	    • Limited (having an insight into one of the character's thoughts and feelings only).
	
	Language:
	✓ Stay in line with the author's style and try to imitate it.
	✓ Consider the amount of narrative, descriptive as opposed to dramatic passages that mainly consist of dialogue.
	✓ Use either long, elaborate sentences or short simple ones like the author.
	✓ Employ imagery (symbolic or metaphorical language) if it occurs in the original text; you need not always think of new images but pick up the ones used and extend them.
	✓ Adopt the author's use of language to place a character in a particular social class or reveal his/her emotions.

B. Change of perspective

You may be asked to consider the fictional situation from the point of view of a different character. This can be done in
- a dialogue
- a diary entry/an interior monologue
- a letter to a friend.

Dos	**Content:** ✓ Consider the relationship between the characters involved, their age, their social standing, the way they might be personally affected by what has happened. ✓ Imagine how they would feel in the circumstances. ✓ Decide how you would comment on other characters and their behaviour. **Language:** ✓ Age, relationship, social class and profession determine the way a person speaks. ✓ Make sure you use an appropriate register (formal, informal, colloquial, scientific, educated). ✓ Emotions may alter a person's behaviour and speech. ✓ Use typical elements of spoken language like exclamations, incomplete sentences (ellipses), questions, etc.
Don'ts	✓ Don't stray from the original text you were given. ✓ Don't create an entirely new universe. ✓ Don't write in your personal style, but adopt the style of the author. ✓ Don't quote when you refer back to instances in the original text. Make the references part of your own narrative.
Language support	✓ In a prose text you can reveal the speaker's feelings not only in his/her words but also in his/her body language, you could even contrast the two levels. ✓ The following verbs can help you: *admit, agree, whisper, shout, cry, scream, deny, accept, convince, persuade, shrug, stammer, nod, wince, declare, laugh, smile, grin, smirk, confide, concede, frown, mutter, mumble, insult, accuse, wink,* etc.

Checklist: Formal letter

There are many different types of formal letters that you could be expected to write, e.g. a letter of request, a letter of inquiry, a letter of complaint, a letter of application, often called a covering letter. Whatever the kind of letter it is, the response you get will greatly depend on the way the letter is written. Formal letters are generally precise and to the point, without unnecessary detail.

It is also important that you adopt the right tone i.e. it should sound business-like rather than emotional. Finally you must also think about the layout of your letter and the type of language you use. The language used in this type of letter should not be chatty and personal but rather formal and reserved.

Before you start writing you should first ask yourself:
- Who am I writing to?
- What do I need to tell them?
- Why am I writing?
- What do I want them to do?

Dos	**Before writing:**
	✓ Observe the rules for the layout of a formal letter (see below).
	✓ Use formal language.
	✓ Choose a more formal font for your letter or email if you use a computer, e.g. Times New Roman or Arial
	✓ Draft and edit your letter or email before you send it. Poor grammar and punctuation or spelling mistakes do not make a good impression.
	✓ Plan the structure of your letter to include the following parts:
	
	Salutation and introduction:
	✓ Address the person you are writing to correctly:
	  • If you know the person's name write: *Dear Ms* (for a woman whose marital status is not known) *Mrs, Mr, Dr Smith,* etc.
	  • If you do not know the person's name: *Dear Sir or Madam,*
	✓ Start the first sentence with a capital letter.
	✓ State the purpose of your letter in the first paragraph.
	✓ Refer to any correspondence that may already have taken place.
	
	Main part:
	✓ Organize your ideas in paragraphs.
	✓ Include important and/or relevant details such as exact names, dates and addresses, e.g. where you saw the job advertised, when and where you bought the defective goods etc.
	✓ Keep to the point and avoid unnecessary details.
	✓ Be polite and tactful.
	
	Conclusion and ending:
	✓ Outline how you expect the recipient to react, e.g. send you information, give you a refund, reply to your application etc.
	✓ End the letter in the appropriate way:
	  • *Yours sincerely* if you address them by name in the salutation
	  • *Yours faithfully* if you use *Sir or Madam* in the salutation
	✓ Type your full name and sign the letter by hand.

Don'ts	✓ Don't write your name above the address. ✓ Don't use inappropriate or informal language, e.g. slang, short forms, abbreviations, …

Checklist: Formal letter

Language support

Say why you are writing:

to reply:
- In response to your letter of September 23rd …

to complain:
- I am writing to express my dissatisfaction with …
- Unfortunately, I am forced to write this letter in order to complain about …

to inquire:
- I am writing to inquire about the possibility of …
- I would be very grateful if you would send me further information about …
- Would you kindly tell me how …?

to apply:
- I wish to apply for the post of …
- I am writing to apply for …
- With reference to your advertisement in the Daily News of March 3rd, I should like to apply for the position of …

Say how you expect the recipient to reply to …

your complaint:
- Under the circumstances, I feel an apology should be offered.
- I would be grateful if you could deal with the problem as soon as possible.
- I must insist that you refund me my money immediately.

your inquiry:
- I would like to thank you in advance for your assistance.
- Please accept my thanks for your help.

your application:
- I look forward to hearing from you.
- I will be glad to supply you with any further information you may require.
- I have attached / enclosed the following documents.

The example formal letter below details the general layout that your letter should conform to.

Write your address and email in the top right-hand corner or on the left above the recipient's address.

> 68, Wood Lane
> Romford RM12 8JY
> sgoodenough@internet.com
>
> November 1, 2015

Leave a line and write the date below your address.

The address of the person you are writing to should be on the left.

> Ms Diane Poole
> Personnel Department
> Debenhams Ltd.
> Romford RM10 6NX

> Dear Ms Poole

Say why you are writing the letter in the first paragraph.

> With reference to your advertisement in the Romford Recorder of October 24th, I should like to apply for a summer job in your Department Store. My final examinations finish on June 23rd and I will be available to start work any time after that date.

The main part of the letter should include any other necessary information.

> I am just completing my final year at Hornchurch Grammar School and have applied to do Business Studies and French at Bristol University in October. Meanwhile, I would like to gain some experience in a large organisation such as yours, and of course earn some extra money to help finance my university course.
>
> Having worked in a local supermarket on Saturdays for the past two years, I have gained a lot of experience in dealing with customers. I also greatly enjoy working in a team and was always a popular member of any group presentation at school because I always do my share of the work. In my last year at school I was a prefect and also captain of the hockey team, which shows I have a sense of responsibility towards others. My teachers have always considered me to be a reliable and conscientious student.

In the last part of the letter, say how you expect the recipient to reply.

> I have attached my CV and will be glad to supply you with any other information you require, for example, the names of referees. Thank you for considering my application. I look forward to hearing from you soon.

End the letter in an appropriate way.

> Yours sincerely
>
> *S. Goodenough*
>
> Sandra Goodenough

Checklist: Letter to the editor

Readers of newspapers often write a letter to the editor to comment on something they have read, usually in the hope that the letter will be published in the newspaper. When writing a letter to the editor, take the aspects for writing a formal letter into account. Use formal language, but include strong statements. Before you start writing the letter, you will need to note down important facts and points from the text you are reacting to. Note down any other ideas you have and arrange all of them in a logical order.

Dos	**Introduction:** ✓ Start with *Sir or Madam:* ✓ Leave out any introductory or closing remarks with which you show your politeness or personal interest. Concentrate on the point you are trying to make. ✓ Name the article you refer to at the beginning of your letter. ✓ Give the reason why you are writing the letter, i.e. what you support/criticize/ would like to comment on about the article. **Main part:** ✓ Follow a clear line of argumentation and stick to the most important point(s). ✓ Explain why you share or oppose the author's point of view. ✓ Support your arguments with evidence and examples. **Conclusion:** ✓ End with a strong statement that sums up your position and/or says what you expect from future articles on the issue. ✓ Just sign your name and state your place of residence at the end.
Don'ts	✓ Don't use *Dear …* at the beginning or *Yours sincerely/faithfully* at the end. ✓ Don't quote from the original article unless it is absolutely necessary. ✓ Don't retell the article and explain it to the editor, but explain your view.
Language support	**Starting the letter:** ✓ I am writing to you in response to the article … ✓ Having read your article …, I would like to point out … ✓ In your article …, you claim that … ✓ Your article … raises the question of whether … **Expressing your opinion in the main part of the text:** ✓ I would like to congratulate you on … ✓ I personally believe that … ✓ I could not have put it better myself. ✓ You are absolutely right when you say …/I utterly agree with you that … ✓ I wholeheartedly endorse … ✓ As a firm believer in …/As a supporter of …, I totally agree/I see no reason why … ✓ Although I understand why …, I cannot accept your overall conclusion that … ✓ I see your point, but I still feel that … ✓ I think you are mistaken if you believe … ✓ What you need to keep in mind is …/You overlook the fact that … ✓ I would question the argument that … **Ending with a strong statement:** ✓ The question can no longer be whether …, but … ✓ However, does the evidence I have cited not prove that …? ✓ All in all, there can be no doubt that … ✓ Ultimately, what matters is (that) … ✓ Consequently, I strongly support/oppose your view that …

Checklist: Speech

When you give a speech, you are aiming to get people to agree with your views. As your speech will only be heard and not read by your audience, you have to be careful how you present what you have to say. Speeches are meant to be spoken, so your language should not be too formal. You may use short forms and contractions like *don't, we're, haven't, I'm,* etc. It may help you to read out aloud to yourself what you have written to check whether your style creates the desired effect.

Dos	**Plan the structure of your speech to include the following parts:** **Introduction:** ✓ Directly address the audience at the beginning. ✓ Begin your introduction with an "attention-getter" to capture your audience's attention, e.g. a story, a rhetorical question, a quotation. ✓ Clearly state the topic of your speech and your personal stance on it. **Main part:** ✓ Explain the topic/problem. ✓ Quote facts and people to persuade your audience. ✓ Show your emotional involvement and appeal to the emotions of the audience. **Conclusion:** ✓ Briefly highlight your main points and end with something strong, e.g. an appeal for support. ✓ Show that the speech has ended, e.g. by thanking your audience for listening.
Don'ts	✓ Don't put too many ideas in your speech, but give the listeners two or three important things to remember. ✓ Don't just read the speech out aloud to your audience. ✓ Don't use too complex expressions. ✓ Don't write very long sentences – listeners must be able to follow you. ✓ Don't use modifiers, e.g. *might be, possibly, probably, more or less,* – you must be very direct and specific to be convincing.
Language support	**Introduction:** ✓ Address the audience: *ladies and gentlemen, fellow students, my friends, members of …, my fellow countrymen, comrades,* etc. **Main part:** ✓ Relate your speech to your listeners. Use receiver-including pronouns and words like *we, us, our, my friends,* etc. ✓ Use connectives to structure your speech: *firstly, finally,* etc. Look at page 159 for help. ✓ Link the different points by using phrases such as: *Having discussed … it is now appropriate to mention …* ✓ Use adverbial phrases to underline your own convictions and win over the audience: *undoubtedly, certainly, undeniably, definitely, indeed, paradoxically, surprisingly, strangely enough, primarily, first and foremost, above all,* etc. ✓ Include rhetorical questions like: *Don't we all agree/want to …?* ✓ Include rhetorical devices like repetitions, exaggerations, alliterations, etc. **Conclusion:** ✓ *Finally, fellow friends of the environment, …* ✓ Clearly indicate the end of your speech: *Thank you for your attention, ladies and gentlemen.*

How to structure a text

When analyzing a text or commenting on an issue, you should not only pay attention to the content and the correct use of language (grammar, choice of words, etc.), but also to the structure of your text.

In order to write a well-structured text you should follow the structure of **introduction – main part – conclusion**. Make sure that you plan how to present your ideas effectively in a sequence of paragraphs before you start writing.

Moreover, you should make the relationships between your points clear by using connectives, e.g. to express cause and effect or to point out contrasts and contradictions.

The outline of a text and paragraph writing

Analysis	
Introduction • Refer back to the task, if necessary. • Make a general statement that sums up what you expect to find out.	**Example:** You are asked to write a characterization of the protagonist and give a general assessment of what he is like. *In this extract, which focuses on John's feelings about his parents, John seems to be a highly ambivalent character who pretends to be friendly to his parents on the surface, but in fact hides how much he dislikes his parents.*
Main part • Develop your interpretation/argumentation in the main part of your analysis/argumentation in a well-structured and logical way so that it is easy for the reader to understand your analysis. • Divide your main part up into meaningful paragraphs before you start writing. • Follow the PEA principle for your paragraph writing. P – point: an introductory sentence that introduces the point that you are trying to make in this paragraph so that the reader immediately knows what you are referring to. E – evidence: examples from the text (including quotations) or arguments and examples that can be used to prove your point (P). A – analysis: the explanation of examples and quotations in order to make it clear how the evidence (E) helps to prove your initial point (P).	**Example:** Characterization of Balram in Adiga's novel "White Tiger": *Judging from his outward appearance, one can initially identify Balram as a typical example of a low-caste servant or a poor Indian in general who slowly becomes aware of the consequences his way of dressing have on his position in society.* (introducing a sequence of paragraphs) *Wearing sandals instead of proper shoes seems to be a distinctive feature separating the rich from the poor in this context as Balram as well as the other drivers all wear sandals. Hence they can identify with the poor man wearing sandals who is refused entry to the shopping mall (cf. ll. 45ff.). As their masters could enter the mall without any problem, Balram and the other drivers realize how the inequality of Indian society manifests itself even in items of clothing.*

Analysis

Conclusion
- Refer back to your opening paragraph.
- Summarize your most important findings concisely.

Example: Characterization of Balram in Adiga's novel "White Tiger":
As a closer look at Balram's character has shown, Balram becomes aware of what makes him recognizable as a lower-caste driver and tries to leave outward appearance as well as other signs like his insufficient command of the English language behind. His new way of dressing, which imitates the style of his master, as well as his recognition that he has to give up old habits that single him out as uneducated and ill-mannered show his determination to rise above his current status.

Comment

Introduction
- Refer back to the task.
  a) If it is a general issue, (example 1), you need to establish a connection to that topic in your opening paragraph.
  b) If you are expected to comment on something that is included in the text you are working on (example 2), you need to refer back to this text.
- Regardless of the context, include a thesis statement which expresses your general view on the issue.

Example 1: You are asked to discuss whether a gap year is worth doing after school.
Thousands of students decide to take a year off from education once they have graduated from school and do not want to start studying straight away. Although this may provide a wide variety of unforgettable experiences, I do not believe that travelling the world for a year is of much benefit for your personal development or your university studies.

Example 2: You are asked to comment on a character's behaviour towards his parents.
As X feels annoyed and humiliated by his parents for not allowing him to live the life of a normal teenager in this situation, it seems highly doubtful that his inability to talk to his parents openly about what bothers him will solve X's problems of unhappiness and isolation.

How to structure a text

Comment

Main part
- Write your comment in a well-structured way so that it is easy for the reader to follow your line of argumentation.
- Structure your arguments beforehand. There are different patterns:
  - from most to least important argument or the other way round
  - first pros, then cons or the other way round
  - topic-oriented (contrasting pros and cons on the same aspect step by step)
- Follow the PEA principle for your paragraph writing.
  P – point: an introductory sentence that introduces the point that you are trying to make in this paragraph so that the reader immediately knows what you are referring to.
  E – evidence: examples from the text (including quotations) or arguments and examples that can be used to prove your point (P).
  A – analysis: the explanation of examples and quotations in order to make it clear how the evidence (E) helps to prove your initial point (P).

Example: Discussing how sensible it is to take a year off for a gap year:
If you choose the place where you are going wisely, you may have the chance to gain some experience in the field you would like to study or work in later. There are definitely some future medical students who assist doctors and nurses in some developing country or those who want to study science and help out in a bird sanctuary or get involved in an environmental project, for example. However, the question is whether everyone already has a clear idea of what they would like to do after their gap year and would maybe prefer to use the year to make up their minds. Even if they would like to gain some experience in the field that interests them, they might not be able to find a suitable place.

Conclusion
- Refer back to your opening paragraph.
- Draw a conclusion by weighing up the pros and cons in your argumentation.

Example: Discussing how sensible it is to take a year off for a gap year:
All in all, I'm utterly convinced that gap years do not really allow you to acquire new skills and prepare for university. Although it may serve as a character-building experience to become more independent and able to adapt to new people and circumstances, I doubt that many situations you experience while travelling around the world are realistic and that these experiences can be applied to everyday life back home. Consequently, I would never do a gap year, but would rather go abroad as part of my degree course.

How to structure a text

Expressing connections between points in the text

Language support	
Adding and ordering points:	• To begin with/First of all/Firstly, … • Secondly, …/Then … • Last but not least … • Finally/In the end , … • All in all/To conclude/To sum up … • The most important point is/Above all … • This also becomes evident when …/… during/… in a scene • Both … and …/… not only …, but also … • This assumption can be supported by … • This is also shown by … • Another point/Another example of … is … • In addition to that/Additionally/Furthermore/Moreover/Besides/On top of that, …
Expressing a contrast:	• In spite of the fact …/Despite the fact … • Whereas … • In contrast to … , … • However, … • But nevertheless, … • On the one hand …, on the other hand … • Although …/Even though …/Even if … • While it is true that …, …
Expressing cause and effect:	• Due to …/Because of …/As a result of … • Therefore, …/For this reason, … • … because … • As/Since … • So/Thus …/Accordingly, … • As a consequence, …/Consequently, …/This results in …
Summing up:	• All in all, …/To sum up, …/As a result, … • In brief, …/In conclusion, …/To conclude, …

How to improve your text

Once you have written your text, read it carefully again and check whether you have considered the criteria listed below. Revise your text accordingly.

a) **Content:**
- Has your text taken all aspects of the assignment into consideration?
- Have you given evidence to support your arguments?
- Have you referred adequately to the text that has to be analyzed (lines, quotations)?
- Have you avoided repetitions?

b) **Structure and logical order:**
Are the following parts included?
- introduction, introductory sentence
- main part, divided up into several paragraphs
- conclusion

Is the text clearly structured and therefore easy to follow with the help of
- connectives? Look at page 159 for help.
- visible paragraphs?
- a clear order of arguments or examples?

c) **Language and style:**
- Have you used the correct tense, e.g. the simple present tense in a summary?
- Have you used the correct language, e.g. formal language in a letter to the editor?
- Are your sentences complete and not too long or complicated?
- Do appropriate linking words connect ideas and sentences to make your text coherent?
- Have you avoided waffling, i.e. excluded all unnecessary words?
- Have you varied your vocabulary by using synonyms?

Language support

Synonyms: Improving your style by expressing yourself more precisely (adjectives and nouns)

Apart from using sentence links to structure and organize a text, there is another way to improve your style: Simply ban the following from your range of vocabulary – at least when writing a formal text like an analysis or characterization:

| SAD | HAPPY | NICE | BAD | INTERESTING | SITUATION |

There are various synonyms you might use instead – here are a few examples:

- For "sad" people you could use:
  downcast, depressed, downhearted, dejected, dispirited, frustrated, discouraged, sorrowful

- For "sad" atmosphere you could use:
  dark, gloomy, dismal, dreary, depressing, desolate, melancholy, hopeless, cheerless, bleak

- For "happy" people you could use:
  cheerful, contented, relaxed, pleased, delighted, light-hearted, jolly, merry, lively, vivacious, animated, buoyant, humorous, spirited

- For "nice" people you could use:
  amiable, kind-hearted, good-natured, gentle, congenial, easy-going, pleasant, sympathetic

- For "nice" atmosphere you could use:
  cheerful, relaxed, pleasant, harmonious, idyllic, picturesque, familiar, friendly, warm

- For "bad" people you could use:
  despicable, contemptible, loathsome, hateful, detestable, reprehensible, awful, vile, mean, repulsive, horrible, dreadful, terrible

- For "interesting" you could use:
  appealing, exciting, fascinating, remarkable, significant, captivating, intriguing, attractive

- For "situation" you could use:
  circumstance, case, state of affairs, condition, predicament, position, dilemma

Language support

Writing about the author's opinion, point of view, bias …

When writing about or referring to the author of the text you have to analyze, you should not only write "the author says" but use more precise alternatives instead. Here are several examples of verbs you could use:

The author …

| refers to … |
| alludes to … |
| talks about/mentions … |
| addresses the issue of -ing … |
| examines … |
| raises the question of whether … |

| claims/maintains/argues that … |
| assumes/supposes/presumes that … |
| asserts … |
| believes … |
| states … |
| insists … |
| emphasizes … |
| sides with … |
| backs up his argument with … |
| is in favour of -ing … |
| puts forward another argument … |

| doubts … |
| attacks/accuses so. of -ing … |
| blames sth./so. … |
| criticizes … |
| reproaches so. for -ing … |
| rejects (the idea of) … |
| abandons the idea of -ing … |
| opposes the idea of -ing … |
| refutes the argument … |

| weighs the arguments … |
| is in two minds about … |

| leaves … unanswered … |
| avoids this issue … |
| does not consider … |

Depending on the type of text you are writing about, there are various synonyms you can use instead of the word "author". Of course, you can also use the author's name or simply "he" or "she".

Synonyms for authors of …
- literary texts: *novelist, playwright, poet, writer*
- newspaper articles: *journalist, reporter, columnist, writer, essayist*

How to work with a dictionary

All competences, but especially reading and writing, often involve the use of a dictionary. There are **monolingual dictionaries,** which provide definitions in English and **bilingual dictionaries,** which give you the German equivalents. Most of the time you will be using a bilingual dictionary.

English – German

When working with texts you may not always understand all the words, so you will need to refer to a dictionary. The use of the dictionary, however, may be determined by the situation you are in.

- Don't look up every single word you don't know but apply the **strategie**s you have learnt **to understand words from the context** first.
- **Limit the number of words to look up** as using the dictionary is quite time-consuming.
- Depending on the task you are given it may be necessary to **check all the words you don't understand**. If you read a novel or a longer text of course, you will need to use your strategies of understanding words from the context, from cognates etc. But sometimes you need to get a detailed understanding of the text.
- Having gone to the trouble of finding the word, try and use it to build and **extend your active vocabulary**.
  - Decide if the word may be useful for later use.
  - Collect the words you have selected in word fields.
  - Add collocations or idioms to avoid possible mistakes in future.
  - Use the newly acquired words and phrases in your homework/written texts. This is the best way to remember them.

How to look the word up properly

- Make sure you look the word up in its **correct spelling** or you may end up with an incorrect translation. Examples of this are: *board-bored, fair-fare, sail-sale*.
- Determine whether the word you are looking up is a noun, a verb, an adjective etc. and read the corresponding part of the entry. With verbs, make sure you look for the basic form.
- There may still be different meanings. Read the complete entry and decide which translation fits the context of your text best.
- Avoid mistakes by checking what grammatical construction is needed with the word you want to use, for example *used to do* as opposed to *get used to doing*.

The phonetic transcription shows you how to pronounce a word correctly. It not only reflects the sound but also gives you the intonation of a word, which may be different depending on the function of the word (e.g. pre'sent *v* – 'present *n*).

n, vi, vt, adj tell you what type of word it is (noun, verb etc.). If there are abbreviations you don't understand, check the explanations in the dictionary.

The headword helps you to find the word more easily.

chest [tʃest] *n* **1.** *(torso)* Brust *f*, Brustkorb *m*; **to fold one's arm across one's** ~ die Arme vor der Brust verschränken – **2.** *(trunk)* Truhe; *(box)* Kiste – **3.** *(treasury)* Schatzkästchen

The different meanings of a word are listed under numbers. Make sure that you read the whole entry to find the meaning that fits the context.

Expressions in bold letters give you examples of how to use the word correctly in typical phrases or idioms (e.g. "heavy: ~ accent, with a ~ heart").

How to work with a dictionary

German – English

When writing texts you will with time want to make your phrasing more precise, varied and differentiated.

Typical needs

- **Spelling:** You are not sure how the English word you want to use is written.
  - Check for changes in spelling in different grammatical contexts.

- **Vocabulary:** You want to use a particular word.
  - Make sure you have the correct German spelling. For example: The word *Widerspruch* will be hard to find if you think it is spelt with *ie*.
  - Read through **all** the possible meanings and consider the specific lexical area in which you want to use the word. For example: The German word *Bank* can mean either *bank* or *bench* in English.
  - If collocations are given, try to use the whole phrase or a parallel construction in your own text.

- **Style: variation (synonyms/antonyms):** When writing a text and editing it you will find that you have repeated certain words.
  - Use the definitions of the German word you have looked up to find other ways in English of expressing it.

Internet dictionaries

/dict.leo.org/

/www.dict.cc/

It may seem the quickest route to use an Internet dictionary, but this often is the quickest way to making lots of mistakes: Internet dictionaries often offer a one-to-one translation which may not always fit. So don't go for the first option but check carefully in which context the respective word can be used.

Tip: Since you will have to work with a non-digital dictionary in your exams, you should practise working with one in class and at home.
  - You will start to get quicker at finding words.
  - You will start to get more confident in choosing the right meaning.
  - You will get used to benefitting from the additional information the dictionary offers you.

How to give feedback / peer-edit

Giving constructive feedback is a helpful way of improving the quality of your own and of your classmates' work.

Feedback on a presentation

Make sure that the feedback you give …
- is worded in such a way that your classmates can accept it without being embarrassed.
- is objective and not personal.
- focuses more on the corrected form and does not dwell on the mistake.
- highlights the use of good language.

Language support	
Here are some phrases you can use to give positive feedback on a presentation by your classmates:	• What I really liked was that you … • What really impressed me was … • I particularly liked … • I think it was a good idea to … • You managed to …
If you need to be more critical, these expressions can help you:	• The explanations/facts given were not (quite) correct. • What could be improved is … • I would have liked to learn more about … • I missed information about … • You did not manage to …

Peer-editing

A good method of improving your writing is peer-editing. It means working with someone from your class to help you to improve, revise and edit each other's writing.

When editing a text check the following aspects:

- **Topic:** Check whether the writer stays on the topic. Information that is not relevant should be left out.

- **Choice of words:** Make sure the writer uses interesting words and not too many "overused" words (e.g. *really, very, nice, interesting*). A writer should also use language which is appropriate for the relevant text type (e.g. register, thematic vocabulary, etc.).

- **Sentences:** Check for sentences that are either too long or too short. A good writer also uses linking words to join his/her sentences.

- **Structure of the text:** A good text should be well organized and easy to understand. An introduction should immediately grab a reader's attention.

How to give feedback / peer-edit

When peer editing a text, you should keep three aspects in mind:

- **Compliments:** The most important rule of peer editing is to BE POSITIVE! Always start with compliments. Remember, you are helping to improve someone else's work. First tell the writer what you think he/she did well. Here are some phrases you can use to give positive feedback:
  This was fun to read because …
  I liked the way you …
  My favourite part was … because …
  I think you used a lot of good details.

- **Suggestions:** Make suggestions by giving some specific ideas about how to improve the piece of writing. Remember to try and stay positive and always try to provide constructive criticism. For example:
  Don't say to your partner: *This paragraph doesn't make any sense.*
  Tell him/her: *If you add more details after this sentence, it will be clearer.*
  Rather than saying: *Your choice of words was boring,* say: *Instead of using the word 'good', maybe you can use the word 'exceptional'.*

- **Corrections:** Only after you and your partner have agreed on how to change your pieces of writing can you actually start with the final step in the peer editing process: making corrections.
  Swap your texts and check your partner's work for
  - spelling mistakes
  - grammar mistakes
  - missing punctuation

Here is some advice on how to spot mistakes:
- Read the text more than once and concentrate on one aspect at a time, e.g. spelling mistakes.
- If you have typed your text on the computer, use the spellchecker in Word.
- After you have finished writing your text, take a break before you check it for mistakes.
- Reading "backwards", i.e. from end to beginning, might do the trick to spot mistakes.

How to quote

When referring to/working with a text, you need quotations from that text to support your statements and findings with evidence.
You can quote directly or indirectly, and you can integrate quotations into your own sentences or quote passages to back up what you have said in your own words.

You may …	Examples
1. … quote indirectly from a text, i.e. say something that can be found in the text in your own words. This is often used when stating facts that need no in-depth interpretation. To show that you haven't quoted directly from the text, use "cf."[1].	Ed works as a taxi driver and plays cards with his friends Audrey and Marvin on a regular basis (cf. p. 58).
2. … integrate direct quotes into your own sentence. But be careful: Don't change the meaning of the quotation, and make sure the resulting sentence is grammatically correct. To show that you are quoting directly from the text, use inverted commas.	Ed comes from one of the parts of the town where the poorer, less educated people live, which he himself describes as a "dirty secret" (p. 59).
3. … quote a short passage or sentence directly to back up what you have already said in your own words. Again, use inverted commas to show that it is a direct quotation.	Ed states clearly that he is not content with his life: "No real career. No respect in the community. Nothing" (p. 58).

When you quote from a text, …

- don't quote very long passages (up to three lines). Quotes should underline or support what you have to say, not say it for you.

- don't use quotes simply to fill paper space – they must refer to your findings.

- quote the exact wording and punctuation from the text. If you leave something out or change something to make it fit into your sentence, you have to indicate that clearly by using […]. You may only make minor changes and mustn't alter the meaning of your quote.

- don't use quotations to retell a text or story.

- make sure the quotes are meaningful – don't quote the first two words followed by "…".

- always refer to lines or pages (l. 1/ll. 5–7/p. 8/pp. 8–9 etc.). Use "l." for one line, "ll." for more than one line, "p." for one page and "pp." for more than one page.

- you should set off the quoted passage further away from the left-hand margin if the quoted text is more than two or three sentences long.

How to listen effectively

Learning a foreign language properly is impossible without learning to listen effectively. Listening comprehension tasks, however, can take very different forms as you may have to listen to a dialogue/interview, a speech, a song, etc. The situations, e.g. parliament, family context, vary as much as the accents, tempo, etc. of the speakers.

a) Preparing for a listening comprehension

Before you start listening, you should make use of all the information that you may already have about what you are going to listen to. So make sure you read the task carefully. Think about the topic you have been discussing in class. If there are photos, headings, additional texts, study them so that you already have some ideas of what the listening text may be about.

b) Listening strategies

- When you listen to an audio clip for the first time, listen for gist, i.e. the main ideas (who?, what?, why?, etc.). Key words that are repeated several times may help you work out what the text is about.
- While listening to the text for the first time, keep the task in mind and try to remember when in the clip there are relevant passages you should concentrate on when you listen to it for the second time.
- Do not try to understand every single word, but the general message. If you listen to a clip a second or even a third time, you will notice that you understand more and more. You will then be able to work out the meaning of words from the context or from similarities they have to other words you know from English (e.g. *high – height, clean – cleanliness*), German or another language (e.g. *deny so. sth.* – French: *dénier*).

c) Working on the tasks

- Use a pencil to take notes or, if it is a multiple-choice test, mark the correct answers.
- Add to your notes when you listen again.
- If it is not a test, check with your neighbour to see if you understood the same things.

How to prepare for an oral exam

Monologue

Oral exams may have different types of assignments that require a monologue. You may be confronted with texts, pictures, cartoons, role cards, statistics or a film sequence and you may be asked to
- summarize a text
- describe and analyze a text or visuals or
- give a presentation prepared at home.

Apart from the content of your statements your language competence will be evaluated.
So it is important that you
- extend your topical vocabulary to make your statements concise and clear which means that you should work on thematic vocabulary lists during course work.
- make sure you pronounce words correctly, so check the pronunciation of new words as you come across them.
- avoid basic grammar mistakes.
- use connectives to link your sentences and make your monologue more fluent.

Phrases that open up a new range of ideas or structure your presentation
may be especially helpful:
> *furthermore, what is more, besides, in addition,*
> *generally speaking, on the whole,*
> *basically, interestingly, surprisingly*
> *as I said before,*
> *considering those facts/character traits/the author's intention/the author's arguments*

It is important to use your presentation time to note down important aspects that you would like to mention in your talk. So highlight words or phrases in a given text, write ideas in the margin and/or list the aspects that seem relevant to you in the order you want to present them. You can use your notes as cue cards during the presentation.

Language support		
To start your talk or presentation you can use the following phrases:	To structure your talk the following phrases may be helpful:	To conclude your presentation you could use phrases like:
• First I'm going to talk about … • I would like to start by … • To begin with, let me describe … • First of all I want to say …	• Secondly … • Next I'd like to point out … • Another important argument is … • On the one hand … on the other hand	• Finally … • To sum up, one could say that … • All things considered, I would say that …

Dialogue

The second part of your exam will be a conversation, either with your teacher or with one or more fellow students.
This situation will test your communicative skills.
So it is important that you are able to do the following:

Language support	
State your view clearly and think of alternative phrases for *I think*.	• I believe that … • I'm convinced that … • I would say that … • In my view … • In my opinion … • As far as I'm concerned …
Clarify your view if necessary.	• What I mean is … • That's not exactly what I mean. • To put it in other words / in other words …
Ask for clarification if you are not sure you know exactly what the other person means.	• Do you (really) mean that …? • I'm not sure I fully understand what you mean. • Does that mean that …? • When you say …, do you mean …?
Use a variety of phrases to agree and disagree in a polite way.	• That's exactly how I see it. • I would say so, too. • I completely agree. • Do you really think so? • I wouldn't say so. • Well, I'm not totally convinced. • You may be right but … • I see your point but …
Use conversational gambits that signal your view but also give you time to think.	• well / sure / definitely / absolutely / exactly / quite / well, perhaps … • I see / Let me see / I know / so?
Involve your partner and bring him/her back into the conversation.	• Well, that's my view. So what do you think? • What makes you so sure? • Don't you think that …? • It's obvious that …, isn't it? • Wouldn't you say so?

How to improve your mediation skills

You are very likely to be confronted with situations where people who do not speak German need your help because some information they need is only available in German. Such situations are very similar to those that you find in mediation tasks.

Step 1: Understanding the task

Before you start working on a mediation task, make sure that you fully understand what is required from you. Mediation does not mean translating the German original word for word.

a) What is the type of text you need to produce?

In the example below, you can see that the German original is an interview, but the text you should produce is a newspaper article. So you must change the way the information is presented to you in German. In order to do this, you need to remember what is typical of that particular kind of text. In the case of a newspaper article, you should remember to include a headline, start with an interesting introduction, write a main part and finish with a final part/conclusion.

Die Internetseite UK-German Connection Voyage, die deutsche und britische Jugendliche einander näherbringen möchte, unterhält ein Onlinemagazin, in dem junge Deutsche und Briten Artikel vor allem über das Verhältnis beider Völker veröffentlichen können. Sie sind eingeladen, einen kurzen Zeitungsartikel über die Gemeinsamkeiten und Unterschiede zwischen deutschem und englischem Humor und Umgang mit Sprache zu verfassen. Als Grundlage nutzen Sie ein Zeitungsinterview mit zwei Journalisten aus Deutschland und Großbritannien, die im jeweils anderen Land leben und arbeiten.

b) What information is needed?

Read the task carefully to find out what information is needed. Certain passages or elements of the German text are likely to be irrelevant to the task. You can leave this information out in your version.

c) Who is the addressee?

In a mediation task, another factor that should influence the way you deal with the text is the addressee that is mentioned in the task. If you write a text for teenagers, your text should be less formal and technical than if you were writing about a difficult topic for experts in a particular field, for example.

How to improve your mediation skills

Step 2: Working on the task

a) Reading

- Highlight all the information relevant to the task (see Step 1b).
- Make notes in English.
- Do not get stuck looking for a literal translation of a German expression. Sometimes it doesn't exist and you can paraphrase the idea you want to express. For example, there may be a German idiomatic expression like "das Zeitliche segnen" which you cannot translate directly. So you need to find either an English idiom that has a similar meaning or go for a more neutral expression, for example "to die".

b) Writing the English text

- Arrange the information you highlighted and noted down in a logical order that fits the type of text you are expected to write. Structure it in such a way that it is easy to understand for the people who are supposed to read your text.
- As stated above, you needn't translate the German text word for word. It is important that all the relevant information is presented clearly. Leave out anything that is not related to the task, but also leave out any personal comments unless you are invited to do so by the task.
- Be careful with expressions and concepts that are very specific to German and Germany. You may have to include an explanation to someone from abroad. For example, a text may include references to people or institutions that most Germans know, but people from abroad do not know. So you need to add a short explanation: *Most Germans watch <u>the news programme</u> "Tagesschau" at 8 o'clock at night on ARD, <u>which is a public TV channel.</u>*

c) Editing the text

- Make sure that you have included all the relevant information required by the task and not used anything that goes beyond it.
- Check that your text fits the criteria of the type of text that the task has asked you to produce.
- Don't forget that the style and register of the text must suit the addressees that the text is intended for. If necessary, make some changes to style and register.
- Check your text for grammatical correctness and the right choice of words.

How to describe pictures

Pictures often say more than words and may be used in many different ways to illustrate a topic. There are many different types of pictures and it is important that you follow these steps, when working with them:

- identify and name the kind of picture you are asked to describe in your introductory sentence.
- describe the different elements in the picture in detail.

Finally, you may be asked to speculate on a particular aspect of the picture or give your own interpretation.

1. Opening sentence.
e.g. *This picture shows an advertisement for OMEGA watches in cooperation with the Bond film "Skyfall".*

2. In the foreground you can see a watch by the exclusive brand OMEGA.

3. in the top left-hand side corner is the title of the Bond film, *Skyfall*. Below it you can see the famous 007-logo.

Next to it at the top you can read OMEGA in capital letters. Below this there is a much smaller subtitle: "James Bond's choice".

5. On the right-hand side you can see actor Daniel Craig as Britain's most famous agent James Bond. He is wearing a jacket, a scarf and gloves. The expression on his face is serious.

4. The background of the advertisement is the London skyline.

6. In the centre you can see the British flag, the Union Jack.

7. In the bottom right-hand corner there is a reference to the brand OMEGA and its logo, the Greek letter omega.

8. Speculation or interpretation.
Possible questions you could ask yourself are:

- What do you associate with James Bond?
- What might be the reason for choosing Bond?
- What is suggested about Bond and Britain by the words/slogans?
- What is the message of the advertisement?
- What is the (intended) effect?
- What atmosphere is createdand how is this achieved?

How to describe pictures

Language support	
Different types of pictures and artists	- *advertisement, caricature, collage, drawing, film still, illustration, (oil) painting, photograph portrait, poster, sketch, watercolour,* - *graphic designer, artist, portrait painter, photographer*
Describing where to find different elements	- *In the top right-hand/left-hand corner* - *In the foreground/background* - *At the top/bottom* - *In the middle/centre* - *On the left/right*
Speculating	- *It would appear that the advertisement is part of a campaign to …* - *It seems likely/probable that …* - *One might assume that …* - *The choice of slogan/photograph might mean that …* - *It seems to be the intention of the artist to …* - *The body language of the central figure suggests …*
Interpreting e.g. atmosphere, tone etc.	- *The atmosphere created by the colours is …* - *There is a certain humorous/mocking/critical/light-hearted tone about the …* - *The choice of … underlines the intention of the artist/graphic designer/photographer to …* - *The painting captures the feeling of …* - *The serious/loving/hateful expression on the face of the figure on the right corresponds with/ contrasts strongly with …*

How to work with cartoons

Cartoons are often used to make a critical comment on a serious issue in a humorous way. They are often published in newspapers or magazines. In order to understand the cartoon it is important to look at the details, and you should consider the connection between the picture, the punch line and any speech bubbles.

Issue
Before you study the cartoon in detail, decide what the issue is.

Presentation of characters
Are the characters in the cartoon caricatures of real people like politicians or other persons of public interest, or do they stand for a particular group?

Scene/Setting
What is the situation depicted in the cartoon? Where is it set? Who are the characters involved? What are they doing?

The cat had figured out how to work Ebay.

Source
The cartoon may be published in a newspaper or a magazine. What is the general attitude represented by the paper? Is it more conservative or more liberal? When was the cartoon first published?

Punch line or written comment
Is the punch line presented as direct speech or as a general statement? Does it contain a play on words or a double meaning? Does it suggest a parallel to past or present situations or events?

Language support	
Describing cartoons	Interpreting cartoons
• At the top/bottom of the cartoon … • In the foreground/background … • On the right/left … • In the centre … • In the top/bottom right-hand/left-hand corner … • The cartoonist shows … • There are … in the picture. • The situation reminds one/me/you of … • The cartoon describes …	• The expression on …'s face shows … • The boys are standing close together. This could mean that … • She is hugging him. That suggests … • By presenting …, the cartoonist …

Glossary – Literary terms

literary terms	definition	example
A addressee	the person to whom something is addressed	
alliteration	emphasis that occurs through the repetition of initial consonant letters of two or more neighbouring words	"bigger box", "red rose"
allusion	a reference to a familiar or famous historical or literary figure or event	"a King who took us to the mountaintop and pointed the way to the Promised Land" (Barack Obama refers to Martin Luther King, who explained his vision of America's future in his "I have a dream" speech.)
anaphora	the repetition of identical words of phrases at the beginning of a sentence or a line	"Nobody hurt you. Nobody turned off the light … Nobody locked the door."
antithesis/ contrast	a contrast between two things; denotes the opposing of ideas by means of grammatically parallel arrangements of words, clauses or sentences so as to produce an effective contrast	"It used to be hot, it becomes cool. It used to be strong, it becomes weak." (Malcolm X)
attitude	The attitude of a character is the way they act which portrays a certain characteristic or emotion they have.	nervous, disdainful, superior, cocky, reassuring, condescending, over-zealous, self-confident, full of anticipation, insecure, in awe, indifferent, defiant, sheepish, arrogant, self-assured
B body language	the movements or positions of your body that show other people what you are thinking or feeling	
C camera angle	The camera angle marks the specific location at which a movie camera or video camera is placed to take a shot.	
character	a person who takes part in the action of a fictional text	Mayor Undersee in Suzanne Collins' 'The Hunger Games'
characterization	the way in which a writer creates characters in a book, play, film etc. The author may present his characters in two ways: directly by describing them (explicit), or indirectly through their actions, thoughts or feelings and words (implicit).	"She has yellow hair, wiry legs, the most beautiful crooked smile in the world." "I was too lazy at school." "Audrey always sits opposite me, no matter where we play." → She seems to be interested
choice of words	a term used to describe the words chosen by an author, using words that are very specific and descriptive of exactly what you want to say	

Literary terms – alphabetical

literary terms	definition	example
cliché	A cliché can apply to almost any situation, person or object. It represents a very simplified understanding of something that has become common among people of the same culture or background because this cliché has been used over and over again.	
close-up	a full-screen shot of a person's face to show emotions revealed by their facial expression;	
comparison	the process of considering how things or people are similar and how they are different	
cross-cutting/ parallel action	combining shots of two or more scenes which are usually taking place at the same time	
cut	a quick move from one shot to the next in a film	
D direct address	when the audience is spoken to in the second-person	
E editorial	relating to the process of editing of books, magazines, newspapers etc	
effect on reader	a lasting impact on the reader which remains with them after having read a text	
ellipsis/ incomplete sentences	leaving out words to avoid repetition	
establishing shot	gives an overall impression of the location at the beginning of a scene	
exaggeration	representing (sth.) as being larger, greater, better, or worse than it really is	"We've heard this complaint a thousand times."
exclamation	something that you say suddenly and loudly because you are surprised, impressed, angry etc	
eye-level shot/ straight-on angle	The camera looks straight at the person. This may suggest a neutral view, however, it can also mean that two people who are not on the same level for some reason (e.g. wealth, age, academic standing, social class) are presented as equal to each other.	
F facial expression	This is how a person uses his/her face to show what he/she is feeling.	
fact	a piece of true information	
field size	the distance between the camera and the object filmed	
first person narration	A first person narrator refers to *I* and *me* and is usually the novel's central character but may also be a minor character who merely observes the action.	

176

Literary terms – alphabetical

literary terms	definition	example
flat characters	a character who does not develop in the course of the action and is often a stereotype (= static character)	Harry in Bali Rai's '(Un)arranged Marriage'
foreshadowing	the technique of hinting at future events in such a way that the reader/viewer is prepared for them or can even anticipate them	
freeze frame	gives a view of the entire figure of a person to show action or to give an impression of a constellation of characters	
full shot	gives a view of the entire figure of a person to show action or to give an impression of a constellation of characters	
gesture	This is how a person uses his/her body to communicate messages.	
group of three	a group of three related ideas or concepts	"our openness, our hospitality and our belief"
high angle shot	The camera looks down on the object so that it seems smaller, less important or inferior.	
introduction	the part at the beginning of any text (exposition)	
intrusive narrator	An intrusive narrator comments directly on events and the behaviour of his characters, often providing a moral judgement or highlighting the general importance of the story.	
inversion	the reversal of the normal order of words	"No longer can we believe in the truth of his words."
ironic, irony	a literary style employing contrasts for humorous or rhetorical effect	"In fact, it was his last big joke before his sense of humour calcified and had to be removed."
limited narrator	The limited narrator's insight into thoughts and feelings is restricted to one of the characters. He sees and judges the development of the story through the eyes of that particular character only.	
long shot	provides a view of the situation or setting from a distance	
low angle shot	the camera looks up at a person so that people seem more important, powerful or even intimidating as it shows them in a superior position	
main body	the main body of a book or document, not including the introduction or the notes	
manner of speaking	the way in which somebody speaks to help influence their aim, such as persuading an audience or portraying a certain emotion	

Literary terms – alphabetical

literary terms	definition	example
match cut	two scenes that are connected by visual or acoustic means, e.g. a door is closed in one scene and opened in the following scene in a different context, someone is crying at the end of the first and the beginning of the second scene	
medium long shot	shows a person or people in interaction with their surroundings	
medium shot	shows a person down to the waist, often used to present two people in conversation	
message	the main idea that you want people to remember from a speech, advertisement, article etc	
metaphor	two ideas that are normally not linked are compared in a metaphor without using "as" or "like". This creates an image in the reader's mind and makes the description more powerful.	"They blazed a trail toward freedom through the darkest of nights." (Barack Obama)
mood (music)	The mood of a piece of music helps portray a certain emotion which is linked to the storyline.	
multiple narrators	The story is told by different characters in the novel so that the events are seen from different perspectives. Thus the reader is presented with different views of an event and the reasons behind it, as each narrator contributes new aspects. This perspective is frequently chosen in modern novels.	
myth	an ancient, traditional story	
N narrative perspective	when a story is told from the narrator's point of view	
O omniscient narrator	a narrator knowing everything about the characters	
opinion	the attitude that you have towards something, especially your thoughts about how good it is	
outward appearance	of or relating to the outside of the body	
over-the-shoulder shot	often used to present two people in conversation. You are looking straight at one person from behind the second person.	
P panning shot	the camera moves horizontally, i.e. to the left or to the right as opposed to tilting	
paradox	a statement consisting of two parts that seem to mean the opposite of each other	"I can resist anything but temptation." (Oscar Wilde)
parallelism	the repetition of sentence pattern often used to contrast	"… look at you. Look at us …"
parathesis	when two grammatically parallel words are used in one case	<u>Who</u> and <u>what</u> are they?

Literary terms – alphabetical

literary terms	definition	example
pathos	a quality in a situation that causes feelings of sadness and pity in an audience	"Even worse than this is the fact that pass laws keep husband and wife apart and lead to the breakdown of family life."
persona	the part of your personality that you deliberately show most people	
playwright	someone who writes plays, especially as their job	
plot	a series of related events that make up the main story in a book, film, etc.	
point of view	the relation in which the narrator stands to the story, a mental viewpoint or attitude	
point-of-view shot	assumes the perspective of one of the characters so that we seem to look through his eyes	
posture	the position that your body is in when you sit, stand, or walk	
prejudice	This is used to refer to preconceived judgments of a group of people or a person because of personal characteristics such as race, gender, class, religion, nationality, etc. It refers to beliefs and attitudes that lack any real evidence and are difficult to change through rational argument. It tends to be negative and to discriminate against certain people.	Unemployed people are just lazy. Black people are better dancers.
quotation	words from a book, play, film etc that you mention when you are speaking or writing	
receiver	directly addressing the audience to create a sense of unity or identity	"we", "my friends", "fellow countrymen"
register	the level of language (degree of formality)	formal, informal, slang, …
repetition	words or phrases that are used more than once in a text, catching the reader's attention	"She knew this though: she loved kites and she loved rainbows. And, above all, she loved her mother."
reported thought	when the audience is informed about what a character is thinking	
reverse angle shot	a sequence of point-of-view shots in which the perspective changes from one speaker to the other	
rhetorical question	a question which expects no answer	"What does it matter now?"
rhythm and pace (music)	the pace or "movement" of a poem. The rhythm is determined by the metre and by the length of sentences.	
round characters	complex characters who may change (= dynamic character)	Manjit in Bali Rai's '(Un)arranged Marriage'

Literary terms – alphabetical

literary terms	definition	example
S sarcasm	comments which are used to mean the opposite of what they say, and are usually made to hurt someone's feelings or to criticize …	"Do they ever shut up on your planet?", "I started out with nothing and still have most of it left."
satire, satirical	Satire is a literary form in which wit and humour are used to expose and criticize flaws or negative tendencies in our society, in institutions or in people. Its aim is to make people laugh, only to then make them realize that they themselves have been unmasked.	
setting	the place and time at which the action of a fictional text takes place	
social background	The social background describes various facts of a person, including how he/she was raised and what ethnic group he/she belongs to.	
stage design	creation of theatrical scenery	
stage directions	notes in a play telling the actors how to speak and act. They also say what the characters and the stage should look like and where and when the action takes place.	"De Clerk's mobile rings." "Tom moves over to de Clerk and massages his shoulders and neck."
stereotype	A stereotype is a simplified and generalised understanding, usually of a person or a group of people, based on what you expect from them or have experienced with them. It is a kind of image that immediately arises in your imagination as soon as you hear a name, for example.	Germans wear leather trousers.
style	the special, often personal and individual way in which a writer expresses ideas depending on personal factors and the type of text he/she is writing	
stylistic devices	techniques used to convince the reader/listener of the author's idea	repetition, enumeration, irony, exaggeration, metaphor, tone
T text type	refers to what kind of text	
third person narration	A third person narrator is not part of the story, so the characters in the story are referred to as he, she, they. The third person narrator can be either omniscient or limited.	
tilting shot	The camera moves vertically, i.e. upwards or downwards as opposed to panning.	
tone	the tone the author uses to convey his/her attitude towards the subject	ironic, sarcastic, serious, sentimental, humorous

Literary terms – alphabetical

literary terms	definition	example
tone of text	The tone of a text reflects the narrator's attitude towards the topic he is dealing with. If the author disapproves of something his tone is likely to be critical.	
tone of voice	a manner of speaking which shows what a speaker is feeling	aggressive, conversational, nervous, uncertain
topic	a subject that you write or speak about	
tracking shot	the camera follows a person or an object	
traits	particular qualities in someone's character	
U unintrusive narrator	Even though the narrator has insight into the thoughts and feelings of his characters, an unintrusive narrator merely reports them without an explicit comment.	
use of unifying pronoun	when a first-person plural pronoun is used which refers to various people	we, us
Z zooming in/ zooming out	A stationary camera seems to move closer to or further away from the object, hereby focussing on it or showing it in its surroundings.	

Names and terms UK

Abramovich, Roman	Russian oligarch famous for being the owner of Chelsea Football Club, an English Premier League team
Act (of Parliament)	law which has passed through parliament and has come into effect
Anglesey (also known as Ynys Môn)	the largest Welsh island off the north-west coast with almost three quarters of the inhabitants speaking Welsh. The Welsh name for the island is Ynys Môn.
Anne Hathaway's cottage	a farmhouse where Anne Hathaway, William Shakespeare's wife, lived as a child
Argos	a British chain of high-street shops which offers lower prices by selling from a catalogue instead of a traditional shop display
Art Nouveau	period of art history at the turn from the 19th to the 20th century, also known as *Jugendstil*. Though present in art, architecture and philosophy, art nouveau is best known for its input in decorative arts such as lamps, glass art, ceramics and jewelry.
Atlantic Alliance = NATO	a military alliance in which member countries agree to defend each other if one of them is under threat
Atlantic Axis	*here:* Britain's relationship with the United States
Austin Reed	upmarket chain of men's tailors
Bath	a city in Somerset, south-west England, 97 miles (156 km) west of London and 13 miles (21 km) south-east of Bristol, well known for being a spa town since the Romans built baths and a temple in the valley of the River Avon around 60 AD.
Beckham, Victoria	an English businesswoman, fashion designer, model and singer (member of the pop band Spice Girls); married to former football player David Beckham, mother of four children.
Belfast agreement (also known as *Good Friday agreement, GFA*)	an important political development in the Northern Ireland peace process of the 1990s • dealing with major issues relating to civil and cultural rights, decommissioning of weapons, justice and policing and • creating a number of political institutions between Northern Ireland and the Republic of Ireland as well as between the Republic of Ireland and the United Kingdom.
Bentley	a very expensive British brand of car
bill	draft law which passes through different stages of parliament
Blackadder	a BBC television sitcom, four seasons set in different historical periods plus a number of Specials, starring Rowan Atkinson (also famous as Mr Bean), Miranda Richardson, Stephen Fry and Hugh Laurie (now famous for playing Dr House)
Blair, Tony	British prime minister from 1997 to 2007
boating jacket	a blazer with very noticeable coloured vertical stripes traditionally associated with the upper classes
Boden	catalogue clothing company popular with the British middle classes
Boy George (born George Alan O'Dowd)	a British singer-songwriter and former member of the band Culture Club, best known for his flamboyant and androgynous appearance. As a result he was one of the most prominent representatives of the English New Romantic movement in the early 1980s.

Names and terms UK

Brer Rabbit	a literary figure. He tricked a fox by telling him to do anything to him, just not throw him into the briar patch. That is exactly what the rabbit wanted to happen because he could then easily get away. And the fox fell for the trick.
BritainThinks poll	a poll of British opinions taken by the company BritainThinks Ltd.
British American Project	a 4-day annual conference attended by over 1,000 British and American leaders and policy makers, intended to strengthen relationships and communication between important people from both countries
Brown, Gordon	British prime minister from 2007 to 2010
Buller Boy	former member of the Bullingdon Club, an exclusive and expensive Oxford University club, the members of which have a reputation for heavy alcohol consumption and destructive behaviour
(the) Cabinet	group of members of a government who are chosen by the leader of the government to give advice and be responsible for its policies
Cameron, David	British prime minister from May 2010 onwards
Cash-4-Gold shop	a shop that will buy unwanted gold items and pay immediately in cash
casual Friday	the policy adopted by many modern offices of allowing their staff to dress in a more relaxed style on Fridays than during the rest of the week
Cecil Gee	upmarket chain of men's tailors
chancellor (of the exchequer)	title of the cabinet minister responsible for financial matters, British equivalent to the role of minister of finance/secretary of the treasury in other nations.
Channel Islands	group of islands situated in the English Channel
Church of England	Both the official Christian church in England and the mother church of the worldwide Anglican Communion that has the British monarch as its leader. Independent from the Roman Catholic Church since 1534: a dispute between Pope Clement VII and King Henry VIII on the annulment of his first marriage led to the excommunication of Henry VIII and finally to the separation of the English Church from Rome. Today the Church of England's doctrinal character is largely a middle way between Catholic traditions and structures on the one hand and principles of the Protestant Reformation movement on the other.
Civil War (in England)	a series of conflicts between the crown and parliament, which took place from 1642 till 1651
cloth cap	working class
Coldstream guards	regiment of the British army with ceremonial duties in London and Windsor
Common Law	an unofficial system of law that has developed from customs/traditions
Commonwealth (of Nations)	an association of countries that mostly used to belong to the British Empire
comprehensive school	a type of secondary school which any child may attend, regardless of ability
Congress	the legislature of the United States government which consists of two houses: the Senate and the House of Representatives.

Names and terms UK

council house	social housing owned by a government agency and rented at a capped price
Council of Europe	an international organisation that aims to promote cooperation between all European countries in the areas of human rights, legal standards and cultural cooperation. It has nothing to do with the European Union (EU). One of its bodies is the European Court of Human Rights. It is based in Strasbourg.
Council of the European Union	is also known as the Council of Ministers. It represents the governments of the EU's member states and is based in Brussels.
Cowes Regatta	a famous series of boat races which take place over a week in August in the Solent (the stretch of water between southern England and the Isle of Wight)
creation of wealth	the act of making a country/group/person richer and more successful
Cromwell, Oliver (1599–1658)	English military and political leader and one of the most controversial figures in British history due to his role as prime mover in the trial and execution of King Charles I in 1649. Cromwell helped to establish the English republic and ruled as Lord Protector of the Commonwealth of England, Scotland and Ireland from 1653–58, followed briefly by his son, who was forced to abdicate and flee after the restoration of the monarchy in 1660.
daffodils	a reference to William Wordsworth's famous poem, which begins 'I wandered lonely as a cloud'
Daily Mirror	British left-of-centre tabloid newspaper
Delage	an exclusive French car company which was founded in 1905 by Louis Delage and closed down in 1953.
detached house	a house which does not share any walls with its neighbours
Disraeli, Benjamin	British writer, aristocrat and politician serving twice as Prime Minister (1868, 1874–80). Disraeli played a central role in the creation of the modern Conservative Party. The belief that societies exist and develop organically, and that members (particularly those of the upper classes) within them have obligations towards each other was an integral part of his political idea known as one-nation conservatism.
Downing Street	street in London where the prime minister (at No. 10) and chancellor of the exchequer (at No.11) officially live
Downton Abbey	popular UK drama series about an aristocratic family and their servants
EastEnders	long running British TV soap, set in the East End of London
Edwardian	dating from the reign of King Edward VII, 1901–1910
EEC (European Economic Community)	the name used up to 1993 for what is now the European Union (EU) and informally known as the Common Market. The EU is an economic and political association of 28 European countries, intended to regulate trade.
electoral reform	a change in electoral systems to make them fairer or more representative of the will of voters
Elton John	an English singer/songwriter, also known for composing film music and musicals such as *The Lion King*. Even before he came out in 1988, he was publicly involved in the fight against AIDS. He was and still is a champion for the LGBT social movement and a supporter of same-sex marriage.

Names and terms UK

environmentalism	an ideological, social and political movement that seeks to influence the political process by lobbying, activism, and education in order to protect natural resources and ecosystems. Though having a long tradition that reaches back to Romanticism and its ideal of protecting and conserving the environment, it has become of more and more relevance since industrialization and its side effects. Today's major issues are global warming and the increase in natural disasters, overpopulation and world hunger, genetic engineering and endangered species.
estuary = *estuary English*	a lower-class style of speech originating from the area around the River Thames and its estuary
Eton	very expensive and exclusive boys' school attended by young royals and future politicians, amongst others
European Coal and Steel Community	an international organization intended to unify European countries after the Second World War by neutralizing competition over natural resources
Euroscepticism	Generally, against European integration and in favour of the national state and its interests. In the UK, Euroscepticism has been a significant and ongoing element in politics, ever since the inception of the European Economic Community (EEC), the predecessor to the EU.
F&M = Fortnum & Mason	a department store situated in Piccadilly in central London. It has an international reputation for high quality goods.
Father Ted	a critically acclaimed Irish TV sitcom (25 episodes) with a mainly Irish cast and crew telling the story of a priest who moves to the remote (and fictional) Craggy Island, off the west coast of Ireland
Fawlty Towers	a BBC television sitcom (two seasons each consisting of six episodes made in 1975 and 1979), both written and starring former Monty Python-member John Cleese
Fellowes, Julian	an English actor, novelist and screenwriter who is also a Conservative member of the House of Lords. He created the series Downton Abbey.
flat cap	type of hat traditionally worn by farmers and other working men in rural areas
Foreign and Commonwealth Office	a department of the UK government, responsible for promoting UK interests and supporting UK citizens and businesses overseas.
Frampton, Peter	an English-American rock musician born in 1950
Fry, Stephen	upper middle-class British comedian, actor, writer, presenter and activist
G8 = Group of 8	a forum attended by the governments of the eight leading advanced economies in the world: Canada, France, Germany, Italy, Japan, Russia, the United Kingdom and the United States. Since the suspension of Russia in 2014 it is now referred to as the G7.
Georgian (architecture)	a name given in most English-speaking countries to the architectural styles current between 1720 and 1830, a period in which the first four British monarchs of the House of Hanover named George (George I of Great Britain, George II of Great Britain, George III of the United Kingdom, and George IV of the United Kingdom) reigned.
Gothic (architecture)	a style of architecture that flourished during the high and late medieval period, best known for features such as pointed archs, ribbed vaults and the flying buttresses characteristic of cathedrals, abbeys and European churches built in that time.

grammar school	a type of secondary school which children must pass an exam to attend
Griffith, Nanci	American singer, musician and songwriter who was particularly popular in the 1990s
haggis	traditional Scottish dish made of sheep's offal mixed with oatmeal packed into and cooked in a sheep's stomach
Harrow	very expensive and exclusive boys' school attended by young royals and future politicians, amongst others
Heritage	English Heritage, an agency of the British government which is responsible for monitoring and protecting listed buildings in England
Holyrood	the Scottish Parliament
Home Counties	the counties of south-east and east England which surround London and which are generally regarded to be relatively wealthy when compared with the rest of the country
housing benefit	money provided by the state to pay the rent of people on a very low income
Hyacinth Bucket	a TV character (from the series "Keeping Up Appearances") famous for social-climbing and snobbery, epitomised in her insistence that her surname is pronounced not "bucket", but "bouquet"
ICM	public opinion research organization that was founded in 1989
IMF = International Monetary Fund	an international organization which aims to stabilize economies, trade and currencies around the world
Ipswich	county town of Suffolk in the East of England
(the) IRA	the Irish Republican Army: organisation which fought, often violently, carrying out terrorist attacks, for Irish independence from the UK
Isle of Man	a self-governing British Crown dependency located in the Irish Sea between the islands of Britain and Ireland
"Jerusalem"	a poem written by William Blake and set to music by Sir Hubert Parry, which is now commonly sung as a patriotic hymn and is sometimes regarded as the unofficial national anthem
John O'Groats	a village which is on the north-east coast of Scotland and is the most distant settlement from Land's End
Kennedy, John	president of the United States 1960–1963
Kleenex tissue	UK's most popular brand of paper handkerchief
Lampard, Frank	English professional footballer
Land's End	the most westerly point of mainland Britain, in Cornwall
League of Gentlemen	a British sitcom with horror elements (1999–2002) set in the fictional village of Royston Vasey in the North of England depicting bizarre happenings in the lives of some of the village's inhabitants.
League of Nations	an intergovernmental organisation formed after the First World War with the aim of maintaining world peace
Lemonheads	an American alternative rock band first formed in 1986 and most successful in the early 1990s.
Lib Dem = the Liberal Democrats	a social-liberal political party in Britain which was created when the two parties the Liberals and the Social Democrats (SDP) merged

Names and terms UK

lowland Scotland	a large area of Scotland adjoining the border with England
Lumley, Joanna	is an English actress, former model and author, who was born in 1946
Lundy Island	small island situated to the north of the UK's south-west peninsula, very close to the coast
Major, John	British prime minister from 1990 to 1997
Mason-Dixie Line	a border that traditionally divides the north of America from the south *here:* a cultural border
McGowan, Alistair	an English actor, singer and writer best known to British audiences for the highly acclaimed comedy programme *The Big Impression*
Miliband, Ed	British Labour politician, member of the Cabinet from 2007 and leader of the Labour Party from September 2010 onwards
mockney	a fake accent, based on the cockney accent famously spoken in the working-class East End of London
Monty Python and the Holy Grail (1975)	film by the British comedy group *Monty Python*, considered a classic parody dealing with King Arthur's legendary quest for the Holy Grail.
MP = Member of Parliament	one of the 650 elected members of the (lower) House of Commons within the parliament of the United Kingdom
National Assembly for Wales	a centralized assembly with power to make legislation in Wales consisting of 60 elected Assembly members created by the Government of Wales Act 1998, which followed a referendum in 1997.
NHS = National Health Service	is a publicly funded health service in the UK which is free at the point of use for people who live in the UK
Neo-Gothic	an architectural movement in the late 1740s in England, reviving the Gothic style by constructing school, college, and university buildings with features well known from Gothic architecture (↑)
New Labour	the Labour Party from the mid-1990s to the early 2000s under the leadership of Tony Blair and Gordon Brown, during which party policy moved more towards the political centre to make the Labour Party more electable
Niemöller, Friedrich Gustav Emil Martin (1892–1984)	a German theologian and Lutheran pastor as well as one of the founders of the Confessional Church, which opposed the nazification of German Protestant churches. He is best known for the following statement/poem that was modified a number of times by himself: „Als die Nazis die Kommunisten holten, habe ich geschwiegen; ich war ja kein Kommunist. Als sie die Sozialdemokraten einsperrten, habe ich geschwiegen; ich war ja kein Sozialdemokrat. Als sie die Gewerkschafter holten, habe ich geschwiegen; ich war ja kein Gewerkschafter. Als sie mich holten, gab es keinen mehr, der protestieren konnte."
Norman Conquest	invasion and occupation of England by an army of Norman, Breton, and French soldiers led by Duke William II of Normandy (later known as William the Conqueror) in 1066.
North Atlantic Treaty Organisation (NATO)	a military alliance between 28 countries across North America and Europe in which member countries agree to defend each other

Names and terms UK

OECD (country)	a signatory to the Convention of the Organisation for Economic Cooperation and Development, which was created after the Second World War with the intention of ensuring economic growth and financial stability and thereby maintaining peace
old Harrovian	former pupil of the exclusive and expensive public school, Harrow
Osbourne House	summer residence of Queen Victoria and her husband Prince Albert on the Isle of Wight.
Oxbridge	the two prestigious universities of Oxford and Cambridge
Pearl Harbour	an American naval base in Hawaii which the Japanese navy attacked on December 7th 1941, causing the USA to enter WWII.
Peep Show	British television sitcom and longest-returning comedy in Channel 4 history. *Peep Show* follows the lives of two men (David Mitchell and Robert Webb) from their twenties to thirties
peer	member of the House of Lords. There are two types: life peers and hereditary peers.
Plaid Cymru	a political party in Wales supporting an independent Wales within the European Union
ploughman's lunch	English pub food. It traditionally consists of a piece of cheese, a slice of bread and an apple. Often pickle is served with it.
Primark	an Irish fashion company selling fashionable clothes at the low cost end of the market in Britain and beyond, expanding rapidly. Primark's working conditions have often been an issue.
prime minister (of the United Kingdom of Great Britain and Northern Ireland)	head of Her Majesty's Government in the United Kingdom, highest ranking minister of cabinet in the executive, while the Queen is the state's official representative limited to non-partisan functions (e.g. appointing the prime minister, bestowing honours etc.) though often with reserve powers.
progressive taxation	a tax where the tax rate increases as the taxable base amount increases. Frequently, the term is applied in reference to personal income taxes, where people with less income pay a lower percentage of that income in tax than do those with a higher income.
public school	a fee-paying school
puffin	stocky black-and-white seabird living in large colonies on coastal cliffs or offshore islands. The Atlantic puffin spends its summer on the coasts of the North Atlantic (e.g. the British Isles) and flies off to Morocco in the winter months.
Quant, Mary	a British fashion designer and fashion icon often considered to be the "inventor" of the mini-skirt and hot pants.
Queen Bess	reference to Queen Elizabeth I's famous speech at Tilbury in 1588 before the English navy defeated the Spanish Armada.
Reagan, Ronald	president of the United States 1980–1988
redistribution of wealth	the transfer of wealth from those who have more to those who have less, but on an economy-wide basis and by means of social mechanisms such as taxation, monetary policies, welfare etc.

Names and terms UK

Ross, Diana	an African-American singer/songwriter and actress. Started her musical career in the 1960s as the lead-singer of the band The Supremes, which became the most successful act of Motown Records (Detroit) and is up to now the most successful vocal group in US history.
Royal Assent	when the king or queen of the UK signs an Act of Parliament, making it an official law
St David's Day	is the 1st March each year. It is in remembrance of the death of St David, who is the patron saint of Wales.
Salmond, Alex	Scottish politician, leader of the Scottish National Party and First Minister of Scotland since 2007.
(the) Scilly Islands	group of small islands situated off the south-west tip of the UK
(the) Scottish independence referendum	a political campaign in Scotland which led to a vote on 18 September 2014: Scottish voters were asked to answer the question "Should Scotland be an independent country?" with "Yes" or "No. The "No" side won, with 2,001,926 (55.3%) voting against independence and 1,617,989 (44.7%) voting in favour of independence.
scouts	a popular movement promoting outdoor activities and skills for children in weekly club meetings which was set up in the early twentieth century
semi-detached house	a house which shares a wall with its neighbours on just one side
Seven Years' War	an imperial war which involved Europe, North America, Central America, the West African coast, India and the Philippines from 1756 to 1763.
Sex Pistols	an English band, formed in London in 1975 that initiated the punk movement and inspired many later punk and alternative rock musicians.
Social Chapter	a part of the Maastricht treaty meant to improve people's living and working conditions
South Shields	a coastal town at the mouth of the River Tyne, England
southern Confederate states	southern American states which disagreed with the northern Union states on policies such as the abolition of slavery
Star Spangled Banner	the national anthem of the United States
state school	a school at which education is provided and paid for by the state
Stella = *Stella Artois*	a Belgian lager which, in the UK, is often considered to be a favourite of violent drunks
Steptoe and Son	a British sitcom (four seasons from 1962 to 1965 and 1970 to 1974) about the inter-generational conflict of father and son and their rag-and-bone business
Stonehenge	One of the most famous sites in the world, a pre-historic monument consisting of a ring of standing stones located in Wiltshire, England.
Suez Crisis	crisis which occurred in 1956 when Egypt nationalized the Suez Canal making it difficult for Britain and France to transport oil from the Middle East
The Sun	British centre-right newspaper
Superdrug	British high-street chemist

Names and terms UK

Tennyson, Alfred Lord	famous English poet (1809–1892)
terraced houses	houses built in rows, sharing walls with their neighbours on both sides
Thatcher, Maggie	Margaret Thatcher, British prime minister from 1979 to 1990
This is Jinsy	classic British comedy programme also famous in America
Tory	An informal term for a member of the conservative centre-right political party in the United Kingdom or for the party in general, formally known as Tory Party/the Tories (= traditionalism and conservatism).
townie	a person who is used to living in an urban environment and not a rural one
Tudorbethan	built in a historically inaccurate mock Tudor or Elizabethan style
Tyneside	is the 7th largest conurbation in England, home to over 80% of the population of the metropolitan county Tyne and Wear in the North of England.
Ugg boots	distinctive sheepskin boots
welfare state	a concept of government in which the state plays a key role in the protection and promotion of the economic and social well-being of its citizens. Services such as healthcare or education are funded by the state and through redistributionist taxation.
West Country	refers to the area of south-western England which includes the counties of Somerset, Dorset, Devon, Cornwall and the City and County of Bristol
William = *here:* William Shakespeare	English poet/playwright (1564–1616).who is generally seen as the greatest writer in the English language.
Wood Green	a district in north London, England.
Wordsworth, William	well-known Romantic poet (1770–1850) who wrote the famous poem "Daffodils"

Copyrights

Bildquellenverzeichnis
Umschlag außen: Keystone, Hamburg/National Pictures/TopFoto
Umschlag innen: Peter Palm, Berlin; Joachim Zwick, Gießen
S. 6: YouTube, LLC – Permission and Rights, San Bruno, CA 94066 (beide)
S. 7: News Group Newspapers Limited, London (The Sun)
S. 9: Peter Palm, Berlin
S. 10: *(1)* ullstein bild, Berlin, *(2)* INTERFOTO, München (Science & Society/National Railway Museum)
S. 11: bpk – Bildagentur für Kunst, Kultur und Geschichte, Berlin (Germin)
S. 18: Cookson, Bernard, Henley-on-Thames/Oxfordshire
S. 22: Andy Davey, London (The Sun/NewsSyndication.com)
S. 30: *(1)* alamy images, Abingdon/Oxfordshire (keith morris), *(2)* Shutterstock.com, New York, *(3)* alamy images, Abingdon/Oxfordshire (David J. Green), *(4)* alamy images, Abingdon/Oxfordshire (Paul Doyle), *(5)* alamy images, Abingdon/Oxfordshire (DuohuaEr), *(6)* alamy images, Abingdon/Oxfordshire (Peter Alvey People)
S. 34: LGP (Lee Gone Publications) Brighton, UK (Martyn Ford)
S. 44: fotolia.com, New York (Robert Kneschke)
S. 45: Getty Images, München (Hulton Archiv)
S. 46: Picture-Alliance GmbH, Frankfurt/M. (Press Association/dpa-Fotoreport)
S. 47: *(1)* alamy images, Abingdon/Oxfordshire (Colin Underhill), *(2)* alamy images, Abingdon/Oxfordshire (Washington Imaging), *(3)* Mirrorpix, London
S. 57: alamy images, Abingdon/Oxfordshire (keith morris)
S. 64: *(1,2)* alamy images, Abingdon/Oxfordshire (keith morris)
S. 69: *(1,2)* Visit Britain, London
S. 70: *(1)* alamy images, Abingdon/Oxfordshire (Cary Clarke), *(2)* alamy images, Abingdon/Oxfordshire (Manor Photography), *(3,4)* alamy images, Abingdon/Oxfordshire (Jon Wilson), *(5,6)* Picture-Alliance GmbH, Frankfurt/M. (Press Association/dpa-Fotoreport), *(7)* ddp images GmbH, Hamburg, *(8)* Kobal Collection, Berlin, *(9)* alamy images, Abingdon/Oxfordshire (Jon Wilson), *(10)* iStockphoto.com, Calgary (stocksnapper), *(11)* Picture-Alliance GmbH, Frankfurt/M. (Yui Mok), *(12)* alamy images, Abingdon/Oxfordshire (John Peter Photography), *(13)* Picture-Alliance GmbH, Frankfurt/M. (PA Wire/Dave Thompson)
S. 71: *(1–6)* Visit Britain, London, *(7)* Picture-Alliance GmbH, Frankfurt/M. (PA Wire/Dave Thompson)
S. 72: *(1)* INTERFOTO, München (Andrew Butler), *(2)* alamy images, Abingdon/Oxfordshire (John Peter Photography), *(3)* INTERFOTO, München (Philip Enticknap)
S. 73: *(1)* Picture-Alliance GmbH, Frankfurt/M. (PA Wire/Dave Thompson), *(2)* Corbis, Berlin (Bettmann)
S. 88: *(1)* Daily Mail, London, *(2)* The Independent, London
S. 89: *(1)* laif, Köln: (Polaris), *(2)* INTERFOTO, München (Mary Evans/Library of Congress)
S. 91: bpk – Bildagentur für Kunst, Kultur und Geschichte, Berlin (Dietmar Katz)
S. 92: Library of Congress, Washington, D. C. (Edwin Marcus)
S. 93: AP Photo, New York
S. 102: Guardian News + Media Limited, London
S. 103: *(1)* Express Newspaper Distr. Bulls , London (Scott Clissold); *(2)* Cartoon Stock Ltd, Bath, *(3)* Zapiro, Cape Town, *(4)* Cartoon Stock Ltd, Bath
S. 105: *(1)* mauritius images GmbH, Mittenwald, *(2)* fotolia.com, New York
S. 106: *(1–4)* wikipedia.org, *(5)* Telegraph Media Group Ltd., London
S. 107: *(1–4)* wikipedia.org
S. 114: *(1)* fotolia.com, New York (nazlisart), *(3–5)* Cartoon Stock Ltd, Bath
S. 116: *(1)* dreamstime.com, Brentwood (Ronfromyork); *(3)* Palm, Peter, Berlin
S. 118: *(1)* Scottish Political Archive, University of Stirling, Stirling, *(2)* alamy images, Abingdon/Oxfordshire (redsnapper), *(3)* Yes Scotland, Glasgow
S. 129: *(1)* Picture-Alliance GmbH, Frankfurt/M. (PA Wire/Dave Thompson), *(2)* Picture-Alliance GmbH, Frankfurt/M. (PA Wire/Dominic Lipinski)
S. 131: Picture-Alliance GmbH, Frankfurt/M. (AP Photo/POOL)
S. 132: Picture-Alliance GmbH, Frankfurt/M. (United_Archives/TopFoto),
S. 133: alamy images, Abingdon/Oxfordshire (Everyday Images)
S. 172: Picture-Alliance GmbH, Frankfurt/M. (Advertising Archives)
S. 174: CartoonStock Ltd, GB-Bath (Plenderleith, Allan)

Copyrights

Textquellenverzeichnis

S. 8: from "How German are you?" by Grant Hollings in *The Sun*, 22.06.2011. © The Sun.
S. 8: from "German efficiency" by Tim Collard in *The Telegraph*, 26.02.2010. © Telegraph Media Group Limited 2014.
S. 8: "German stereotypes: über-efficiency" by Helen Pidd in *The Guardian*, 18.03.2011. © Guardian News & Media Ltd 2014.
S. 12–13: from "These Strange German Ways and the Whys of the Ways" by Susan Stern. © Atlantik-Brücke, Berlin, 2000, S. 3–7.
S. 20–21: from "Keeping up with the Germans" by Philip Oltermann. © Rogers, Coleridge and White Lit Agency, London, 2011, S. 236–242.
S. 23: from "German stereotypes: Don't mention the sense of humour" in *The Guardian* 16.03.2011. © Guardian News & Media Ltd 2015.
S. 26–27: "Was deutschen und britischen Humor verbindet" by Martina Goy in *WELTonline* 14.07.2012.
S. 28–29: "Ende einer Städtepartnerschaft" by Marco Evers in *Spiegel Online* 17.12.2011.
S. 30: from "What does Britishness mean to you?" by Tim Stephen Moss in *The Guardian*, 05.02.2012. © Guardian News & Media Ltd 2014.
S. 31: from "We have surprised ourselves – and our potential is unlimited" by Tim Lott in *The Independent*, 12.08.2012. © The Independent 2014.
S. 35: from "Pyrenees" in "Selected Plays 1999–2009" by David Greig. © Faber & Faber Ltd, London, 2010, S. 260.
S. 36–38: from "Pyrenees" in "Selected Plays 1999–2009" by David Greig. © Faber & Faber Ltd, London, 2010, S. 261–269.
S. 41: from "Testing the Echo" by David Edgar. © Nick Hern Books, London, 2008, Scene Two.
S. 42–43: from "Testing the Echo" by David Edgar. © Nick Hern Books, London, 2008, Scene Twenty-two and Twenty-Three.
S. 45–46: from "Mind the Gap: The New Class Divide in Britain" by Ferdinand Mount. © Short Books, London, 2005, S. 36–38.
S. 48–51: from "Three views from across Britain's class divide" by Kevin Maguire, David Randall and Matthew Bell in *The Independent*, 20.03.2011. © The Independent 2014.
S. 56–57: "How to Become a Chavette (Female Chav)" on *WikiHow*.
S. 57–58: from "Chav: the vile word at the heart of fractured Britain" by Polly Toynbee in *The Guardian*, 31.05.2011. © Guardian News & Media Ltd 2014.
S. 60–61: from "Money busts the convenient myth that social class is dead" by Polly Toynbee on *guardianonline*, 29.08.2011. © Guardian News & Media Ltd 2014.
S. 66: from "No such thing as the British class system any more? That's rich" by Paul Routledge in *The Mirror*, 05.04.2013. © The Mirror 2014.
S. 66–67: from "Classing Britain: why defining social status is so difficult" by Mona Chalabi and Ami Sedghi in *The Guardian*, 03.04.2013.
S. 67: from "What did I learn from this class survey?" by Mark Steel in *The Independent*, 04.04.2013. © The Independent 2014.
S. 74: from "England, England" by Julian Barnes. © Vintage Books, London, 2012, S. 61–63.
S. 78: from "England, England" by Julian Barnes. © Vintage Books, London, 2012, S. 178–182.
S. 80–81: from "High Fidelity" by Nick Hornby. © Riverhead Penguin Group USA, New York, 1996. S. 55–58.
S. 82–85: from CHART THROB by Ben Elton. Published by Bantam Press. Reprinted by permission of The Random House Group Limited.
S. 88: from "William Hague on the EU membership vote: We won't leave Europe, but it won't rule us" by William Hague in *The Telegraph*. © Telegraph Media Group Ltd 2014.
S. 88: from "Awkward partners … but still married" by Kirsty Hughes on *EuropeanVoice.com*, 26.07.2007. © EuropeanVoice 2014.
S. 116–118: "A timeline of devolution" by Ros Taylor in *The Guardian*, 09.04.1999. © Guardian News & Media Ltd 2014.
S. 119–120: from "Scottish independence: the other One Nation debate" in *The Guardian*, 15.10.2012. © Guardian News & Media Ltd 2014.
S. 122: Open letter reply by Mark Austin in *The Guardian*, 16.10.2012. © Guardian News & Media Ltd 2014.
S. 124–125: "Wales: drumbeat of devolution" in *The Guardian*, 01.03.2012. © Guardian News & Media Ltd 2014.
S. 127: from "Das neue Heilige Römische Reich" by Joachim Fritz-Vannahme on *Zeit Online*, 05.12.2007. © Die Zeit 2014.
S. 134–137: from "She Shall Not Be Moved" by Shereen Pandit. © Shereen Pandit 2014.
S. 142–144: from "Loose Change". © Andrea Levy, in *Six Stories and an Essay*, Tinder Press 2005.